Music Scenes

Local, Translocal,

and Virtual

Music Scenes

Local, Translocal, and Virtual

*Edited by Andy Bennett
and Richard A. Peterson*

Vanderbilt University Press
NASHVILLE

This book is printed on acid-free paper.
Manufactured in the United States of America

"Jazz Places" © Howard Becker, used with permission.

Library of Congress Cataloging-in-Publication Data

Music scenes : local, translocal & virtual / edited by
Andy Bennett and Richard A. Peterson.—1st ed.
p. cm.
Includes bibliographical references and index.
ISBN 0-8265-1450-2 (cloth : alk. paper)
ISBN 0-8265-1451-0 (pbk. : alk. paper)
1. Popular music—History and criticism.
I. Bennett, Andy, 1963–
II. Peterson, Richard A.
ML3470.M895   2004
781.64'09-dc22   2003018798

*Dedicated to all those
who keep music alive
in scenes
around the world*

Contents

Acknowledgments   xi

Notes on Contributors   xiii

Introducing Music Scenes   1
Richard A. Peterson and Andy Bennett

Jazz Places   17
Howard Becker

> Becker shows that the social space in which music is performed shapes the music that is produced by focusing on two innovative periods in the development of jazz—the first, the earliest days of bebop in the 1930s gang-controlled underworld of Kansas City, and the second, the university tours and concerts that helped shape cool jazz in the 1950s.

Part I
Local Scenes

1   **The Symbolic Economy of Authenticity in the Chicago Blues Scene**   31
David Grazian

> Drawing on years of ethnographic research, Grazian shows how the signifiers of authenticity in the Chicago blues scene of the past are manipulated by contemporary artists, bartenders, and club owners to satisfy the expectations of today's fans and tourists, who differ sharply in their expectations of what "real" Chicago blues is.

2   **Behind the Rave: Structure and Agency
     in a Rave Scene**   48

Ken Spring

Spring uses participant observation and interviews to trace the rise
and fall of an intense rave scene in a small industrial city. He focuses
on the interests behind the rave scene—bar owners, promoters,
DJs, drug dealers, police, and city officials—who, for a brief period,
made it possible to put on raves in a risk-free environment.

3   **"Scenes" Dimensions of Karaoke
     in the United States**   64

Rob Drew

Much like early punk, karaoke encourages the liberating sensibility
that "anyone can do it." While for many in the United States
karaoke is an excuse for drunken self-expression, Drew shows that
for a goodly number it is a regular social activity that gives great
personal satisfaction and knits participants together in a number of
overlapping scenes, each appropriate for its locale.

4   **"Tween" Scene: Resistance
     within the Mainstream**   80

Melanie Lowe

Using focus groups, Lowe explores the realm of youthful fandom
that surrounds Britney Spears, which exists worldwide and in
fans' own rooms. Girls gush over their favorite and simultaneously
challenge her overly sexualized media image, revealing a reception
strategy that allows them to take pleasure in music often at odds
with their budding feminist consciousness.

5   **"Doin' It Right": Contested Authenticity
     in London's Salsa Scene**   96

Norman Urquia

Urquia shows that questions of authenticity operate at several levels
in the London salsa scene. Non-Latin dancers offer a variety of
claims on salsa as their own, while salsa dance teachers continually
strive for more exhibitionist personal styles to attract students.
Over time, ironically, the original Latin form has lost its identity as
authentic salsa.

Part II
Translocal Scenes

6   "Riot Grrrl Is . . .": Contestation over Meaning
     in a Music Scene   115
     Kristin Schilt

Schilt describes how widely dispersed scenes devoted to feminism and punk music came together to create the Riot Grrrl movement, in which every girl could be a riot grrrl. She shows how this fusion rapidly made the translocal scene visible and led to its fissuring, as musical and political differences came to the fore.

7   Translocal Connections in the Goth Scene   131
     Paul Hodkinson

With the collapse of the worldwide mass media–promoted genre of goth music in the early 1990s, numerous groups of goths linked up to form a translocally connected movement. Hodkinson shows how goth fans mutually reinforced each other through their symbols of goth identity, frequent travel to distant goth events, compilation of goth records, fanzines, Internet communication, and mail-order specialty stores.

8   Music Festivals as Scenes: Examples from
     Serious Music, Womyn's Music, and SkatePunk   149
     Timothy J. Dowd, Kathleen Liddle, and Jenna Nelson

Dowd, Liddle, and Nelson explore the Yaddo Festival, devoted to serious (art) music, the Michigan Womyn's Festival, and the Vans Warped Tour to illustrate the ways in which festivals—large organized events in which scenes periodically reproduce themselves in a cloistered area protected from the gaze of outsiders—can be scenes.

9   "Not for Sale": The Underground Network
     of Anarcho-Punk   168
     Tim Gosling

More than their local counterparts, translocal scenes depend on recordings and those who make them to get the music known and to build the sense of a scene. Gosling shows the role of band-owned record companies in the anarcho-punk scene of the 1980s and explains why the U.S.-owned companies were much more effective scene builders than were their English counterparts.

Part III
Virtual Scenes

10   **Internet-based Virtual Music Scenes:**
      The Case of P2 in Alt.Country Music   187
      Steve S. Lee and Richard A. Peterson

      Using the example of a group based on a listserv devoted to
      alternative country music, Lee and Peterson show how the Internet
      can be the locus of a long-lasting music scene, using a case study of
      Postcard Two to compare virtual scenes to local scenes.

11   **New Tales from Canterbury:**
      The Making of a Virtual Scene   205
      Andy Bennett

      In the development of a scene devoted to the memory of the music
      of a group of 1960s bands associated with Canterbury, England,
      Bennett finds that promoters and fans have used the Internet
      effectively to construct a virtual scene that perpetuates the notion
      that there was once a local scene built around the Canterbury
      Sound.

12   **The Fanzine Discourse over Post-rock**   221
      James A. Hodgkinson

      In his critical analysis of post-rock, Hodgkinson explores the
      dynamics of a virtual scene based on music reviews in fanzines and
      in the commercial music press. In doing so, he demonstrates the
      power of journalistic discourse to provide the musical terms and
      other forms of categorization central to the formation of a scene.

13   **Kate Bush: Teen Pop and Older Female Fans**   238
      Laura Vroomen

      Kate Bush, who had several teen-oriented hits in the late 1970s,
      has recorded sporadically since. Interviewing and interacting
      with a number of Kate Bush fans, Vroomen shows how Internet
      communication helps fandom continually reinvent itself as fans and
      artist mature.

      Index   255

Acknowledgments

The initial idea for this book came from a conversation between the editors following the IASPM U.K. and Ireland conference at the University of Surrey, Guildford, U.K., in July 2000. We are grateful to all who attended this conference and, in particular, to those who subsequently submitted papers for our consideration as chapters in this book. We would also like to express our thanks to those who have paved the way for the current academic interest in the "scenes" perspective—notably the pioneering work of Howard Becker and Simon Frith and the more recent studies of Will Straw, Sara Cohen, and Barry Shank.

We also wish to thank Moni Schuster, Anne and Herbert Bennett, and Claire and Ruth Peterson for their continuing support and encouragement. Both editors say thank you to the fellow musicians—too many to mention by name—with whom they have had the privilege to share the stage over the years, helping them get an insider's feel for what it means to be part of a scene. Thanks also to Global Communication, Yo La Tengo, Boards of Canada, Glenn Gould, amusia, and Henryk Góreki for providing an inspiring soundtrack during long hours of editorial work on this project.

Finally, heartfelt thanks to the individual chapter authors, who have given of their time, energy, and special expertise, and to the Vanderbilt University Press, especially Betsy Phillips, who has been an unerring source of advice and support throughout the editing of this book.

Notes on Contributors

Howard S. Becker has taught at Northwestern University and the University of Washington. The author of *Outsiders, Art Worlds, Writing for Social Scientists,* and *Tricks of the Trade,* he lives and works in San Francisco.

Andy Bennett is Senior Lecturer in Sociology at the University of Surrey. He has published articles on aspects of youth culture, popular music, and local identity in such journals as *British Journal of Sociology; Sociological Review;, Media, Culture, and Society;* and *Popular Music.* He is the author of *Popular Music and Youth Culture: Music, Identity, and Place* (Macmillan, 2000) and *Cultures of Popular Music* (Open University Press, 2001) and coeditor of *Guitar Cultures* (Berg, 2001). Andy is chair of the U.K. and Ireland branch of the International Association for the Study of Popular Music (IASPM) and is coconvenor of the British Sociological Association Youth Study Group.

Timothy J. Dowd received his Ph.D. from Princeton University and is Associate Professor of Sociology at Emory University in Atlanta. His research deals with cultural sociology, media sociology, sociology of music, and organizational sociology. His publications have appeared or are forthcoming in such journals as *American Sociological Review, Social Forces, Administrative Science Quarterly, Sociological Forum,* and *Comparative Social Research.* He has also edited special journal issues, including "Explorations in the Sociology of Music" (*Poetics,* 2002) and "Creative Industries" (*Poetics,* forthcoming). Tim currently serves on the editorial boards of *Poetics* and the *International Journal of Sociology and Social Policy.*

Rob Drew is Associate Professor of Communication at Saginaw Valley State University, University Center, Michigan. His research centers on the ethnographic study of popular music consumption. His work has appeared in the *Journal of Contemporary Ethnography, Popular Communication, Bad Subjects,* and several edited collections. Rob is the author of *Karaoke Nights: An Ethnographic Rhapsody* (AltaMira Press, 2001).

Tim Gosling is a freelance writer in Zagreb. He has written for a variety of publications in the United Kingdom and in Europe. Previously Tim was the managing editor of the "In Your Pocket'" cultural city guides to Prague and Zagreb.

David Grazian is Assistant Professor of Sociology at the University of Pennsylvania in Philadelphia, where he teaches courses on popular culture and urban nightlife. He is the author of *Blue Chicago: The Search for Authenticity in Urban Blues Clubs* (University of Chicago Press, 2003), in which he provides an ethnographic account of the musicians, audience members, bar regulars, and club owners who make up Chicago's blues scene. David is conducting research for a book on sex segregation and the role of women in the U.S. music industry.

James A. Hodgkinson is Senior Research Officer in the West Midlands Regional Research Team in the Home Office, U.K. Previously he was Research Lecturer at the Centre for Research in Primary and Community Care, University of Hertfordshire, and studied for a Ph.D. at the University of Surrey, analyzing the role of language in the development of the "post-rock" music scene. James's current research interests are crime reduction, fear of crime, and community safety, and he has coauthored a chapter in *Crime in England and Wales 2002/03*. He retains a keen interest in both consuming and making experimental electronica and avant-rock.

Paul Hodkinson is Lecturer in Sociology at the University of Surrey. He researches the relationships between media, commerce, and collective forms of identity, issues he explores via a comprehensive reworking of the notion of subculture in *Goth: Identity, Style, and Subculture* (Berg, 2002), a book that gave rise to national media reviews and interviews. He has also published papers and chapters based on his extensive doctoral research of the goth scene. Paul is newsletter editor for IASPM U.K. and Ireland, and in 2003 he was co-organizer of an international conference, "Scenes, Subcultures, and Tribes."

Steve S. Lee is a graduate student in the Department of Sociology at Vanderbilt University. His research focuses on cultural sociology, with an emphasis on understanding how critical discourse reinforces cultural classification systems. He is also interested in looking at the role of social networks among artists in facilitating career longevity. A current paper investigates the effects on music diversity of market consolidation in the broadcasting industry.

Kathleen Liddle is a doctoral student in sociology at Atlanta's Emory University and earned a degree in music from Oberlin College. In addition to the sociology of music, her research interests include culture, organizations, and social movements. Her dissertation examines feminist bookstores in the United States.

Melanie Lowe, Assistant Professor of Musicology at Vanderbilt University, holds a secondary appointment in Vanderbilt's Program in American and Southern Studies. Melanie has published articles on early adolescent girls and teen pop, classical music in U.S. media, and the music of Joseph Haydn in such journals as *Popular Music and Society, American Music,* and the *Journal of Musicology.* She is completing a book on pleasure and meaning in late-eighteenth-century symphony for Indiana University Press.

Jenna Nelson is a doctoral candidate in women's studies at Emory University in Atlanta. She holds an MA in Literature from Université de Montréal and an undergraduate degree from the University of Pittsburgh. Her dissertation research examines the production of children's entertainment.

Richard A. Peterson is Professor of Sociology at Vanderbilt University and founding chair of the Culture Section of the American Sociological Association. He is the author of *Creating Country Music: Fabricating Authenticity* and *The Production of Culture* and coeditor of *Sounds of Social Change.* A member of the board of directors of the U.S. branch of the IASPM, he has researched rock, pop, classical, country, jazz, and dance music and continues his work on the use of culture in status displays. Richard has several research projects under way in the sociology of music.

Kristen Schilt is a graduate student in sociology at the University of California Los Angeles. Her research interests include youth culture, sexuality, and gender in the workplace. She has published articles on Riot Grrrl in

Popular Music and Society and on zines and cultural resistance in *Youth and Society*. She is working on her dissertation, which explores the experiences of transsexuals in the workplace.

Ken Spring is a Ph.D. candidate at Vanderbilt University. His dissertation is entitled "The Development of Risk-Free Environments: Structure and Agency in Music Scenes." An active participant in the scenes he studies, Ken is also an Instructor of Sociology at Belmont University in Nashville, where he teaches theory and culture.

Norman Urquía is a doctoral student at the University of Surrey, where his research was funded by the Economic and Social Research Council. His upcoming research will examine how the consumption of a whole package of cultural products other than music and dance may contribute to the construction of identity in a multicultural city.

Laura Vroomen lectures in popular culture at the United Kingdom's Open University and in literature at Warwick University, where she completed her Ph.D. In addition to subcultural phenomena and expressions of fandom on the Internet, she is interested in film music and film adaptations of literary texts.

Introducing Music Scenes

Richard A. Peterson and Andy Bennett

It is widely said that something over 80 percent of all the commercial music of the world is controlled by five multinational firms. It is good that this is not the whole story, because then music would deserve no more attention than do men's shoes or shower fixtures. Instead, music is an important way that millions of people find enjoyment, define who they are, and affirm group membership. While the music industry is global, most music is made and enjoyed in diverse situations divorced from these corporate worlds. The concept "music scene," originally used primarily in journalistic and everyday contexts, is increasingly used by academic researchers to designate the contexts in which clusters of producers, musicians, and fans collectively share their common musical tastes and collectively distinguish themselves from others. We have commissioned the chapters in this book especially to illustrate the diversity of musical worlds currently being investigated using a scenes perspective. Each chapter focuses on a distinct aspect of scenes, from how individuals construct and negotiate scenes to the behind-the-scenes activities needed to sustain them. In the process, a number of different methods of analysis are illustrated. No chapter aims to be a complete description of a music scene; each highlights an aspect of scene life, and together they present something that approaches a complete view of scenes.

Scenes in Journalistic Discourse

The term "scene" was first widely used by journalists in the 1940s to characterize the marginal and bohemian ways of life of those associated with the demiworld of jazz. In the years since, journalists have applied the term loosely to a wide range of other situations—"Venice West poetry scene," "East Village beatnick scene," "this year's London theater scene," "goth scene," "punk scene," "hip-hop scene," and the like. This journalistic discourse not only has served to describe the music, dress, and deportment appropriate to a scene, but also has functioned as a cultural resource for fans of particular musical genres, enabling them to forge collective expressions of "underground" or "alternative" identity and to identify their cultural distinctiveness from the "mainstream." Many scenes go unacknowledged by the press, but as Thornton notes, the music press and associated niche media can "baptize scenes and generate the self-consciousness required to maintain cultural distinctions" (1995, 151).

The contemporary tourist industry helps perpetuate some music scenes that respond to the expectations of what Urry (1990) calls the "tourist gaze." That is, tourists travel to particular regions or cities with a stock of expectations based on visual, print, and other media-generated information to vicariously experience their expectations about a scene. Music often figures centrally in these efforts, as local promoters for the tourist industry exploit the distinctive aspects of their city's music scene. A notable example of this is Liverpool in the United Kingdom, which, partly in an attempt to revive its local economy in the 1980s, created a number of tourist venues, including an interactive museum, an inner-city shopping mall, and a series of tours, all based around the lives and work of the Beatles. Artifacts associated with Elvis Presley serve the thriving tourist industry of Memphis in the United States, and country music and jazz draw thousands of tourists to Nashville and New Orleans, respectively. Writing in this volume, David Grazian illustrates how the global image of Chicago blues as an authentic musical expression of the black urban experience is maintained through a series of blues clubs and bars, many of which, according to blues purists in the city, have been created purely to satisfy tourists' desires for what they define as an "authentic" blues experience.

Scenes in Academic Research

Since the early 1990s, the concept of scene, first mentioned in academic discourse by Will Straw (1991), has increasingly been used as a model for academic research on the production, performance, and reception of popular music. Work in the scenes perspective focuses on situations where performers, support facilities, and fans come together to collectively create music for their own enjoyment. In many ways the organization of music scenes contrasts sharply with that of the multinational music industry, in which a relatively few people create music for mass markets. The scenes and industrial ways of making music of course depend on one another. The industry needs scenes to foster new forms of musical expression and to give its products the veneer of authenticity, while scenes take advantage of technology, from the CD to the Internet, created by the music industry.

What we and others call "scenes" have often been called "subcultures" (see Clarke 1990; Bennett 1999). We use the term "scene" here rather than "subculture" because the latter term presumes that a society has one commonly shared culture from which the subculture is deviant (Gelder and Thornton 1997). In addition, we avoid "subculture" because it presumes that all of a participant's actions are governed by subcultural standards, while the scene perspective does not make this presumption. To be sure, a few at the core of the scene may live that life entirely, but, in keeping with a late-modern context in which identities are increasingly fluid and interchangeable (Chaney 1996), most participants regularly put on and take off the scene identity (Bennett 2000). Our formulation of the scene concept draws heavily on Pierre Bourdieu's (1984) idea of "field" and Howard Becker's (1982) idea of "art worlds," which both make many of the same assumptions we do.

There are already a number of studies of particular music-making sites that exemplify important aspects of the scenes perspective, even though their authors may not employ the term "scenes." Here we mention only a few to illustrate their range. In *Dissonant Identities,* Barry Shank (1994) looks at the various music scenes that have developed in Austin, Texas, from the cosmic cowboys of the mid-1970s to the alternative punks of the 1990s. He focuses on how the bands, clubs, critics, and university students of Austin generated a series of scenes over these twenty years. In "The Local Economy of Suburban Scenes," Donna Gaines (1994) describes the ways in which kids stuck in the wasteland of suburban America spawn their own music scenes and subcults in an effort to invest their lives with new meaning. Focusing on youth and music making in a single city, Sara Cohen's *Rock Culture in Liverpool* shows that the depressed socioeconomic conditions of Liverpool engendered in many young people the feeling that "you might as well pick up a guitar as take exams, since your chances of finding full-time occupation from either were just the same, being in a band was an accepted way of life and could provide a means of justifying one's existence" (1991, 3). Four chapters in Andy Bennett's *Popular Music and Youth Culture* (2000) are devoted to how music scenes that originally developed in quite different locales can be shaped to fit specific local sensibilities of quite a different sort. These include hip-hop in Newcastle, England, and Frankfurt, Germany, as well as Punjabi Bhangra and DJ-based dance music in Newcastle. In his discussion of the development of rap in a number of distinct places across the United States, Murray Forman (2002) shows how "place" moves from being a source of identity to being a merchandising tool for bands.

In a kaleidoscopic focus that ranges across the world from New York City to New Zealand, Tony Mitchell (1996) shows how local music is expressed, appropriated, and recombined to fashion local identities through music. In the 1990s, widely scattered music scenes devoted to extreme metal music existed in Brazil; San Francisco; Tampa, Florida; Stockholm; Chile; Malaysia; Norway; and Israel. Keith Harris (2000) calls the links that bind these "global," but here we will describe such networks of local music scenes as translocal. Finally, Marjorie Kibby (2000) describes how an Internet-based music scene devoted to a particular folk artist, John Prine, flowered and died within two years. Participants in Internet chat rooms were delighted to find other fans scattered across the world with whom they could exchange information and opinions online, as well as via phone and in person if they so chose. In the process, they were able to create what Kibby (2000, 93) calls a "virtual place of music community" and what we will call a "virtual music scene."

Scenes and the Culture Industries

Scenes are often regarded as informal assemblages, but scenes that flourish become imbedded in a music industry. Typically, as Ken Spring shows in his chapter on the making of a rave scene in Ruston, this form of "industry" contrasts sharply with the corporate form dominated by a handful of media conglomerates. In the established corporate model, large firms produce, market, and distribute music, routinely referred to as "product," to an atomized mass of individual "consumers" (see Peterson 1990; Negus 1999;

Bennett 2000). Quite a different sort of music industry typically develops where there are music scenes at its core. This scene-supporting industry is largely the domain of small collectives, fans turned entrepreneurs, and volunteer labor. This sort of Do-It-Yourself (DIY) industry is an important site for researching the dynamics of music scenes and the music they produce (Smith and Maughan 1997).[1]

Much early research on the DIY industry focused on bands in Manchester in northwest England. During the early 1990s, research carried out by the Manchester Institute of Popular Culture (MIPC) on the local rave scene noted that illegal warehouse parties relied on informal networks of entrepreneurs who found and organized DJs and secured and transported the necessary sound and lighting equipment (see Redhead 1993; Hemment 1998). Further research by Smith and Maughan (1997) has demonstrated more fully the extent to which music production and performance at the local level has become an entrepreneurial activity. According to Smith and Maughan, the scale of such local music-making activities and various support networks is such that they constitute an alternative form of transnational music industry, coordinated by young people for whom such informal means of making a living are becoming an accepted norm as more conventional routes to vocational and economic success are increasingly blocked by unemployment and the casualization of labor. In his chapter in this volume, Tim Gosling shows how DIY band-driven record companies in the United States and the United Kingdom played a central role in the international spread of the anarcho-punk music scene.

The 1980s digital revolution and its impact upon the nature of the recording process facilitated the rapid development of this DIY music industry. Whereas high-quality recording facilities were once the sole property of extremely costly professional studios, digital and computer technology opened up new levels of access to the recording process. The creative potential of "amateur" musicians and producers has also been substantially enhanced by relatively cheap state-of-the-art technology (Ryan and Peterson 1994). Important in this respect is the digital program called Musical Instrument Digital Interface. It enables a musical instrument or sound to be electronically connected to a computer so that sounds can be manipulated and combined with an infinite number of *samples* of sounds made by other instruments or generated electronically. Thus, with relatively inexpensive equipment that can easily be set up and used in a bedroom or living room, it is possible to create a full band sound. "Studio quality" recording can now be made inexpensively in any location and without the need for supporting technical staff (Negus 1992; Ryan and Peterson 1994).

Easy access to such cheap but high-quality recording equipment has democratized the recording process and has allowed songwriters, solo artists, groups, and nonperforming music samplers to record their music without the financial backing of record companies. Such grassroots musical activities have been matched by the growth of an informal infrastructure designed to give the music of home and bedroom recording artists exposure in the public sphere. Thus, as Smith and Maughan explain, in addition to music making itself, the informal music industry comprises a range of support services, including "record labels, distribution companies, specialist record shops, agencies, artwork etc." (1997, 21). While researching dance music in Newcastle, U.K., Bennett (2000) discovered an alternative dance-music scene in the city generated entirely by informal economic networks. These networks were comprised of young people who, tired of the restrictive club-licensing laws in the city, created their own scene around house parties and local DJs.

The rapid development of the Internet beginning in the mid-1990s has facilitated the democratization of music making, its distribution, and increased fan communication. It has also made possible music file sharing among musicians and fans around the world. Internet-based Web pages make it possible for any enterprising band to get the latest word out about upcoming appearances and to promote its latest self-produced recordings without having to sign with a major record company. As a result, a lively scenelike exchange among fans can flourish, as is shown in the chapters by Steve Lee and Richard Peterson and by Andy Bennett.

Types of Scenes

Each scene is unique. Nonetheless, it is useful to recognize in this scatter several distinct types that share a number of characteristics in common. Of course many classifications are possible, but for the sake of this discussion and for the organization of the chapters that follow, we define three general types of scenes. The first, local scene, corresponds most closely with the original notion of a scene as clustered around a specific geographic focus. The second, translocal scene, refers to widely scattered local scenes drawn into regular communication around a distinctive form of music and lifestyle. The third, virtual scene, is a newly emergent formation in which people scattered across great physical spaces create the sense of scene via fanzines and, increasingly, through the Internet.

Local Scenes

Initial academic work on popular-music scenes considered the relationship between local music-making processes and the everyday life of specific communities, where the forms of music in question were seen as imbedded in long-standing local cultures. Cohen's (1991) research on the local music scene in the city of Liverpool, U.K., provides a highly insightful account of the ways in which local music-making practices correspond with issues of socioeconomic hardship, male camaraderie, creative desire, and spiritual escapism. Shank (1994) also focuses on a specific urban location in his study of the local music scene in Austin, Texas. Shank, however, refines Cohen's analysis of the relationship between music and locality through his consideration of the local as a space for multiple expressions of musical life, characterized by a series of coexisting scenes. He shows that while such scenes may conflict musically, visually, or both, each corresponds, albeit in different ways, with particularized local sensibilities of the city and the state. This is demonstrated by Shank through his examination of cowboy song and punk rock, musical styles which have very different historical and cultural associations with Austin, but which are linked through their offering of parallel, yet conflicting, discourses on Texan identity and local political attitudes.

Much recent work on local music scenes is less concerned with "organic" relationships between music and the cultural history of the locale than with the ways in which emergent scenes use music appropriated via global flows and networks to construct particular narratives of the local. Besides music, such narratives of emergent local identity incorporate aspects of other local cultural forms (Williams 1965), such as local dialect, dress, and history, as well as diverse forms of local knowledge, that are often used as strategies of resistance to local circumstances. For example, socioeconomic hardship, racism, sexism, personal identity, and the like, as these are experienced at a local level, are illustrated by Rob Drew in his chapter on karaoke in the United States and by Norman Urquia in his chapter on Salsa in London. In each case, music becomes part of a creative process whereby members of particular local scenes construct shared narratives of everyday life. As Harris observes: "Industrialisation and globalization have made available an increasingly large range of musical resources that have enabled a growing range of groups and individuals to use them in the construction of identity and location" (2000, 26).

A notable consequence of this approach to the study of scenes has been the equation of "scene" with "community." This device has been frequently employed in journalistic accounts, notably in relation to punk (see Frith 1983), to suggest that there are locally situated pockets of grassroots musical creativity distinct from global mainstream music styles. Thus, as Straw observes, while emergent musical styles in specific urban or rural locations may on the surface appear to constitute "moments of disengagement from the functioning of the international music industries," in reality such styles are the result of an "interlocking of local tendencies and cyclical transformations within the international music industries" (1991, 396, 370).

Recent work on hip-hop culture offers examples of such uses of global musics to construct particularized forms of local identity. Although early theorists suggested that hip-hop can be regarded as translocal culture, projecting urban U.S. black culture around the world (see, e.g., Gilroy 1993; Lipsitz 1994; Rose 1994), more empirically grounded studies of hip-hop have demonstrated highly particularized local reworkings of hip-hop that are used to engage with issues of race, identity, and place in various national and regional settings (see Mitchell 1996; Bennett 2000; Forman 2002).

To summarize, we view a local scene to be a focused social activity that takes place in a delimited space and over a specific span of time in which clusters of producers, musicians, and fans realize their common musical taste, collectively distinguishing themselves from others by using music and cultural signs often appropriated from other places, but recombined and developed in ways that come to represent the local scene. The focused activity we are interested in here, of course, centers on a particular style of music, but such music scenes characteristically involve other diverse lifestyle elements as well. These usually include a distinctive style of dancing, a particular range of psychoactive drugs, style of dress, politics, and the like.

Translocal Scenes

Often the most self-conscious local music scenes that focus on a particular kind of music are in regular contact with similar local scenes in distant places. They interact with each other through the exchange of recordings, bands, fans, and fanzines.[2] These we call translocal scenes because, while they are local, they are also connected with groups of kindred spirits many miles away. (See Harris 2000 and, in this volume, Kristen Schilt, Paul Hodkinson, and Tim Gosling on Riot Grrls, goths, and anarco-punks, respectively, as seen in these terms.)

Kruse (1993) considers alternative rock of the 1980s what we here call a translocal scene. While face-to-face interaction may form one aspect of the scene-building process—for example, in clubs and other local urban spaces—Kruse argues that equally important are the translocal properties of the music and its associated stylistic innovations. These serve to produce affective communities that transcend the need for face-to-face interaction as a necessary requirement for scene membership. A further example of the power of such translocal processes in the building of scenes is evident in the evolution of contemporary dance-music culture, which, as Laing observes, is sustained as much by "the flow of affinities across national and continental borders" as through a sense of belonging to a particular club crowd (1997, 130).

Ironically, global media messages can be the catalysts for what become intensely local scenes. The Beatlemania of the mid-1960s is an excellent case in point. Within months, teens around the world became acquainted with the band's sound, look, and deportment. At the same time, the teens reinterpreted the Beatles to fit the image and music of the band into their own cultural experience. Accordingly, a number of popular-music theorists reconsidered the relationship between the global and the local to recast the link between the localized innovations and the stream of globally available media products (Gebesmair and Smudits 2001). Slobin, for example, uses the concept of transregionalism to illustrate how such innovations emerge simultaneously in disparate local scenes across the world. Thus, argues Slobin: "Transregional musics have a very high energy that spills across regional boundaries, perhaps even becoming global. This category of musics is increasing rapidly due to the mediascape, which at any moment can push a music forward so that a large number of audiences can make the choice of domesticating it" (1993, 19). The complex interplays among local and global musics are represented by the authors anthologized by Gebesmair and Smudits (2001). The worldwide diffusion of hip-hop and its incorporation into a wide range of local scenes is an excellent case in point (see Mitchell 1996; Bjurström 1997; Condry 1999; Bennett 2000, 133–165).

The music festival is a special sort of translocal scene. While most such scenes involve the interconnection of several local scenes, festivals draw dispersed individuals together on designated occasions. "Festivals," as we mean the term here, are large multiday events that periodically bring together scene devotees from far and wide in one place, where they can enjoy their kind of music and briefly live the lifestyle associated with it with little concern for the expectations of others. Events are most likely to take on the characteristics of a scene if festivals take place over a number of days in a risk-free environment, such as a rural area, so that participants have a chance to enact the ways of life idealized within the scene free of the usual supports of urban life and away from other people and from the agents of social control. The rock festivals of the late 1960s and early 1970s were the largest and most spectacular (Peterson 1973), but the practice of festivals goes back to the early eighteenth century, when religious congregations held massive singing revival conventions. Adherents of bluegrass and other roots musics are most likely to hold festivals, but as Timothy Dowd, Kathleen Liddle, and Jenna Nelson show in their chapter here, feminists and marginalized devotees of classical music have regularly held festivals as well.

Another kind of translocal scene is created when a band's fans regularly follow their favorite musicians around the country from tour date to tour date and energize local devotees of the music and lifestyle. Such tours might best be called "music carnivals." The caravans of Deadheads who trek with the Grateful Dead are the model of such a scene, but a number of other jam bands have devoted followers who follow their tours. To date, such carnivals have not been studied from a scenes perspective, but the chapter by Dowd, Liddle, and Nelson describes a commercialized version of a carnival scene in the section on the SkatePunks who follow the annual Vans Warped Tour with their boards and BMX bikes and enjoy thrash punk over a weekend.

Virtual Scenes

In this age of electronic communication, fan clubs dedicated to specific artists, groups, and subgenres have proliferated by using the Internet to communicate with each other. Like the participants in translocal scenes, participants in virtual scenes are widely separated geographically, but unlike them, virtual scene participants around the world come together in a single scene-making conversation via the Internet. A chat room–based group devoted to the folk artist John Prine has been studied by Marjorie Kibby (2000). In this volume, Laura Vroomen also focuses on a virtual scene devoted to a single artist, Kate Bush; Lee and Peterson explore the dynamics of a listserv-based scene built around a subgenre, "alternative country music"; James Hodgkinson shows that fanzines fostered a post-rock virtual scene; and Bennett's chapter on the revival of the Canterbury Sound of the 1960s by Internet-based enthusiasts illustrates a virtual community whose focus is the nostalgia for rock associated with a particular English city.

Whereas a conventional local scene is kept in motion by a series of gigs, club nights, fairs, and similar events where fans converge, communicate, and reinforce their sense of belonging to a particular scene, the virtual scene involves direct Net-mediated person-to-person communication between fans, and the scene is therefore much more nearly in the control of fans. This may involve, for example, the creation of chat rooms or listservs dedicated to the scene and the trading of music and images online. Much chat room communication quickly descends into name-calling and flame wars, but the listservs of virtual scenes that last for any length of time evolve norms of communication; novices to the group are informed about the norms of civility, and there is the exchange of the kind of knowledge that Thornton (1995) refers to as "subcultural capital." Lee and Peterson in their chapter here explore the dynamics of this process as they study the life of a listserv-based virtual scene that has thrived since 1996. Among other findings, they learn that group members are sensitive to attempts by musicians and music industry members (the latter called "weasels") to promote their own work or the work of their artists via the listserv. Thus to a far greater extent than in other kinds of scenes, virtual scenes are devoted to the needs and interests of fans, and Net-based media that try to influence them tend to be quickly found out and censured.

Although the concept of virtual scene has been highlighted by the advent of the Internet, fanzines (Duncombe 1997) and other forms of niche media (Thornton 1995) have long served as an important resource for fans of particular genres of music, offering a channel of communication, for example, for the exchange of information about their favourite performers, performances, production techniques, and so on. Such media of communication can become the focus for intense local scenes. For example, McRobbie and Garber identified a strong teeny-bopper culture among teenage girls in Britain of the 1970s. Denied access to male subcultures and subject to paternal control stricter than that for their male peers, teenage girls constructed a teeny-bopper scene "around the territory available, . . . the home and the bedroom" (1976, 219). In such domestic spaces, teenage girls met, read pop-music magazines such as *Smash Hits* and *Jackie,* exchanged posters and pictures of pop stars, and discussed their personal preferences. In her chapter here, Melanie Lowe shows the continuing relevance of such scene formations; members of these scenes now use the Internet to talk about the appeal of contemporary pop artists such as Britney Spears. Similarly, Vroomen examines an Internet chat group to understand the taste patterns of the older female music fans of U.K. singer Kate Bush.

Introducing the Chapters

Since some people are more involved in a scene than others, and because scenes ebb and flow with time, there is no hard line between what is and what is not a scene. Consequently it is not useful to try to draw a hard line between scenes and nonscenes and between members and nonmembers. It seems more appropriate to see the degree to which a situation exhibits the characteristics we have discussed. The chapters in this volume describe situations with varying degrees of "sceneness." The three main parts of the book are devoted to the three types of scenes just discussed: local, translocal, and virtual. The article by Howard S. Becker, "Jazz Places," precedes the section on local scenes because his early ethnographic work on jazz musicians and the "worlds" in which they work was a major inspiration in the development of subcultural studies and of the scenes perspective.[3]

Notes

1. For our purposes it is sufficient to contrast the corporate music industry with the scene-based DIY industry. In fact, they are highly interdependent. The corporate industry needs the scene-based DIY industry to supply a steady flow of new talent that gives a veneer of authenticity to their "product," and the DIY industry relies on the technologies created by the corporate industry. The two forms intertwine and merge at a number of points. Some of the best work on these processes has focused on hip-hop and rap (see Negus 1999, 83–102; Forman 2002; Lena 2003).
2. Fanzines are newsletters created privately by fans who seek to share their opinions about a particular kind of music, musicians, or social concerns of common interest. Print runs are generally no more than a few hundred copies, and few last more than a couple of issues. This said, a few have importantly shaped particular scenes, as Kristen Schilt notes in her chapter on Riot Grrrls.
3. For an introduction to Howard Becker's relevant work, see Becker 1951, 1963, 1976, 1982.

References

Becker, Howard S. 1951. "The Professional Dance Musician and His Audience." *American Journal of Sociology* 57: 136–44.

———. 1963. *Outsiders: Studies in the Sociology of Deviance.* New York: Collier-Macmillan.

———. 1976. "Art Worlds and Social Types." In Richard A. Peterson, ed., *The Production of Culture.* Beverly Hills, Calif.: Sage.

———. 1982. *Art Worlds.* Berkeley: University of California Press.

Bennett, Andy. 1999. "Subcultures or Neo-Tribes? Rethinking the Relationship between Youth, Style, and Musical Taste." *Sociology* 333: 599–617.

———. 2000. *Popular Music and Youth Culture: Music, Identity, and Place.* London: Macmillan.

Bjurström, Erling. 1997. "The Struggle for Ethnicity: Swedish Youth Styles and the Construction of Ethnic Identities." *Young: Nordic Journal of Youth Research* 5: 44–58.

Bourdieu, Pierre. 1984. *Distinction: A Social Critique of the Judgement of Taste.* Translated by R. Nice. London: Routledge and Kegan Paul.

Chaney, David. 1996. *Lifestyles.* London: Routledge.

Clarke, Gary. 1990. "Defending Ski-Jumpers: A Critique of Theories of Youth Subcultures." In Simon Frith and Andrew Goodwin, eds., *On Record: Rock, Pop, and the Written Word.* London: Routledge. First published 1981 by University of Birmingham Centre for Contemporary Cultural Studies.

Cohen, Sara. 1991. *Rock Culture in Liverpool: Popular Music in the Making.* Oxford: Clarendon Press.

Condry, Ian. 1999. "The Social Production of Difference: Imitation and Authenticity in Japanese Rap Music." In H. Fehrenbach and U. Poiger, eds., *Transactions, Transgressions, Transformations: American Culture in Western Europe and Japan,* Providence, R.I.: Berghan Books.

Denisoff, R. Serge, and Richard A. Peterson, eds. 1972. *The Sounds of Social Change.* Chicago: Rand-McNally.

DeVeaux, Scott. 1997. *The Birth of Bebop: A Social and Musical History.* Berkeley: University of California Press.

Duncombe, Stephen. 1997. *Notes from Underground: Zines and the Politics of Alternative Culture.* London: Verso.

Forman, Murray. 2002. *The Hood Comes First: Race, Space, and Place in Rap and Hip-Hop.* Hanover, N.H.: Wesleyan University Press.

Frith, Simon. 1983. *Sound Effects: Youth, Leisure, and the Politics of Rock.* London: Constable.

———. 1996. *Performing Rites: On the Value of Popular Music.* Cambridge: Harvard University Press.

Gaines, Donna. 1994. "The Local Economy of Suburban Scenes." In Jonathon S. Epstein, ed., *Adolescents and Their Music: If It's Too Loud, You're Too Old.* New York: Garland.

Gebesmair, Andreas, and Alfred Smudits, eds. 2001. *Global Repertories: Popular Music within and beyond the Transnational Music Industry.* Aldershot, U.K.: Ashgate.

Gelder, Ken, and Sarah Thornton, eds. 1997. *The Subcultures Reader.* London: Routledge.

Gilroy, Paul. 1993. *The Black Atlantic: Modernity and Double Consciousness.* London: Verso.

Harris, Keith. 2000. " 'Roots?' The Relationship between the Global and the Local within the Extreme Metal Scene." *Popular Music* 191: 13–30.

Hemment, D. 1998. "Dangerous Dancing and Disco Riots: The Northern Warehouse Parties." In George McKay, ed., *DiY Culture: Party and Protest in Nineties Britain.* London: Verso.

Jarviluoma, Helmi. 2000. "From Manchuria to the Traditional Village: On the Construction of Place via Pelimanni Music." *Popular Music* 191: 101–124.

Kibby, Marjorie D. 2000. "Home on the Page: A Virtual Place of Music Community." *Popular Music* 191: 91–100.

Kruse, Holly. 1993. "Subcultural Identity in Alternative Music Culture." *Popular Music* 121: 31–43.

Laing, Dave. 1985. *One Chord Wonders: Power and Meaning in Punk Rock.* Milton Keynes, U.K.: Open University Press.

———. 1997. "Rock Anxieties and New Music Networks." In Angela McRobbie, ed., *Back to Reality: Social Experience and Cultural Studies.* Manchester, U.K.: Manchester University Press.

Lee, Steven. 1995. "Re-examining the Concept of the 'Independent' Record Company: The Case of Wax Trax! Records." *Popular Music* 141: 13–32.

Lena, Jennifer C. 2003. "From 'Flash' to 'Cash': Producing Rap Authenticity, 1979 to 1995." PhD diss., Columbia University.

Lipsitz, George. 1994. *Dangerous Crossroads: Popular Music, Postmodernism, and the Poetics of Place.* London: Verso.

McRobbie, Angela, and Jenny Garber. 1976. "Girls and Subcultures: An Exploration." In Stuart Hall and Tony Jefferson, eds., *Resistance through Rituals: Youth Subcultures in Post-War Britain.* London: Hutchinson.

Mitchell, Tony. 1996. *Popular Music and Local Identity: Rock, Pop, and Rap in Europe and Oceania.* London: Leicester University Press.

Negus, Keith. 1992. *Producing Pop: Culture and Conflict in the Popular Music Industry.* London: Edward Arnold.

———. 1999. *Music Genres and Corporate Cultures.* Routledge: London.

Olson, Ted. 1999. "Hippie Hootenanny: Gram Parsons and the Not-Quite-Nashville Cats." *Journal of Country Music* 203: 26–36.

Peterson, Richard A. 1973. "The Unnatural History of Rock Festivals: An Instance of Media Facilitation." *Popular Music and Society* 2: 1–26.

———. 1978. "Disco! Its Distinctive Sound Isn't Just Another Fad." *Chronicle of Higher Education,* 21 May, sec. 2, 26–27.

————. 1990. "Why 1955? Explaining the Advent of Rock Music." *Popular Music* 9: 97–116.

————. 1994. "Culture Studies through the Production Perspective: Progress and Prospects." In Diana Crane, ed., *The Sociology of Culture*. Oxford: Blackwell.

————. 1997. *Creating Country Music: Fabricating Authenticity*. Chicago: University of Chicago Press.

Redhead, Steve, ed. 1993. *Rave Off: Politics and Deviance in Contemporary Youth Culture*. Andershot, U.K.: Avebury.

Rose, Tricia. 1994. *Black Noise: Rap Music and Black Culture in Contemporary America*. Hanover, N.H.: Wesleyan University Press.

Ryan, John, and Richard A. Peterson. 1994. "Occupational and Organizational Consequences of the Digital Revolution in Music Making." In Muriel Cantor and Sherell Zollars, eds., *Creators of Culture*. Greenwich, Conn.: JAI Press.

Shank, Barry. 1994. *Dissonant Identities: The Rock 'n' Roll Scene in Austin, Texas*. London: Wesleyan University Press.

Slobin, Mark. 1993. *Subcultural Sounds: Micromusics of the West*. London: Wesleyan University Press.

Smith, Richard, and Tim Maughan. 1997. "Youth Culture and the Making of the Post-Fordist Economy: Dance Music in Contemporary Britain." Occasional paper. London: Department of Social Policy and Social Science, Royal Holloway, University of London.

Straw, Will. 1991. "Systems of Articulation, Logics of Change: Communities and Scenes in Popular Music." *Cultural Studies* 53: 368–388.

Thornton, Sara. 1995. *Club Cultures: Music, Media, and Subcultural Capital*. Cambridge: Polity Press.

Urry, John. 1990. *The Tourist Gaze: Leisure and Travel in Contemporary Societies*. London: Sage.

Wellman, Barry, and Milena Gulia. 1999. "Virtual Communities as Communities." In Marc A. Smith and Peter Kollock, eds., *Communities in Cyberspace*. London: Routledge.

Williams, Raymond. 1965. *The Long Revolution*. London: Pelican.

Jazz Places

Howard S. Becker

> Still, there will come a time . . . when nothing will be of more
> interest than authentic reminiscences of the past. Much of it
> will be made up of subordinate "memoirs," and of personal
> chronicles and gossip—but we think every portion of it will
> always meet a welcome from the large mass of . . . readers.
> —Henry M. Christman, *Walt Whitman's New York*

Every artwork has to be someplace. Physical works, like paintings and sculptures, have to be housed someplace: a museum, a gallery, a home, a public square. Music and dance and theater have to be performed someplace: a court, a theater or concert hall, a private home, a public square or street. Books and similar materials take up space too—in bookstores and distributors' warehouses and people's homes. What places are available to exhibit or perform or keep and enjoy works in? Who is in charge of them and responsible for them? How does this organization of place constrain the work done there? What opportunities does it make available? I'll restrict myself to the case of twentieth-century jazz, for the most part in the United States, for the somewhat unrespectable reason that this is a subject I know well. And I will rely on my own memory, as well as on what scholarship is available.

Jazz has always been very dependent on the availability of places to perform it in. For much of its existence, jazz was played in bars and nightclubs and dance halls, places where the money to support the entire enterprise came mostly from the sale of alcohol and secondarily from the sale of tickets. So the availability of places for the performance of jazz depended on the viability and profitability of such places. Thus, one of the great centers of jazz development—Kansas City in the 1920s and 1930s—drew its vitality from the political corruption which made nightlife profitable:

> Kansas City jazz prospered while most of America suffered the catastrophe of the Great Depression, largely because of the corrupt but economically stimulating administration of Boss Tom Pendergast. Through a combination of labor-intensive public works programs (many of which closely resembled later New Deal programs), deficit spending, and the tacit sanction of massive corruption, Pendergast created an economic oasis in Kansas City. Vice was a major part of this system and gave a strong, steady cash flow to the city. Jazz was the popular social music of the time, and the centers of vice—nightclubs and gambling halls—usually hired musicians to attract customers. The serendipitous result was plentiful, if low-paying, jobs for jazz musicians from throughout the Midwest and an outpouring of great new music. (Pearson 1987, xvii)

Pearson says that "over three hundred Kansas City clubs featured live music, and many also included floor shows." And he explains the consequence: "the constant jam sessions and warm socializing that thrived in nightclubs. K.C. in the thirties enjoyed a remarkable musical community that largely existed in and around its clubs" (ibid., 107). He quotes Count Basie:

> Oh my, marvelous town. Clubs, clubs, clubs, clubs, clubs, clubs, clubs, clubs. As a matter of fact, I thought that was all Kansas City was made up of, was clubs at one time. . . . I mean, the cats just played. They played all day and tomorrow morning they went home and went to bed. The next day, the same thing. We'd go to one job we'd play on, then go jamming until seven, eight in the morning. (108)

In a setting like that, musical innovation flourished. The jam sessions allowed an experimentation with new forms and ideas, and the chance to improvise at length, to play far beyond the time allowed by a disc or a dance set. There was no audience or the audience no longer cared what they were listening to.

The setting for Kansas City jazz changed radically in later years. Boss Pendergast went to prison for corruption and, by the 1950s, when I arrived there, that thriving jazz scene was comparatively dead.

Innovations in venues can lead to new playing opportunities. Musical innovation began to move out of clubs. Jazz was becoming an art music, no longer an accompaniment for dancing and drinking, but rather a music people listened to attentively in a quiet setting, supported entirely by the synergistic sale of recordings and tickets—the concert hall, where people came to hear the groups they had learned to appreciate from recordings. I don't know whether the claim is justified, but Dave Brubeck's biographer traces this development of the "college tour," in which a small musical group could travel around the United States performing on the college campuses found everywhere, to Brubeck's wife's desire to see more of him at home:

> Iola one day came up with an entirely new concept that quite incidentally revolutionized the old one-nighter, road-trip concept. She searched the list of colleges and universities in the *World Almanac* for every institution on the West Coast, and personally wrote to more than one hundred of them, suggesting the Brubeck Quartet as a great entertainment for campus concerts, citing their recordings and reviews. So successful did these events become that they spread nationwide and opened an entirely new avenue for expression and income for jazz groups everywhere. Before that, many bands had played college dances and fraternity parties, but very few concerts. (Hall 1996, 50)

College campuses contained large numbers of bored young people, most of whom had an interest in popular music and some of whom were jazz fans. Between the two, you could sell enough tickets to fill a medium-sized auditorium and thus pay the expenses and salaries of such a traveling operation. And students came to the concerts because they wanted to hear Brubeck play the kind of jazz they had become acquainted with through his recordings. The recordings created an audience for live performance, and the live performances created an audience for the records. In these university concert halls, Brubeck could play music that was undanceable, like his experiments with unconventional (for jazz) time signatures like 5/4 ("Take Five") or 9/4 ("Blue Rondo à la Turk"). He could play at whatever length pleased him and indulge the experiments of his colleagues as well. The people who bought the tickets had come to hear him do just that. The place made the musical opportunity.

Now I'll add my own memories, which take place on a smaller stage and deal with more specific, detailed, and much less impressive variations and results, but which illustrate further the general point that where jazz players perform affects what they perform.

Before I do that, I should define, informally, what I mean by a "place." It is, first of all, a physical place: a building (or part of one), or an enclosed place in the open air. But it is also a physical place that has been socially defined: defined by its expected uses, by shared expectations about what kinds of people will be there to take part in those activities, and by the financial arrangements that underlie all of this. And defined further by a larger social context that both provides opportunities and sets limits to what can happen. A place, so defined, can be as large as a city (as large as Kansas City in the earlier descriptions) or as small as a nightclub or concert hall. And, of course, we must recognize, as the story of Kansas City illustrates, that places change more or less continuously. What can be played in a place will vary as well.

I played the piano in Chicago in the '40s and early '50s, a time when live popular music was performed in hundreds of public places by professional players who were paid for their services. The entrepreneurs who owned and managed these places (the word "venue" has now become a general term for performing places) had a variety of motives for their activity, but in general the presentation of music was a business activity undertaken for profit. To be profitable, these places had to attract patrons who would pay something to hear the music played, either directly or by buying liquor. So the music my colleagues and I played had to be acceptable to the bosses we worked for and to their customers. If it wasn't, we were fired, or not hired again, and someone who played more acceptably took our place.

What kinds of public places were there in Chicago then for the performance of jazz? Who went to them and what did they want? What kinds of music did we get to play? I will present this picture in some detail and discuss some alternative ways of organizing jazz performance that existed then or have grown up since, and how those changes affected what was played. It's important to understand that the organizations I will describe no longer exist and that much of what now seems "natural," the only possible way these things could be done, was not then in existence.

A preliminary point. There were very few places then devoted to playing jazz without apology or disguise, "jazz clubs" where you went because some form of jazz was being played and you wanted to hear it. There were almost no "jazz concerts" or presentations. A few clubs presented Dixieland music (I have forgotten their names, since this was not a kind of music I cared for), and one or two clubs in the Loop (the city center), such as the Blue Note, presented small jazz groups. Several large clubs, some of them in the major hotels, presented big bands, many of whom played one or an-

The Bobby Lain Trio, appearing at the 504 Club, 504 W. 63rd St. Chicago, circa 1950. Bobby Lain, saxophone; Dominic Jaconetty, drums; Howie Becker, piano.

other version of big-band jazz, although always for dancing, as well as for listening. So Duke Ellington occasionally appeared at the Boulevard Room of the Stevens Hotel, and a succession of major bands—Woody Herman, Benny Goodman, Count Basie, Cab Calloway, Tommy Dorsey, among others—appeared at the Sherman Hotel's Panther Room. Les Brown and Bob Crosby occasionally played at the Blackhawk. In the late '40s and early '50s, a number of bars presented well-known players fronting small groups of five or six players—Miles Davis at the Crown Propeller Lounge on Sixty-third Street, Charlie Parker at the Argyle Show Lounge. These groups did play for people who paid especially to hear them play some form of jazz. All these places presented performers from outside Chicago, groups more or less well known to the relatively small group of Chicago jazz fans, many of whom were themselves working musicians.

I did not play in any of the places that presented jazz, nor did most of my colleagues. We performed (we would have said, "We worked") in a variety of commercial entertainment venues, which took several forms. We played for "private parties," that is, entertainments presented by private persons or groups for the pleasure of their members and guests: Weddings, bar mitzvah parties, and parties given by organizations for their members were the most common kinds. These typically took place in establishments rented for the occasion: a country club, a hotel ballroom, an ethnic meeting hall, a church social hall. The hosts typically provided food, most often prepared by a commercial caterer, and music, provided by a small band made up (though our employers usually didn't know this) of musicians hired for the occasion, who might never have worked together before.

We called these performances "jobbing dates." Or, more simply, "jobs." (The term varied from city to city; in other cities they might be called "casuals" or "club dates.") The bandleader the party givers had hired had a stake in providing suitable entertainment, because he hoped to have the hosts recommend him to other party givers. But the musicians themselves (the "sidemen") only wanted to do a good enough job that the bandleader would hire them again or recommend them to some other leader. The band could be as few as three people or as many as fifteen. The smaller groups mainly improvised; the larger groups often had a large library of arrangements written for their extended instrumentation. (You could buy printed arrangements that could be played by groups of from five to fifteen instrumentalists; these were known as "stock arrangements.") There were, of course, many more jobs for small groups than for large ones.

What we played on such occasions varied with the class, age, and ethnicity of the group attending the party. Wedding customs of ethnic groups vary substantially, often requiring special music. If we played for an Italian wedding, we had to be prepared to play "Come Back to Sorrento," "O Sole Mio," and some tarantellas, to which the older people danced enthusiastically. A Polish wedding called for polkas. Some ethnic groups' musical requirements were too exotic for the average player, and a special ethnic band might be hired in addition. So one night when I played for an Assyrian wedding, an Assyrian band made up of a tenor banjo and a tambourine alternated with us. We played for "American" dancing, and they played for the more traditional dances, in which the families of the bride and groom competed to give money to dancers from "their side." Greek music was difficult for most of us too, since most of it was played in unfamiliar—to us—time signatures like 5/4 (which became more familiar after Dave Brubeck recorded "Take Five").

Many kinds of bands existed in this setup. Some came together for only the one occasion, that night's job, the personnel being chosen ad hoc, perhaps even, in those days, at the local union hall, where musicians would assemble to look for work, and leaders for players. Some groups were more established, and much the same personnel assembled night after night to play the same material.

The usual party lasted three hours. That, at least, was what we were usually hired for, although a lively party might provoke the host into splurging on an extra hour or so. We played perhaps forty-five minutes or more out of every hour, and played music that people could dance to (which meant not too fast) and that they recognized. We usually played a mixture of currently popular songs from the "hit parade" and older "standards" chosen from the ever-growing collection of tunes musicians liked to play, often ones that had been played on recordings by jazz players we liked. We almost never played "straight" jazz songs, that is, songs like the ones Count Basie's band invented for itself and recorded, which were not known to the general public.

Because people were dancing and might want to change partners, we stopped and started frequently, seldom playing more than three choruses of anything (which is to say three times thirty-two bars, that being the number of bars in the conventional popular songs we played, or ninety-six bars). We varied the tempos but of course never played the very fast tempos a lot of jazz players liked to play. And we usually played the melody or something that didn't depart too much from it. This limited how much "jazz," however defined, we could play on a jobbing date. Not much. At best, one of us might improvise a chorus of the song we were playing, never straying too far from the melody.

There were some exceptions to this rule, reflecting the influence of ethnic and age differences. I worked for perhaps a year with a band called Jimmy Dale, actually led by Harold Fox, who had a custom-tailoring establishment where he made suits mainly for criminals, police, entertainers, and musicians. Harold was a (very bad) trumpet player, but his shop brought him into contact with many well-known bands, for whom he made matching suits that they wore as uniforms. He persuaded many bandleaders to let him use their bands' arrangements (we called them "charts") for the fifteen-piece band that was his hobby. (I call it a hobby because he often lost money on an engagement, getting paid for ten or twelve people although he hired and paid fifteen.) We thus played the same arrangements as several of the well-known jazz-oriented big bands of the era, especially Basie, Woody Herman, and Stan Kenton.

The band was racially mixed, which in segregated Chicago in 1950 was unique. Places that catered to white audiences seldom wanted black players, and never wanted a racially mixed band, which openly defied well-understood patterns of segregation. As a result, we played only for black dances and parties (with the exception of the meat cutters union, which was also racially mixed). These difficulties were increased, in ways I never completely understood, by the racial segregation of the musicians union.

This band mainly played for large dances in ballrooms. On occasion we played for a formal dance (tails and evening gowns) given by one of the fraternities for adults that were a feature of the upper reaches of Chicago's black society. Mainly, however, we played in places where people paid at the door and bought drinks from the bar, for instance, the Savoy Ballroom, the Parkway Ballroom, and the ballroom at the Sutherland Hotel. The audiences were entirely black and usually young and enthusiastic. They liked our hip big-band sound. There were some difficulties for me, because the audiences often had favorites that had to be played exactly as they were played on the recordings that the originating bands had made. So I was required to play Eddie Heywood's solo on "Begin the Beguine" exactly as Heywood had played it, and similarly with Avery Parrish's famous piano solo on Erskine Hawkins's "After Hours," and Stan Kenton's grandiose solo on "Concerto to End All Concertos."

But this was unusual. A smaller variation from the standard pattern, which allowed some accommodation between our desire to play jazz and what our audiences wanted, occurred when we played for Jewish audiences. Stereotypically, and often enough in fact (for reasons I don't know), these audiences liked to dance to Latin American music: rumbas, sambas, mambos. Bands like Tito Puente had made the mambo, especially, desirable to jazz players; we felt that these songs "swung" in a way that ordinary popular music, played as people wanted to hear it, didn't. The same thing happened some years later when the bossa nova became popular enough for that Brazilian form of jazz to be acceptable to dancers.

We (I'm still talking about the ordinary, nonfamous musicians, of whom I was one) also played "steady jobs," or "gigs," in bars and taverns and clubs, which were open to the general public, and which made their money by selling drinks. The numbers and kinds of such bars and clubs varied from city to city, as a result of local laws that governed the sale of liquor, and the general demand for these services. Chicago, laid out on a grid, had eight parallel streets to the mile, both east-west and north-south. Every half mile, the street was a "major" street, wider than the others and usually with some form of public transportation on it. Where major streets, and their accompanying transportation facilities of buses and trams, crossed, a "major intersection" provided commercial facilities. These intersections often had several bars and—in the time I am speaking of, before television provided the major form of entertainment in bars—at least one and often more had live music, usually a trio or a quartet.

None of the musicians who played in these neighborhood bars were well known enough to attract people who wanted to hear them play jazz in sufficient numbers to satisfy a club owner. So we played for whoever came into the bar, people who had come there to drink and see their friends. Many of the bars we played in catered to a very local trade, people who knew one another and who "hung out" in this club, among others. We provided background noise for the socializing that went on in the bar.

Such venues had their advantages for us as would-be jazz players. People did sometimes request a specific song, which we then had to play so that it could be recognized, which meant no extensive improvising, staying close to the melody. But people sitting at the bar usually paid very little attention to the band or to what we played. Since they weren't dancing, tempos didn't matter and we could play as fast as—well, as fast we could play, if we wanted to.

People in the bar sometimes really didn't care at all what we played, and therefore the bar owner didn't care either, and we could indulge ourselves in playing the kinds of jazz we wanted to play. I worked in a few clubs where, late in the evening, the boss let us welcome to the stand other musicians who had finished their jobbing dates, and an old-fashioned jam session would take place. Then we would play like people did in the legendary jazz clubs of the East or West Coasts. Every player on the stand took long solos, several choruses at least, just like on the records made by the famous players we idolized. We played songs no one in the audience had ever heard of in styles that were unfamiliar to them as well. This didn't happen often, but when it did we prized our luck.

We played a lot in these clubs. At the time I speak of, some Chicago clubs had a license that allowed them to stay open until two in the morning; others had a more expensive license that let them stay open until four. So we played, usually, from nine in the evening until two or four in the morning, either six nights a week or just the three weekend nights. For a young player like me, this was a form of practicing, and it was crucial to the development of technical skills and, more importantly, improvising skills. We played over and over the songs that were the basis of the jazz repertoire, hundreds of times in a year, so that improvising on their chords became effortless and we had countless opportunities to experiment with melody and harmony and rhythm.

Some of the clubs we played had "entertainment," mainly striptease dancers. This was a sophisticated and legal way of extracting money from members of the army and navy on temporary leave, from convention goers out for a big night on the town, and from people who for whatever reason wanted to look at some almost nude women. The dancers might request certain songs but never had actual scores for us to play from. Still, we had to play in a sort of stop-and-start pattern, accompanying the removal of their costumes, that wasn't really conducive to jazz improvisation.

I occasionally worked at places that had real entertainment: "acts," which is to say people who performed as singers, "real" dancers, magicians, jugglers, or comedians. They sometimes had written or printed scores we had to play more or less as written, without rehearsal. Since their music was usually quite conventional, that was never difficult, except when the scores were so faded we couldn't read them. There was seldom any room for anything resembling jazz.

A few venues featured well-known jazz players from elsewhere, but those jobs were never available to people like me. I studied jazz piano with Lennie Tristano, a Chicagoan who soon moved to New York, where the opportunities were somewhat better, and I don't think he ever worked more than a few nights anywhere in Chicago.

But most of what musicians like me played was "commercial" music, meant for dancing (at a party or in a club or ballroom) or as background noise in a bar or club. We played most of the jazz we played by sneaking it into the performance of other kinds of music we had been hired to play.

In short, our repertoire and style of playing were completely dictated by the circumstances of the places we played in. We knew what we wanted to do, which was to play like our heroes—in my day, the big bands of Basie, Herman, and others, the small bands of Gillespie, Parker, Stan Getz, and so on. But we seldom could do that. Most of the time we played what the "place"—the combination of physical space and social and financial ar-rangements—made possible.

That was Chicago as I knew it. Shortly after I left Chicago in the early '50s, everything changed. Television became the major form of entertain-ment in neighborhood bars, and the places that had formed the basis of my brief career were no longer available.

The obvious and important conclusion to be drawn from this lengthy exposition of the possibilities for jazz playing in Chicago is that a big city can house a great variety of smaller places, each providing its own combination of circumstances that affect what the musicians in it can do. Most of them, almost all, will be places neither totally hospitable to jazz as its most enthusiastic adherents would like to hear it nor devoid of possibilities for occasionally playing "the real thing." Which means, in turn, that most musicians, playing in the full range of places available, played in a complex and varied repertoire of styles, each its own variation on what the popular music of the day offered.

And it means that it would be wise to guess, in trying to understand the output of any player or group, that what they did in one place affected what they did in another, so that the music of even a very serious jazz group might bear the traces of the less than pure music they had played in some other place on some other night. Careful listening usually reveals some traces of all those other kinds of music, from strip joint to church, in any jazz player's output.

And that means, finally, that it is not accurate to divide musicians into such groups as jazz players, commercial players, and so on. These are better thought of as ways of playing, ways of doing the job. Some people might have engaged in only one form of that activity, like the "honorable" one that is called "jazz," and never have participated in the less honorable versions of the trade, the playing for weddings and bar mitzvahs and fashion shows and dances that were the customary fare of someone who made a living playing popular music. Generalized, this is an empirically based warning against too facilely substituting a classification of people for one of activities.

Notes

The chapter epigraph is from Henry M. Christman, ed., *Walt Whitman's New York: A Collection of Walt Whitman's Journalism Celebrating New York from Manhattan to Montauk* (New York: Macmillan, 1963).

References

Hall, Fred M. 1996. *It's About Time*. Fayetteville: University of Arkansas Press.

Pearson, Nathan W., Jr. 1987. *Goin' to Kansas City*. Urbana: University of Illinois Press.

PART I

Local Scenes

1

The Symbolic Economy of Authenticity in the Chicago Blues Scene

David Grazian

During the first half of the twentieth century, Chicago blues music helped to define a certain kind of urban life for local blacks seeking refuge and entertainment in the South Side and West Side neighborhoods where they worked and resided. But during the 1960s, blues music would develop as a viable moneymaker in a handful of the city's white neighborhoods as well. In the 1960s, the emergence of the folk music revival brought many of Chicago's bluesmen to pseudobohemian pubs and countercultural clubs in gentrifying neighborhood areas such as Lincoln Park. By the mid-1980s, the patronage of these clubs gave way to a flood of suburbanites and tourists in search of the globally diffused cultural images made popular not only by internationally successful blues legends like Muddy Waters and Junior Wells, but also by blues-rock icons such as Eric Clapton and the Allman Brothers, and Hollywood motion pictures like *The Blues Brothers*. In recent years, the commodification of the city's local blues scene has exploded into a full-blown tourism industry, and the blues music once made popular by classic standards such as Robert Johnson's "Sweet Home Chicago" can be heard throughout the week in more than fifty venues located not just in predominantly black neighborhoods, but in all areas of the city: South Side, North Side, West Side, and the downtown area, known locally as the Loop.

Urban entertainment zones are dense commercial areas of the city that feature a concentration of businesses oriented toward particular kinds of leisure activities, such as dining and dancing. From Bronzeville to the Loop, entertainment zones have always served as anchors for Chicago's blues clubs (Reckless 1933). In part, these clubs rely on the reputation and drawing power of their entertainment zones to attract patrons with specific kinds of consumer tastes. Downtown clubs attempt to draw affluent tourists and business travelers; established clubs in neighborhoods that surround the downtown hub attract a mix of tourists and city residents; off-the-beaten-path venues draw on an exclusive patronage of Chicago residents; and small local bars serve regulars who reside on neighboring streets. By establishing niche-based commercial districts that consist of businesses that offer similar kinds of social and aesthetic experiences, local entrepreneurs transform urban neighborhoods into nocturnal playgrounds ripe for specific kinds of cultural consumption.

However, to fully comprehend how cultural commerce operates in the city, one must also understand how consumers *themselves* invest entertainment zones and other spaces in the city with personal significance and import. Urban dwellers adopt neighborhood terrains for themselves by reconstructing their spatial identities and reputations through active strategies of consumption. In the case of the Chicago blues scene, tourists and residents alike evaluate local clubs according to the reputations and images which their entertainment zones evoke vis-à-vis other areas of the city, and organize their consumption accordingly. Because consumers frequently grow anxious and skeptical about the intense commercialization of tourist-oriented clubs, they often seek out what they perceive to be the "authenticity" found in venues in neighborhoods outside the city's central entertainment district, and they value those clubs over their downtown counterparts.

The search for authenticity in the urban milieu presents a fascinating example of the social production of collective meaning and myth. In spite of the importance placed on authenticity by cultural consumers in the postmodern era, sociologists and historians serve us well by reminding us that authenticity itself represents little more than a "fabrication" and "invention" (MacCannell 1976; Hobsbawm and Ranger 1983; Peterson 1997). Like similarly loaded terms such as "community," "authenticity" is not so much an objective quality that exists in time and space as it is a shared belief about the nature of the places and moments most valued in any given social context. Likewise, since authenticity is as subjective as any other

Photo by Joe Carey

social value, it follows that different kinds of audiences measure authenticity according to somewhat divergent sets of criteria, and therefore find it in somewhat remote types of cultural experiences (see Cohen 1988). As authenticity, like beauty, can truly exist only in the eye of the beholder, the search for authenticity is rarely a quest for some actual material thing, but rather for what consumers in a particular social milieu imagine the symbols of authenticity to be.

Along these lines, participants in Chicago's blues subculture invest in a network of signs and spaces that one could call a *symbolic economy of authenticity*, in which various interpretative communities evaluate local music scenes according to multiple definitions of authenticity. According to many consumers, clubs located in transitional entertainment zones with romantic and storied reputations seem less commercialized and thus more special than those in the downtown area. Since local tastemakers organize the city's blues clubs and their entertainment zones along a sliding scale of authenticity from the most seemingly "mainstream" to those they consider the most authentic and hip, tourists begin their search by patronizing clubs located downtown and work their way toward the outer limits of the city center until they reach what they imagine to be a satisfactory level of authenticity.

This sliding scale of authenticity not only represents how musicians, consumers, and cultural critics manufacture authenticity through their reliance on stereotypes and urban myths, but also demonstrates how they rank venues and their locales in relation to one another according to those subjective measures. For example, *spatially* marginalized entertainment districts in transitional areas may depend on *socially* peripheral yet romantic identities for their survival by serving as ideological counterpoints to more centrally located and less risqué nocturnal zones. Likewise, just as working-class subcultural scenes frequently establish reputations based on what consumers imagine to be a heightened sense of exoticism and authenticity, late-night revelers frequently seek out these dramatic spaces of entertainment in the hopes of increasing their own nocturnal status as consumers. In the case of Chicago blues music, consumers draw on highly elaborated images of local place and racial difference when comparing local clubs in terms of their alleged authenticity, and direct their consumption on the basis of those stereotypes.

Studying the Chicago Blues Scene

I first discovered the world of the Chicago blues for myself during my first year of graduate school as a student at the University of Chicago. In a way, the city's blues clubs represented a place where I could take a break from the world of sociology, free from the rigorous demands of the academic world and the drabness of the university library. But despite my best efforts, over time I discovered that the Chicago blues scene provided an ideal laboratory for analyzing cultural processes in the urban milieu, at least in comparison to the sterile and bookish environment of the university. Consequently, I began conducting intensive ethnographic fieldwork at a local North Side blues bar, appropriately (if unimaginatively) named B.L.U.E.S. That activity transformed the world of the blues club from my space of leisure into a research site for social inquiry.

On multiple evenings during the week, I would arrive at the club shortly after its house band began its first set, order a beer, and strike up open-ended barroom conversations with musicians, bartenders, tourists, bar regulars, and club owners, during which I would ask them about their tastes in music, expectations of the club, and reflections on the contemporary Chicago blues scene. At the same time, I would document the club surroundings, with special attention to the onstage performances of the entertainers. After a certain point in the research, I began playing the alto saxophone at a number of jam sessions at various nearby clubs, and that participant-observatory fieldwork offered me the opportunity to observe the world of the blues club from the point of view of its stage musicians.

At a certain point, I realized that my emphasis on B.L.U.E.S., while providing me with an increasingly familiar space in which to conduct my research, could hinder my ability to accurately depict the variation among blues clubs in other regions of the city. To supplement my ethnographic study of this venue, I conducted additional observations in thirty-six blues-oriented bars, nightclubs, restaurants, and cafés in an ethnically diverse range of neighborhoods and entertainment zones throughout the city. This expansion of the study brought me to places like the Checkerboard Lounge, a well-worn tavern in Bronzeville, one of the city's historic black districts, as well as a series of downtown tourist attractions such as Blue Chicago, Buddy Guy's Legends, and the House of Blues. By extending my research to these clubs, I intended to compare and contrast how audiences and participants experienced their different environments, and where they located these clubs within their own mental maps of the city's entertainment landscape. (For a further elaboration of my methodological approach, see Grazian 2003.)

I rely on the ethnographic research in this chapter to explore how cultural producers and consumers in different spatial contexts within Chicago generate myths of authenticity through appropriating and exploiting symbols of black culture and urban space. Specifically, I compare the reputations of blues clubs located in three entertainment zones: the downtown area surrounding the Loop, the affluent North Side neighborhood of Lincoln Park, and the black working-class neighborhood of Grand Boulevard on the city's South Side. At clubs ranging from B.L.U.E.S. to the Checkerboard Lounge, observations and barroom conversations reveal how participants rely on stereotypical images of authenticity when comparing local clubs and their entertainment zones along a sliding scale of urban authenticity, and draw on such definitions of place when consuming blues music in these areas.

Downtown Blues

The bright lights of downtown Chicago draw tourists into a world of consumption, where theme-park restaurants and crowd-pleasing entertainment meccas like Planet Hollywood and the Hard Rock Cafe (see Sorkin 1992; Hannigan 1998) have transformed a once homegrown commercial zone into a playground of brand-name kitsch. This commodified milieu envelops the city's downtown blues clubs, which, like their nearby counterparts, rely on themed images, logos, and catchy menu selections to attract tourists into their nonthreatening environments. As just one example, Joe's Be-Bop Cafe and Jazz Emporium hosts vacationers who enjoy blues piano and jazz combo sets over Duke Ellington Baby Back Ribs with Joe's Sideman Be-Bop BBQ Sauce, Blow Hard Garlic Bread, and Banana Lama Ding Dong Smoothies.

Elsewhere, local blues performers exploit their celebrity to market tourist-oriented clubs, ranging from the popular Buddy Guy's Legends to the recently revived Koko Taylor's Celebrity. Meanwhile, in the sleek atmosphere of Blue Chicago, affluent international tourists from Germany and Italy sip cocktails while listening to local characters like Eddy "the Chief" Clearwater sing the blues. Posters and framed photographs cover the walls, along with paintings that feature black caricatures of shouting blueswomen and carnivalesque scenes of southern juke joints. On the outside of the club, a large mural depicts a black blues guitarist who plays his instrument with a cigarette dangling from his mouth and a bottle at his side. In its efforts to market culture and place, the club sells T-shirts displaying images like these for eighteen dollars each, along with a special soundtrack collection of compact discs produced by the club.

As for the music itself, downtown clubs rotate the same blues bands for their nightly bookings, and so while the music often seems fresh to weekend visitors, it grows somewhat predictable for regular customers. The repertoires of these local Chicago bands typically include well-known blues standards, as well as rhythm-and-blues and pop hits; local favorites such as the aforementioned "Sweet Home Chicago," Muddy Waters's "I'm Your Hoochie Coochie Man" and "Got My Mojo Working," B. B. King's "The Thrill Is Gone" and "Every Day I Have the Blues," Albert King's "Crosscut Saw," and the perennial favorite "Call It Stormy Monday" draw enthusiastic applause from audience members, who lip-synch and play air guitar to the music, bouncing on their barstools all the while.

Among these songs, the most popular are those that encourage audience involvement through singing along, dancing, or trading off lyrics with the band, such as Wilson Pickett's "Mustang Sally" and Sam and Dave's "Soul Man." When performed at B.L.U.E.S., these songs energize nightclubbers, who rush the dance floor and growl aloud to their dates, "Ride, Sally, ride!" and "I'm a soul man!" Since many of these songs have been popularized by pop stars with broad crossover appeal, including, not coincidentally, the Blues Brothers, they tend to be much more familiar to a mass audience than lesser-known hits by more traditional blues recording artists like Junior Wells or Howlin' Wolf. In fact, a rather wide range of pop songs, particularly those by black artists, finds its way into the set lists of local blues performers at the club, including Otis Redding's "(Sittin' on) The Dock of the Bay," Chuck Berry's "Johnny B. Goode," Bob Marley's "No Woman No Cry," and James Brown's "Get Up (I Feel Like Being a Sex Machine)."

Perhaps not surprisingly, blues players tire of performing these same songs week after week. According to Philip, a local guitarist:

> We usually play the same songs. . . . You know, we add a new one every three or four months, and we don't have a set order or anything. But yeah, we mostly play the same songs, and man, I get so tired of playing them, you know, like "Got My Mojo Working," "Sweet Home Chicago," and let's see, um, "Crosscut Saw." . . . But, you know, we have to play them, because they're the songs that people know and they want to hear. I'm so sick of playing those songs.

Finally, it is significant to note that audiences not only demand to hear these standards performed early and often, but also expect that they will be played by black musicians, as authenticity in the Chicago blues scene is almost always evaluated in accordance with coarse racial stereotypes of black culture. Elliot, a white singer and guitarist who performs in several downtown clubs, explains:

> It's because white audiences and owners are ignorant. The owners know that tourists will ask at the door, "Well, is the band playing tonight a *black* band, or is it a *white* band?" Because the tourists only want to hear black bands, because they want to see an authentic Chicago blues band, and they think a black band is more *real*, more *authentic*. When they come to Chicago, it's like they want to go to the Disneyland of the blues. You know, it's like this: People want German cars, French chefs, and, well, they want their bluesmen black. It's a designer label.

The consequences of this audience demand are startling, according to Shawn, a black bass player:

> I've always been treated okay, but a lot of times the owners will try to break up your band if you have too many white guys. Like, if a band has three black guys, the owners sometimes let them have two white guys, but a lot of times they'll say there's too many white guys on the stage, because, well, you know, the blues is supposed to be the music of blacks, and they're doing it for the tourists, and it's all about business.
>
> But if you can play the blues, it doesn't matter who you are—anyone can play the blues. It doesn't take a certain kind of person to play the blues. . . . Everybody *gets* the blues, right? So, either you can play the blues or you can't, and it doesn't matter if you're white or black or whatever. . . . But the owners, they'll try to break up your band if you've got too many whites.

Urban Authenticity and the Sliding Scale

But while many tourists in Chicago accept such racial stereotypes as given, one should not downplay the role which additional definitions of authenticity play in structuring their experiences of consumption in local blues bars. For example, many consumers patronize clubs outside the central commercial district because they imagine that such places provide a heightened sense of the authentic. In their quest to consume urban spaces that suggest the romanticized allure of the so-called underground city, rather than the more traditional renderings of metropolitan sophistication, many contemporary consumers fashion themselves as urban pioneers involved in a constant project of cultural colonization as they venture through entertainment zones as imagined frontiers of the city (Smith 1996). For these tourists, clubs in neighborhoods outside the city center seem attractive because they are thought to offer a more authentic Chicago experience than more theme-oriented entertainments indicative of the downtown area, such as the House of Blues.

For some cultural consumers, this turn to a postmodern brand of slumming involves a search for the prototypical urban community as a symbolic space of authenticity. Tourists often measure a club's authenticity according to its ability to project a sense of intimacy, imagined or otherwise. For example, *global* travelers evaluate clubs favorably by envisioning tourist attractions as unassuming and anticommercial nightspots where *locals* regularly fraternize, instead of tourists like themselves. By internalizing myths that celebrate these clubs as bastions of community and social solidarity in contrast to the asphalt jungle of the city at large, these "anti-tourists" (see MacCannell 1976) take pleasure in locating and experiencing what they imagine to be islands of authenticity in a sea of urban anomie and commodified culture.

B.L.U.E.S., a club located just outside the downtown area in the affluent North Side neighborhood of Lincoln Park, serves such a purpose for many of its patrons. On weekends, a well-heeled crowd of tourists, business travelers, and international exchange students crams inside the club's long, narrow interior under the glow of yellow lamps and a haze of cigarette smoke. The intimate and modest décor of the club, exemplified by its worn bar stools and cheap plaster walls, accentuates the kind of run-down environment that symbolizes authenticity to consumers of the Chicago blues scene. Suchi, a tourist from Iowa, explains her appreciation of B.L.U.E.S.: "It's smaller here, and it's cozy, you know, people seem to know each other, it's less touristy." Lisa, a seasoned visitor from California, favors peripheral clubs like B.L.U.E.S. over larger downtown clubs like Blue Chicago, and characterizes them as informal havens indicative of the iconic urban community in contradistinction to the sprawl of Los Angeles nightlife:

> I go to clubs to hear music all the time in L.A., and especially in
> Hollywood, . . . but there's really nothing like this out there. . . . I mean,

out in L.A. all the clubs are so huge. . . . There's just nothing like this, you know? This place is just smaller and has a real neighborhood feel to it, . . . and after going to Blue Chicago, this place seems much cooler, much more homey.

Likewise, Maria, a student from Barcelona on a ten-day tour of Chicago, explains her touring group's decision to attend B.L.U.E.S.:

Maria: Well, today we saw Les Miserables . . . it was really wonderful, . . . and we wanted to go someplace typical for Chicago, so we wanted to hear blues and jazz, and somebody told us this would be a good place. First we went to the House of Blues, . . . you know the House of Blues? But we left, because it was too big and, you know, for tourists, so we came here, and it's much better, it's smaller and more personal. . . . Do people from Chicago come here a lot?
David: Yes.
Maria: Oh, good! The House of Blues was just so big, and we wanted a place that was small and more, um, typical, ah, more, um—
David: Real?
Maria: Ah, yes! Real! That's it!

For an international tourist such as Maria, B.L.U.E.S. provides a means of experiencing the authenticity suggested by local neighborhood life, and thus she romanticizes the "personal" aura of B.L.U.E.S. by imagining that "real" Chicagoans take their pleasures there. Meanwhile, the House of Blues disappoints Maria because she finds that its self-conscious hubris in tourist-ridden downtown Chicago contradicts the subaltern, populist meanings she attributes to urban blues music. She envisions B.L.U.E.S. to be an authentic blues club and neighborhood bar, set miles away from the centrality of downtown. Likewise, Hiroshi, a blues fan from Japan, revels in the intimacy he attaches to B.L.U.E.S as he carefully remarks: "I like this club very much. . . . Some places, they are too big. But here, it is small, and the music and the people and the beer are all together." He clasps his hands to express this intimacy and adds: "And when the musicians come off the stage, they are right here, and you can talk to them."

In contradistinction to the enthusiasm of many tourists, local regulars and musicians often evaluate the club differently. For example, Darryl, a harmonica player, suggests how the club's popularity among tourists has dampened his impression of its communal atmosphere in the 1970s:

Back in those days, B.L.U.E.S. just had more authentic bands, you know, guys who were really big in the '50s would play there, like Sunnyland Slim, Smokey Smothers, Big Walter Horton, Floyd Jones, Big Leon, and I just remember the music was really great. . . . Of course, the audience was basically white, because it was a North Side club, but for some reason, the crowds never seemed as shallow or loudish as they do today. . . .

Then one day, I came to this realization that these audiences at these clubs had changed, they were really shallow now; . . . it had become a kind of culture for fraternity guys and tourists. . . . At B.L.U.E.S., they had become much more concerned with maintaining a glossy image. . . . Like one night, I remember we found Good Rockin' Charles a few blocks away from the club, and he was really drunk and had hit his head and was just bleeding everywhere, and we realized that we had to get him inside and we wanted to call an ambulance, and so we thought we could bring him into B.L.U.E.S. and take him into the back room, and the bouncer knew us, and he gave us a really hard time and he almost didn't let us in, and it was just terrible, because Charlie's head was really bleeding badly, and the bouncer just stood there arguing with us, and after that he *finally* let us in.

While North Side bars like B.L.U.E.S. appeal to tourists and many locals, musicians like Darryl find even these clubs too commercialized and inauthentic for their taste. According to Jack, another musician:

Well, back then the audience was a lot older. I mean, there were hardly any kids at all; most of the crowd was in their midthirties and older, and there were some seniors here too, and a lot of old hippie types. They were people who were really acquainted with the music; . . . on any given night, you could imagine overhearing a thorough discussion in the back about the styles of Blind Lemon Jefferson or Sunnyland Slim, because these people knew all about the traditions of the music. Today, the audiences don't know anything about blues; . . . if you mentioned Sunnyland Slim, they might think it was a drink or something.

Longtime regulars at clubs like B.L.U.E.S. frequently echo the same concerns. During a Tuesday night show at B.L.U.E.S., Sean, a former regular, suggests how the experience of attending the club has changed for him over the past decade:

I've been coming here for, well, twelve years now, yeah, since 1987. . . .
Back then the crowd was really into it, and now the audience seems
like, I don't know, it's more for "the masses." Like now, the blues is
more "chic," and coming out to hear blues is more the "thing to do." For
them, it's just about going out for "blues," instead of going to hear one
particular artist, while back then the audience really knew about the
music, and the names of people they wanted to see, and it was more
authentic.

And so, even as tourists like Lisa, Maria, and Hiroshi enthusiastically
praise B.L.U.E.S. for its intimate atmosphere, musicians and former regulars
frequently denounce such clubs for their *lack* of authenticity.

Selling the Urban Ghetto as a Tourist Attraction

In the 1950s, Chicago's black residents and southern migrants patronized
countless blues clubs spread throughout the South and West Sides of the
city. But as the number of tourist-oriented clubs like B.L.U.E.S. and Blue
Chicago proliferated in North Side areas of Chicago during the 1970s and
1980s, the city's black neighborhoods witnessed a steep decline in their
ability to maintain operational and successful blues bars. During the past
thirty years, several black community areas where blues clubs had once
thrived, including Grand Boulevard, Englewood, and Washington Park,
have suffered drastic increases in concentrated unemployment, poverty,
depopulation, and community instability (Wilson 1987, 1996; Wacquant
and Wilson 1989; Massey and Denton 1993; also see Chicago Fact Book
Consortium 1995). As these neighborhoods fell into decline, and North Side
and downtown clubs began competing for the attention of local talent and
affluent audiences, it became increasingly difficult for their blues taverns
to remain in operation; today, many of these clubs face severe difficulties
attracting enough customers to support even the occasional booking of a
band. For instance, while the Cuddle Inn remains open to serve whisky and
cheap beer to a dwindling group of local residents, its deteriorating walls,
lack of live entertainment, and large supply of empty barstools on weekend
nights testify to the decline of a once prosperous blues culture.

However, in a strange twist of fate, this decline has increased the value
that audiences place on the urban authenticity suggested by the few remaining blues clubs in the city's black ghetto neighborhoods, since such clubs
are thought to represent a more genuine alternative for consumers who

seek to avoid the intensified commercialism and popularity suggested by more upscale North Side establishments. As a result, Chicago's most racially segregated and impoverished areas have been transformed into commodified tourist attractions. For example, the Checkerboard Lounge attracts a sizable pool of white consumers, largely made up of business travelers and graduate students. In their search for the rugged authenticity which they associate with images of urban poverty, these patrons derive satisfaction from the grittiness of the Checkerboard's cheaply fashioned interior—its ripped orange booths, tables lined with contact paper, walls covered with tinsel strips and posters of gowned black women, and bathroom floors tiled with flattened cardboard boxes. In comparing the Checkerboard to a local jazz club known for its elegant interior, Rajiv, a conventioneer, explains, "The Green Mill was very polished; I like this place a lot more—*especially* the decor.*"

Like travelers in search of authenticity in other cultural contexts, many visiting patrons find the Checkerboard attractive because they imagine it to be an authentic space untainted by voyeuristic audiences such as themselves. They reveal this bias in their offhand remarks at the club. On a wintry Saturday night, I escorted a white professional couple from the suburbs to the Checkerboard. As our waitress wrote down our drink order on a napkin, the gentleman turned to me to ask: "So, would you call this club more authentic? Is the music more authentic?" Meanwhile, his partner peered across the bar with an unsatisfied expression on her face, disappointed by the number of whites at the club; they included a spirited pack of middle-aged men from New York and a gaggle of college-age drunks bounding across the length of dance floor.

As a result of its emergent popularity among affluent audiences, the Checkerboard does its best to pander to its mostly white customers by providing racially and sexually charged entertainment within its deteriorating walls. Local black acts playfully tease their female audience members with innuendo rife with hypermasculine bravado, explicit allusions to oral sex, and X-rated versions of otherwise innocuous songs such as "Hold On, I'm Comin' " and "She'll Be Comin' Round the Mountain When She Comes." Meanwhile, before his recent death, a popular local character dubbed the "Black Lone Ranger" strolled around the club selling home-recorded tapes that featured his renditions of blues standards such as "I'm a Man," and invited customers to pay to have their Polaroid photograph taken with him in his contemporary minstrel regalia, complete with white ten-gallon hat and black mask.

At the same time, since the 1960s, local journalists and other cultural critics in Chicago have drawn on the popularity of these South Side blues taverns by evoking traditional racial stereotypes to depict these clubs as decidedly more authentic than their downtown counterparts. Illustrating a long-standing stereotype, in *Chicago: An Extraordinary Guide,* author Jory Graham celebrates the history of the black migration to Chicago's ghettos, where the blues articulate "hard, driving sounds of inner-city pressures," by arguing that this tradition continues in surviving clubs on the contemporary South Side, where "soul—the raw emotion, the pain of being black—is not withheld." Graham continues by relying on an essentialist portrait of blackness to promote her vision of authenticity: "Since 'soul' is the one inalienable possession of the Negro, the one thing whites may comprehend but never possess, it's perfectly natural that the places to hear the blues nightly are in the Negro ghettos of the city" (1967, 85).

Like Graham, *Living Blues* magazine editor and local critic Jim O'Neal relies on folk-based characterizations of race to promote the relative authenticity of the city's black neighborhoods in his *Chicago Reader* review of the city's blues clubs:

> Really, nothing can compare with a night of blues in a real blues club. The atmosphere, the crowd, the way the band sounds, everything is just—bluesier. At most South and West Side blues lounges, the door charge (if there is one) is $1.00; I.D.'s are checked irregularly. Beer is usually 75¢ a bottle. Big Duke's two clubs, Pepper's and others serve ribs, chicken, and other soul food from their own kitchens as well. The accommodations aren't deluxe, and the washrooms may be smelly, but it doesn't matter. . . . The dancing, drinking, talking and laughing of the crowds may be loud in comparison to the polite attention and applause the artists receive on the North Side, but the music is loud too. And funky. (1973, 29)

O'Neal privileges the experience of visiting a "real" South Side or West Side blues club for its "soul food," cheap beer, "funky" music, and "bluesier" authenticity. Indeed, although he claims otherwise, that at such clubs the "accommodations aren't deluxe, and the washrooms may be smelly" *does* matter to North Siders who regard such things as true markers of authenticity. O'Neal's consequent reviews for the *Reader* rely on similar racially charged rhetoric, which describes the authenticity of black *audiences* as well as musicians: "There are more reasons for hearing blues in a black tavern than just the quality of the music. For one, the natural ambiance of the crowds adds a dimension to the blues experience that's missing in more formal settings" (1975, 31).

Meanwhile, many local critics and promoters draw on the anxious fears and fantasies of white audiences by exoticizing the city's black regions as romantically dangerous places, thereby heightening the "thrill" of entering racially segregated neighborhoods and their "natural ambiance." For example, one guidebook wholeheartedly promotes evening trips to the South Side on the basis of its urban authenticity and perceived risks: "The neighborhood bars tend to be more modest, of course, and often more rough and tumble" (Banes 1974, 69). The book adds that "getting there, and staying in one piece once you've gotten there, is often half the fun," animating the fantasies and fears held by middle- and upper-class whites and blacks alike regarding the "risk" of entering the city's racially segregated neighborhoods. Rather than encouraging potential consumers to put such misgivings aside, these narratives feed on their anxieties about race and crime to depict an evening in a South Side blues bar as an authentic experience exactly *because* such an outing might seem intimidating to newcomers. In this manner, Chicago's black ghetto itself has emerged as an authenticated tourist attraction by offering the promise of urban danger as well as "bluesier" cultural experiences to responsive audiences.

Discussion

As in other popular music scenes, participants in the world of the Chicago blues consume culture as a kind of focused activity in which shared meanings are collectively imagined and diffused within a specific spatial context. But perhaps more important, they demonstrate how popular-music scenes attract participants of *differing* tastes and dispositions. While authenticity may represent a common goal among consumers in search of its cultural power, in reality different kinds of audiences approach the issue of authenticity with varying degrees of intensity and focus, and they sometimes rely on contradictory sets of criteria when evaluating a particular place or performance. The search for authenticity is an exercise in symbolic production in which participants frequently disagree on what specific kinds of symbols connote or suggest authenticity, and even those who agree on the symbols themselves may share different views on how they might manifest themselves in the world.

The case of the Chicago blues also suggests how global and local cultures might interact with one another in the urban milieu. From records to film, the international dissemination of authentic images of the "local"—the elderly black songster, the smoke-filled neighborhood blues bar, the sounds of the city's black ghetto—help frame the expectations which "global" tourists and travelers maintain concerning the look and feel of the Chicago blues scene. But at the same time, club owners, musicians, and other cultural producers rely on those expectations as a guide for manufacturing authenticity within local clubs. Insofar as Chicago blues clubs represent a local response to a globally diffused set of criteria for the evaluation of authenticity, it is ironic that consumers identify the presence of those signifiers as evidence of local authenticity. Of course, this process of cultural transmission and exchange is not really unusual at all, given that the authenticity of tourist attractions, national monuments, and regional entertainments is often contrived, or "staged" (MacCannell 1976), to meet the expectations of outsiders.

In fact, it is telling that the interaction between local subcultures and the commodification of global culture in this context produces a symbolic economy of authenticity, because this process seems indicative of a larger set of dynamics that operates in many other types of entertainment landscapes and urban art worlds. For instance, the desire to experience authenticity in a postmodern world increases the popularity not only of the blues, but also of other forms of black music. As is true for the blues, the popularity of hip-hop music, fashion, and style encourages musicians and other cultural producers to cater to the expectations of an increasingly internationalized audience in local scenes, as well as in more virtual arenas of mass culture, such as MTV. Perhaps ironically, this heightened popularity drives consumers to search even *more* vigilantly for signs of authenticity untainted by the blemishes of commercialism. Indeed, the desire to "keep it real" in hip-hop (Kleinfield 2001; McLeod 1999) hardly seems very different from the hunt for authenticity in the Chicago blues scene; in both cases, it appears unlikely that such a quest could ever come to a satisfying resolution, insofar as the search for authenticity in the world of popular culture may always seem just over the next horizon but is never truly within reach. And so, in the end, it may make more sense to think about this search for authenticity in the Chicago blues as best represented not merely as a sliding scale, but as an onion whose paper-thin layers can be forever peeled away, always masking the hollow and empty core that resides at its center.

References

Banes, Sally. 1974. *Sweet Home Chicago.* Chicago: Chicago Review Press.

Chicago Fact Book Consortium. 1995. *Local Community Fact Book: Chicago Metropolitan Area 1990.* Chicago: Academy Chicago.

Cohen, Erik. 1988. "Authenticity and Commoditization in Tourism." *Annals of Tourism Research* 15:371–86.

Graham, Jory. 1967. *Chicago: An Extraordinary Guide.* Chicago: Rand McNally.

Grazian, David. 2003. *Blue Chicago: The Search for Authenticity in Urban Blues Clubs.* Chicago: University of Chicago Press.

Hannigan, John. 1998. *Fantasy City: Pleasure and Profit in the Postmodern Metropolis.* London: Routledge.

Hobsbawm, Eric, and Terence Ranger, eds. 1983. *The Invention of Tradition.* Cambridge: Cambridge University Press.

Kleinfeld, N. R. 2001. "Guarding the Borders of the Hip-Hop Nation." In *How Race Is Lived in America: Pulling Together, Pulling Apart.* New York: Times Books.

MacCannell, Dean. 1976. *The Tourist: A New Theory of the Leisure Class.* New York: Schocken Books.

Massey, Douglas S., and Nancy A. Denton. 1993. *American Apartheid: Segregation and the Making of the Underclass.* Cambridge: Harvard University Press.

McLeod, Kembrew. 1999. "Authenticity within Hip-Hop and Other Cultures Threatened with Assimilation." *Journal of Communication* 49: 134–50.

O'Neal, Jim. 1973. "Reader's Guide to Blues." *Chicago Reader,* 28 September, 29.

————. 1975. "Reader's Guide to Blues." *Chicago Reader,* 26 September, 31, 33.

Peterson, Richard A. 1997. *Creating Country Music: Fabricating Authenticity.* Chicago: University of Chicago Press.

Reckless, Walter C. 1933. *Vice in Chicago.* Chicago: University of Chicago Press.

Smith, Neil. 1996. *The New Urban Frontier: Gentrification and the Revanchist City.* London: Routledge.

Sorkin, Michael, ed. 1992. *Variations on a Theme Park: The New American City and the End of Public Space.* New York: Hill and Wang.

Wacquant, Loic J. D., and William Julius Wilson. 1989. "Poverty, Joblessness, and the Social Transformation of the Inner City." In Phoebe H. Cottingham and David T. Ellwood, eds., *Welfare Policy for the 1990s.* Cambridge: Harvard University Press.

Wilson, William Julius. 1987. *The Truly Disadvantaged.* Chicago: University of Chicago Press.

————. 1996. *When Work Disappears.* Chicago: University of Chicago Press.

2

Behind the Rave: Structure and Agency in a Rave Scene

Ken Spring

To the casual observer, music scenes probably seem to emerge more or less spontaneously: jazz in New Orleans, 1914; be-bop jazz in New York, 1943; rock in Liverpool, 1963; psychedelic rock in San Francisco, 1967; grunge in Seattle, 1991. This view may be sufficient for discussing the experience of a scene, but it is a bit like describing a movie as the interaction among a group of actors preserved on film. It fails to examine the required interactions of many individual specialists, such as directors, set designers, music score writers, lighting experts, scriptwriters, film editors, and others who work behind the cameras and contribute their skills to make a film. Likewise, for music scenes to flourish, a variety of types of people need to cooperate in order to take advantage of opportunities for scene building in a particular place and time. First drawing on Goffman's (1959) concept of backstage, then borrowing from Becker's (1982) analysis of backstage contributors, I focus here on the individuals who have played a role both in the rise and in the fall of a music scene.

So why do scenes happen? Why do scenes occur where and when they do? And in particular, what is the role of those working backstage in creating a risk-free environment that facilitates the appearance of a spontaneous music scene? Here I discuss the circumstances within which a local scene was launched, hit cruising altitude, and then came crashing to earth. In many ways this flight is not unlike that of innumerable local scenes, such as the rock scene of Austin, Texas, described by Shank (1994), rave in Wisconsin (Champion 1997), and contemporary dance club culture (Thornton 1995).

I describe the ebb and flow from 1987 to 1996 of a rave music scene in a largely Eastern European ethnic working-class satellite city near Detroit, Michigan. The city, which I call Ruston, proved an ideal site for this study. (The name of the city has been changed, as have the names of the key actors, so that I can report events candidly while protecting the confidentiality of the informants.) This is an ethnographic account made by a participant observer who was involved in the Ruston scene in a variety of roles over the course of seven years. My roles ranged from checking identification and taking money at the door to promotions, from bartending and bouncing to setting up and breaking down the space. I have refreshed these observations by using journals I made at the time, as well as those of peers, co-workers, and friends. I have supplemented these with recent interviews and correspondence with several former club kids, DJs, promoters, drug dealers, and club managers familiar with the Ruston scene.

The Ruston scene flourished when it did because many elements that complemented one another came together in one particular place in time. Some may argue that it "just happened"; however, the Ruston scene occurred as the result of a rather complex social structure in conjunction with a few exceptionally driven individuals who set goals and followed them through to the end. While the music played a vital role in establishing an overall atmosphere and rationale, an underlying complex of social networks that involved money, power, and status was essential for the rave scene to emerge. So while music is central to the scene, the focus here will remain on the elements of the supporting apparatus that in combination allowed the scene to flourish. To establish this context, I focus on the particular urban setting, the actors associated with building the rave scene, and the sociopolitical structure that provided capital and political cover.

What Is Techno? Who Are Its Fans?

Techno music lies at the heart of the Ruston scene. One in the family of genres associated with dancing that evolved out of 1970s dance music, it developed in Detroit in the early 1980s and spread across the United States to Europe and Southeast Asia.

Techno requires a disc jockey (DJ) who plays especially produced vinyl albums that typically have a deep bass-driven beat mixed with diverse forms of electronic sound. Using two turntables mounted side by side and equipped with record-speed equalizers, sound faders, and diverse sound-altering devices, the proficient DJ continually switches the sound between the two turntables or blends the sounds coming from each. These recorded sounds are periodically augmented by manually pushing the revolving disk backward, creating a distinctive scratching sound. While one turntable is being played, the record on the other can be replaced; the result is a song with a steady beat that continually changes but need never end.

Typically, DJs stand on a raised platform over the dance floor, and their continual activity takes on the look of an intensely self-absorbed dance. Proficient DJs regularly watch the dancers and interact with them from time to time, while shaping the sound to maximize the number of people actually dancing. The resulting block of continual music (called a set) is a unique performance that can last from forty-five minutes to several hours. Typically, a set begins softly and builds to an intense peak, then mellows out to bring the dancers down and signal the set's end.

The vinyls that DJs spin are especially produced for them from sounds generated electronically or acoustically and augmented with music sampled from diverse sources. These samples range from familiar dance music to themes from old TV shows and movies to world music. The most proficient DJs have signed with independent record companies that cater to the techno market, so they can make their own mixes into vinyls. These they use as the raw material for making live mixes at dances. DJs regularly share their vinyls with label mates, and they are sold to other DJs, so a new mix can spread around the world in a matter of weeks.

This genre of music was not played on MTV or mainstream radio in the 1990s, so it was not widely embraced by the mainstream U.S. audience. Rather it remained unique to a marginalized population that consisted predominantly of white urban "club kids," that is, people between eighteen and thirty who participate with others like themselves in activities associated with urban nightlife that revolve around dance, alcohol, and drugs.

The Rave Scene as a Risk-free Environment

Throughout this chapter I will refer to the ambiance of the rave scene as a risk-free environment. This sort of environment was essential for a vibrant rave scene, because much of the activity was transgressive or illegal. Raves are associated with several styles of electronic music, including techno, house, trance, jungle, and other forms that came and went more rapidly. Many of the nightclubs that played this music in the United States were exclusionary in the sense that only a few kinds of people were welcome. This was due to regulations regarding age, dress, looks, and finances. As a result, DJs took their music to abandoned warehouses, old churches, and other evacuated areas where kids could escape and be themselves in a world that seemed separate and entirely their own.

The environment created, one of mutual toleration, sharing, and anti-competitiveness, allowed freedom of dance, sexual expression, and drug use. The most common drug was Ecstasy (called "E" or "X"), because it created euphoria and facilitated dancing for extended periods of time, but other drugs such as marijuana and cocaine were used. Other characteristics of the rave scene, which over the course of the Ruston scene changed a number of times, are colorful lights, "smart" drinks (herbal juices thought to enhance the mood, as well as the environment), dancers (called ravers or partiers), lightsticks, and stylistic clothing. (For a more in-depth discussion of the characteristics of rave culture, see Reynolds 1997, Champion 1997, or van Veen 2002a, 2002b.)

Flow and Ebb of the Rushton Rave Scene

Few of the many small cities like Ruston developed an active rave scene, so what set this city apart? In fact, for the Ruston rave scene to develop, a number of structural factors had to come together in this small Midwestern city, which was not widely known for its music or nightlife. Just as Stanley Cohen (1980) speaks of the necessity of bridging structure and culture through biography to understand the [sub]cultural scene, this chapter will flesh out the relationship between structure and agency through a biography of the Ruston scene. This process can be described in three stages: founding days, functioning scene, and collapse.

Founding Days of the Ruston Scene

As Phil Cohen (1972) points out, the relationship of the subculture (scene) with the physical territory or community is important in a scene's development. In Ruston, the characteristics of the neighborhood and the management of the venue where the scene began were vital in shaping the scene. The setting was a four-block-long, two-block-wide urban environment. It was a run-down area with houses converted to cheap apartments, along with abandoned buildings, vacant stores, a few small, locally owned stores, and three biker bars. The area, referred to here as "the Strip," was cut off from the more prosperous part of town except for one connecting street that formed its focus.

The one remaining local restaurant/bar was on this street. Johnny's Bar and Grill had been in one family for three generations, and the rising owner-manager, Bill, then in his early twenties, instituted Saturday-evening music shows in the early 1990s that featured "alternative" bands such as the Smashing Pumpkins, Kid Rock, the B-52's, Babes in Toyland, and the Goo-Goo Dolls—all before they became famous and pricey—as well as other bands supported by kids in the area. The club's location was far from the town's entertainment district on the "other side of the tracks" and had poorly lit streets and little police protection, which might seem to make it an unlikely place to draw hip young people. However, Bill was able to use this negative stereotyping to his advantage and marketed Johnny's Bar and Grill as the Beat, which became the nucleus of an underground scene.

By catering to the stereotype of the other side of the tracks, Bill was able to attract a select group of alternative kids. By day he ran an ordinary working-class neighborhood bar and grill, but at night, when all the regulars had gone home, Bill's bar turned into a hip place for the college-age crowd attracted to trendy live music by local and national alternative rock bands, as well as other popular college groups. This was music that spoke to the kids and gave them a voice—angst-driven punk rock, soul-searching acoustics, and so on. The Beat fit the stereotype as well. It was dark, slightly seedy, and yet a cutting-edge oasis that was nestled in a run-down commercial area that kids considered dangerous because of the nearby biker bars. Adding to the rough underground stereotype, the Strip was located on the run-down and shabby industrial side of the city.

An important factor in the creation of the scene was that Bill was from the neighborhood, and everyone was delighted to see him do well. In the daytime, locals would file in to have a few drinks at lunch or before making their way back home. Consequently, the Beat was well established and supported in the area. As a neighborhood boy who grew with the business, Bill not only developed the managerial skills needed to run such a business, but also learned how to deal with members of the local community, the police, fire and sanitation inspectors, and the political authorities downtown.

The residents of the community supported Bill's efforts because they had hopes of more money being spent in their community, while new tax

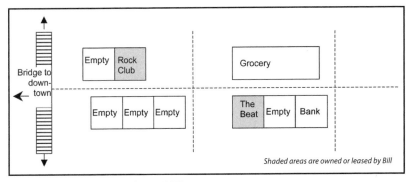

Ruston scene in early stages (1989–1992)

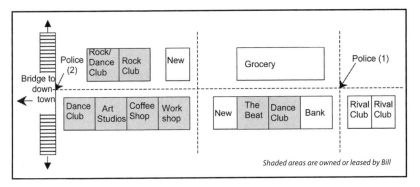

Ruston scene full development (1994–1996)

dollars would translate into more funds for police protection, road repair, and other activities that would affect the development of the neighborhood and raise land values. As a result, building owners gave Bill the chance to purchase properties before they were officially advertised for sale. And because Bill seemed to have a vision and a genuine interest in the community, the community was more likely to turn a blind eye to inappropriate or illegal activities going on behind the closed doors of the club; it was not a public nuisance, and all that was visible were the immediate benefits, such as new facades on buildings, better roads, and increased police patrols. Having local community support also translated into solid backing from the precinct alderman, the police, and city political authorities. Bill received city money earmarked for urban renewal and, though young, was officially cited for his civic contributions. He reciprocated by giving generous contributions to political officials.

Developing the Ruston Music Scene

After experiencing early success with alternative rock bands playing nightly in the bar, in 1989 Bill opened up the previously unused basement of the Beat as an underground dance club devoted to playing vinyl records mixed by DJs. From the outset, much of the music that was being played in the warehouses and studios of Detroit found its way to the Basement of the Beat. While most of the Basement's music had been played widely for weeks, the last two hours of every night were set aside for the DJs to play their new musical inventions. In addition, about once a month, the club would close down at the regular time, only to reopen its back door to continue as a private party. This was a time for the DJs to really share their new techno music with the audience.

Detroit DJs and their music heavily influenced this scene, but the Ruston scene flourished as a result of a handful of individuals, many of whom had begun as party kids themselves, growing into full-time jobs step by step. It was run as a private party, where in exchange for not charging rent, Bill the bar owner kept all of the bar receipts and paid no one. Bartenders worked for their tips; DJs played for free drinks and the promise of a good time; active clubbers were comped in (that is, got in without paying an entry fee). In addition, two of the bartenders took it upon themselves to play the role of promoters and bring rave music to Ruston. One told me of the beginning of the scene:

> When we opened up Monday nights, I took twenty bucks out of the drawer; we chipped in a few more bucks and bought a cooler full of imports and a bag of weed. I could get four DJs to show up—a couple from Detroit, and a few locals. If I got four DJs to show up, each would bring about five people with them at least. At first we would style everyone down with alcohol, two-dollar cover, joints, and a lot of extras passed out at a nominal fee (Ecstasy was big, mushrooms, acid).

The other bartender, an MBA student at a local university, gave me a good idea of how the rave scene was introduced to Ruston: "I introduced the music 'risk free' to the DJs and people I considered the early adopters. A good marketer knows that the early adopters get things for free at first and then, well, you know, [prices] go up."

As another promoter said: "Anyone who wanted to get involved in the scene could get good drugs, and get laid." This programming and style of operation apparently worked, because in a few weeks the word of the late-night parties got around, and club kids were coming in from all over that part of the Midwest. Ruston now had an after-hours dance-party scene known to those in the dance club world. Monday nights drew several hundred participants from around the Midwest.

The Functioning Ruston Scene

Over the course of the next four years, from 1989 to 1993, the Strip added two all-night eateries, four nightclubs, a tattoo parlor, and a coffeehouse/record and clothing store. Bill owned and operated most of the venues or leased them to a business or an individual. All leases had clauses that stipulated either that the lessees could not compete with Bill or that he would be cut in on a percentage of their profits. Apartments over the stores owned by Bill were filled with artists' studios and semi-stabilized vagrants. Vacant buildings were condemned and demolished to make way for well-lit parking lots. In addition to all of Bill's enterprises, new nonrelated chain-store businesses popped up, such as drugstores and pizza places. This structure of the Strip existed for about four more years, until early 1997.

In the heyday of the scene, two clubs specifically targeted the underground-club crowd, and the largest of the new clubs, the Center Stage, set aside an off night (Monday) for rave music. Bill never asked about the events that took place at the Center Stage on Monday nights. It was easy money, and the club was becoming more profitable each week. Participants entered through the back door, and neither the police nor liquor control officials interrupted the party. In addition to the Beat and Center Stage, the coffeehouse offered kids much more than coffee: rave clothing, a showcasing of graffiti art, vinyl records and turntables to try them out on, bootleg tapes of their favorite DJs latest party mix, and a well-equipped basement that frequently housed after-hours dance parties. While the upstairs was a mellow environment for kids to grab a coffee or water to help control their buzz, the downstairs was just the opposite. In the basement, they could find everything to maintain or enhance their music- and drug-induced "high."

Beyond the ravers, others essential to maintaining the Ruston rave scene included DJs, promoters, drug dealers, politicians, fire marshals, and police.

DJs

DJs provided the mix of music the kids wanted to hear and introduced new music the dancers would come to want to hear. When I asked how the Ruston DJs went about introducing people to techno music, the answer given by one of them is representative: "I always try to keep the crowd guessing. And I always try to educate by introducing a new sound in between a couple of tracks which the crowd may already be familiar with. This way they are pumped at the point that the new sound comes on and pumped again when it goes off. It's sort of like programming them to like it."

Beyond sharing their music, the Ruston DJs maintained established social networks with other DJs and promoters in the music industry, advising each other about good places to spin. As a result, when the Ruston Monday-night raves became established, they drew headline DJs from major cities such as Toronto, London, Chicago, and Detroit. Local DJs used the experience to educate themselves in both the music and the culture, and in time many of them became draws in other cities around the United States; several are still in demand around the world.

Advertising visiting name DJs became unnecessary, because it was understood by the kids that the Strip always had good DJs and that the range of styles would meet or exceed their expectations. As one club kid said:

> The promoters always had a well-balanced line-up of DJs for the evening; they would spin house, techno, trance, and maybe a hip-hop artist to kick things off. Promoters were known, and if their names were associated with the party, people knew that the best DJs, the best drugs, and the best time would be had. The convenience and security of the Strip was the perfect fit for their cause.

Promoters

Promoters' prime role was to introduce people to one another, including club managers, DJs, club kids, and drug dealers. The promoters of the Ruston rave scene were all well educated; some were in various stages of earning MBAs—master of business administration degrees—with a focus on marketing and were therefore well versed in the tools of marketing and networking. At the same time, they had a genuine interest in the music and could profit financially by connecting others in the scene.

The most influential promoters in the Ruston scene took advantage of the risk-free space to cash in on some of these events with their own safe venue. They leased the coffee shop from Bill and threw parties that complemented the other events on the Strip. Bill demanded that they not compete with his bar business, and they agreed that their parties could not begin until the legitimate clubs were closing. The promoters complied because violation of this stipulation would result in their lease being revoked.

Drugs

Drugs were prevalent at parties, as well as within the bar scene. As one club kid remarked, "The same five people were always holding, and once you knew, you could count on it every time." When I asked a promoter if it was easy for a newcomer to find out who was holding drugs, he said it was easy for them "if they personally knew one of the promoters or DJs. The drugs were part of the business and vital for making money to support upcoming events." Thus it was an unspoken certainty that anyone who wanted to extend or enhance the party mood had the opportunity to do so. Many of my informants mentioned that not only were you assured that you could find the drugs you wanted, but also you had a place to use them with little chance of being arrested or negatively sanctioned for your actions. They agreed with my assumption that the risk-free environment increased both attendance and drug use. DJs and promoters stated that while "drugs have always been a part of the rave culture, now it seems to be the main part of the culture, dominating even over the music." They also agreed that most parties in most cities operate in a similar fashion.

Security guards hired by the management or promoters were essential to the regular availability, quality, and price of drugs. By the time everything was set up and ready to start, security would arrive to work the door. Even for "underground" parties, some form of security would be present. Sometimes the security would be off-duty police officers or bouncers from one of the clubs; sometimes the promoters would hire out friends to work security. In all cases, security would be at the parties, patting down people and checking bags prior to entry. Security guards would not typically go beyond the front door of the party, and in most instances they would be located outside. In addition to checking IDs for age, a major part of their job was to take drugs away from kids seeking access to the party.

How then did drugs get on the premises? One of my informants explained:

A few selected dealers with a reputation for high-quality drugs were allowed in before opening of the party, perhaps during set up. The dealers would have the night's supply inside the party before anyone came. Then security would only catch the 'unlicensed' dealers who tried to smuggle in the goods, guaranteeing that the selected dealers would sell out and owe the promoters a percent of what was sold.

Thus an absolute monopoly was formed. There was no direct agreement as to how large a cut promoters would receive, and in some instances it was the promoters themselves who made the drugs available. Some of the benefits of the drug sales for club goers were a decrease in the cost to get into the party, better-known DJs, better lighting, and better sound, as well as a better quality of drugs.

According to knowledgeable respondents, drugs were chosen for their reputed mood-control effects. Marijuana was not considered a real drug, any more than were nicotine or caffeine. Recreational drugs included LSD, E or X, mushrooms, cocaine, and various types of speed. Alcohol was always present. As one observer said: "In the beginning, alcohol was important to gain critical mass; a lot of people won't come out if they can't drink." An experienced raver told me: "Alcohol was important as a stabilizer—you do enough drugs, you need something to calm you down." When I inquired about the percentage of people who were using recreational drugs at the parties, safe estimates were between 50 and 60 percent; from my observations, these estimates are low.

While the drugs were indeed pervasive, people seemed to be aware of their personal limits. This does not suggest that people sometimes did not use in excess, but most would not push their limits, and in my seven years on the scene, there was no instance when an ambulance needed to be called to cope with a drug problem. As one promoter said:

> The majority would take what they could get without crossing their personal limits. However, a lot of people know better than to use the harder drugs like coke, crystal meth, or crack, and they would simply say "No thanks" if offered those. The hard-core ravers used E. For the mullet heads [outsiders], who found themselves at a party uninvited, it was a free-for-all.

Officialdom

The political structure of the Ruston community in the early 1990s aided in the creation and continuation of the rave scene. In this rust-belt industrial city in a postrecession era, there was a dire need to encourage new businesses. The Strip was located in a run-down area that offered low rent for a large amount of space, and one could purchase a building for much less than in other areas of town. In addition, the city was eager to have new businesses take over the otherwise vacant spaces on the Strip, which generated tax revenues and ensured the viability of the area. Bill, the club owner, approached the mayor and city councilman with requests for urban-development money and for a tolerant attitude regarding what was happening in his clubs. City officials were eager to help him succeed, in part because his success facilitated their efforts to bring the city back to economic prosperity. The political alliances that were created by Bill, a local boy, with the local ward alderman and city officials made possible the risk-free environment. I suggest that an official blind eye with regard to the events was essential to the establishment and smooth functioning of the Ruston rave scene, and Ruston city officials, police, and fire marshals worked with Bill to create a structure that allowed marginalized deviant activity to occur without the threat of sanction.

Bill established close ties with the local councilman and had a scattering of other political figures either on his payroll or with a vested interest in the success of the Strip. Whenever concerns arose in the mayor's office, the councilman for the district where the Strip is located would typically attempt to persuade a majority of the council to withdraw their objections to the permit renewals. Bill received honors from the city for his renovation of the Strip and was praised by the mayor, the councilman, and local police.

Fire Marshals and Police

Police and fire marshals had the job of accommodating the rules of the city to the needs of the rave scene. While policing was increased in areas around the Strip, the same rules did not necessarily apply to everyone equally. The maximum attendance set by the fire code was 300 for the Beat and 250 for the Center Stage, yet crowds at those bars would typically exceed capacity three and four times over; neither club was ever served a formal citation for its violations. When the fire inspectors came on their infrequent inspections, they would give the manager a verbal warning along with an order to clear the premises in a timely fashion (the time conveniently coinciding with the party's planned ending time). Thus Bill and his enterprises appeared to be bullet proof, adding to the feeling of the Strip as a risk-free space.

Bill's close connections with the fire marshals and police allowed him and his associates to use these officials for their own ends. Thus, for example, in order to terminate a profitless night, the party promoters would sometimes call the fire inspectors and ask them to preemptively close the place. Bill used the authorities against his rivals as well. Two clubs that opened on the street within a few hundred yards of the Beat to cash in on the Strip's success were closed by city officials within a year for the same violations that occurred in Bill's clubs on a regular basis. These raids were often initiated by anonymous phone calls that informed police about violations in these other locations. In this way, Bill used his political power to have the competition removed. In another example of differential treatment, police set up DUI (driving under the influence) checkpoints at the intersection just past the Strip, essentially shutting down any traffic to the rival clubs.

Some violations that occurred at Bill's bars were brought to the attention of public officials, but the citations seemed to get set aside, or perhaps even lost in the paperwork. Violations such as serving liquor to a minor, making excessive noise, urinating in public, exceeding fire code limits, operating without a liquor license, selling alcohol after hours, and others added up in Bill's clubs on the Strip, but citations for these violations did not make it to court, let alone result in the clubs being closed. In fact, as these violations were adding up, Bill received official accolades from the mayor and city council members as one of the outstanding businessmen in the city.

City authorities were also helpful in protecting Bill's bars from state liquor-control agents who might stop by for a "surprise" inspection of underage drinking and other violations. Advance warning allowed the operation to run squeaky-clean while the agents were in the building. Youngsters were asked to leave, and security guards closely checked the age identification of customers. Bouncers would be sure to check hand stamps, as well as recheck the IDs of customers they thought were suspect. In addition, through a set of signals, bartenders knew the exact moment that the agents entered the building, as well as when they left, and would tip off the crowd to keep it under control while they were present. It was back to business as usual as soon as they left.

The scene benefited not only those already mentioned but also the community surrounding the Strip. Ruston community residents benefited from higher tax revenues, better roads, higher property values, and increased police patrol.

The Day the Music Died

The scene's demise began when all of the important actors began to compete for a greater share of the profits, causing the structure of mutually supportive arrangements to collapse. For example, the resident house DJs came to feel underappreciated as well as underpaid so, given the opportunity, would play a private party, which left the club managers scrambling to find a no-name substitute, thus disappointing the club kids. As one DJ said: "DJs prefer to play after-hour parties versus being a resident at a club. When you are a resident, you have owners and managers telling you what to do, what to play." Furthermore, the good DJs could make four to five times the amount of money playing a party instead of working at one of the clubs. On several occasions, DJs would leave in the middle of the set, or leave early, to go play a party across town. This would force the club either to shut down early or to improvise with a bartender or manager playing some CDs, which cast a pall over the rest of the evening.

To give another example, several promoters decided they could manage the drugs directly, cutting out the politically well-established dealers. The promoters who leased the coffee shop started cutting into Bill's hours of operation. They had parties every weekend, and they started their billing earlier in the evening, sometimes as early as nine or ten o'clock. As a result, attendance at the Beat and the Center Stage, as well as at Bill's other clubs, dropped significantly. Bill retaliated by evicting the coffee shop owners for violations of their lease agreement and for allowing suspect activity within his building, thus eliminating one of the prime attractions to the Strip.

Bill's decision not to support the political campaigns of the precinct alderman and city officials had swift and devastating results. One night without warning the police set up DUI checks at the only convenient railroad crossing, where 90 percent of the clientele traveled into the Strip. In subsequent weeks, the police checkpoint was announced on the evening news. Though few arrests were made, at a stroke these actions destroyed the sense of a risk-free environment that had been so carefully nurtured. This news spread rapidly among club kids across the Midwest, and the Strip no longer was a place to be.

Many of the city officials who had supported Bill in the past became vocal participants in the destruction of his empire. The city clerk found the piles of official citations that had been filed against Bill and his establishments—several of Bill's clubs were closed immediately. City officials publicly decried the types of activities that occurred on the Strip and denounced Bill for allowing them to occur. In the ensuing investigation, the state liquor-control agents put together a case against Bill that cost him high fines and barred him from having a license to sell liquor in the entire state. The police and city officials received acclaim from the media for "cleaning up" the Strip and saving Ruston youth from sex, drugs, and techno music.

The Ruston case provides a solid example of the complexities that exist between organizational structure and entrepreneurial agency. These are highlighted when entrepreneurial agents in Ruston attempted to bend the existing structure to create a risk-free rave scene in this small Midwestern city. The rapid demise of the scene again reflects the complex interdependency of these elements. As we have seen, the scene would not have flowered without the cooperation of a bar owner, club kids, DJs, promoters, drug dealers, police, fire marshals, and city politicians, and the scene fell apart when the cooperation was overtaken by personal greed. The Strip is gone now, and perhaps the scene's only tangible echo is in the careers of several local DJs who have gone on to establish custom record companies and international acclaim in the worldwide techno music scene.

A number of studies have shown officialdom to be hostile to raves (Thornton 1995; Champion 1997; Hollands 1995), but I wonder to what extent the story they report is only the one that authorities and the media want to project. This observation suggests one other significant actor in the making of the Ruston rave scene: the media, who played an important role by doing nothing. The local newspaper must have had some idea of the collusion of public officials. At the very least, members of the paper's staff were in regular attendance at events on the Strip, but it was not until city officials attacked Bill that the media attacked him, and they never asked how he had been able to operate in this manner for all those years.

References

Becker, Howard. 1982. *Art Worlds*. Berkeley: University of California Press.

Champion, Sarah. 1997. "Fear and Loathing in Wisconsin." In Steve Redhead, Derek Wynne and Justin O'Connor, eds., *The Clubcultures Reader: Readings in Popular Cultural Studies*. Oxford: Blackwell.

Cohen, Phil. 1972. "Subcultural Conflict and Working Class Community." In Ken Gelder and Sarah Thornton, eds., *The Subcultures Reader*. London: Routledge.

Cohen, Stanley. 1980. "Symbols of Trouble." In Ken Gelder and Sarah Thornton, eds., *The Subcultures Reader*. London: Routledge.

Goffman, Erving. 1959. *The Presentation of Self in Everyday Life*. Harmondsworth: Penguin.

Hollands, Robert. 1995. "Friday Night, Saturday Night: Youth Cultural Identification in the Post-Industrial City." Department of Social Policy Working Paper No.2, University of Newcastle, Newcastle-upon-Tyne, U.K.

Peterson, Richard A. 1990. "Why 1955? Explaining the Advent of Rock Music." *Popular Music* 9, 1: 97–116.

Reynolds, Simon. 1997. "Rave Culture: Living Dream or Living Death." In Steve Redhead, Derek Wynne, and Justin O'Connor, eds., *The Clubcultures Reader: Readings in Popular Cultural Studies*. Oxford: Blackwell.

Shank, Barry. 1994. *Dissonant Identities: The Rock 'n' Roll Scene in Austin, Texas*. London: Wesleyan University Press.

Thornton, Sarah. 1995. *Club Cultures: Music, Media, and Subcultural Capital*. Cambridge: Polity Press.

Van Veen, Tobias. 2002a. "Turntables, Warehouses, Drugs, and Revolution: A Rave in Vancouver, 1994, and the Flight from May '68." *www.shrumtribe.com*.

———. 2002b. "Vinyauralism: The Art vs. the Craft of DJing and Turntablism: The DJ School." *www.shrumtribe.com*.

3

"Scenes" Dimensions
of Karaoke in the United States

Rob Drew

In 1995, Lenny Stoute reported in the *Toronto Star* that Clinton's, the venerable Toronto rock club that hatched the careers of acts like the Cowboy Junkies and Jeff Healy, was "succumbing to what many say is a fate worse than disco, . . . the final frontier of live musical insult"—it was becoming a karaoke bar. Asked about the changeover, the club's talent booker and sound man, Bo Cairo, blamed it on an influx of Korean immigrants in the neighborhood, as well as on the preferences of the bar's new owner, himself Korean. Commenting on the pending karaoke system, Cairo complained: "I have to say that it hurts. Because it's so anti-music, so anti-life" (Stoute 1995).

Other urban rock clubs have taken up karaoke with less of an uproar. After falling out of fashion for several years, karaoke made a comeback in downtown clubs in the late 1990s, as indie-rock venues like the Elbow Room in New York and the Lounge Ax in Chicago introduced karaoke nights. But from all accounts, the crowds at these clubs took up karaoke only in a tongue-in-cheek spirit (Chaplin 1998; Ratliff 1998; Williams 1998). Journalist Ben Ratliff describes the Elbow Room karaoke night as "a new place where baby celebrities and rock musicians hang out to be goofy" (1998) and recounts performances that involve mad screeching, mock sex, and guitar solos played on broomsticks. Such venues share little with the small-town neighborhood bars and suburban strip-mall bars that have been home to karaoke for more than a decade.

Live-music scenes, particularly rock-based scenes, have for the most part maintained their (ironic or geographic) distance from karaoke. In my research on karaoke, I've often found that "serious" rock fans react to it with the most disdain. Rock fans and musicians say it involves a high degree of technological mediation, which rockers tend to distrust despite their own dependence on technology (Frith 1986), consisting of "cover versions," which are traditionally subordinated in rock; worse yet, they are cover versions of pop hits and stars, which goes against rock's taste for the alternative.

Most of all, karaoke seems to violate all the rules of what defines an authentic live-music scene. Despite popular music's increasing ties to global communication and its often diffuse conditions of production, many fans (particularly rock fans) cling to a myth of gemeinschaft that values music as an organic outgrowth of a community. Will Straw (1991) points to a "musical localism" among rock scenes that emphasizes the organic relationship between musical sounds and styles and the places in which they are produced and consumed. Exhibits at Cleveland's Rock and Roll Hall of Fame, for instance, are organized not around musical subgenres or subcultural styles, but around scenes: early Memphis rockabilly, Detroit's Motown sound, San Francisco psychedelia, and so on. Within this logic, scenes are rated by their apparent stability, coherence, and distinctiveness, and musicians are rated by their local knowledge, commitment, and status within scenes.

If musicians and music scenes are judged in these terms, then karaoke may not seem to qualify as the basis for a scene, and karaoke performers hardly seem to merit the title of musician. Karaoke's supporters hew to a democratic conviction that "anyone can do it," and at most karaoke bars pretty much anyone *can* do it, regardless of vocal ability or criminal history or legal sanity. As a result, "most perceptions of karaoke . . . involve images of drunken businessmen wreaking havoc with a show tune, ties askew, faces red, highball glasses in hand" (Williams 1998, 41). With its standardized song repertoires and machine-driven accompaniment, karaoke comes off as a musical practice that can happen anywhere but sounds about the same everywhere, a practice that demonstrates no competence and implies no commitment.

Over the past decade, I've done ethnographic research on karaoke in three cities: Philadelphia; Albany, New York; and Tampa, Florida. I've observed performances as well as offstage behavior, interviewed performers and other interested parties both formally and informally, and performed myself on many occasions. In this chapter, I'm most interested in demonstrating some of the "scenic" qualities that the most vibrant karaoke events have in common. At its best, karaoke gains a stable position within certain of a community's venues and within the lives and relationships of the people who frequent these venues. Karaoke breeds competence and commitment among its devotees and rewards them with higher status within its hierarchy. And karaoke develops distinctive meanings and functions within different bars and localities, reflected in different song repertoires, selections, performances, and responses. I hope to show that in all these defining ways, karaoke's local manifestations are not very different from more familiar live-music scenes. At the same time, my conclusion will confirm that karaoke's scenes *are* different in important ways, and that these differences reflect karaoke's particular appeal in a highly mobile society fraught with complex social demands.

Stability of Karaoke Scenes

Unless they participate in it on a regular basis, most people are likely to encounter karaoke only on special occasions or on vacations. Indeed, karaoke tends to be particularly popular in those neither-here-nor-there places that are off the beaten track of people's everyday lives, such as hotels, resorts, roadside inns, and airport lounges. Some of the most riotous karaoke scenes I've witnessed are at places like the dingy after-hours bar a block off the boardwalk in a New Jersey resort town, or the motel lounge across the highway from a Florida theme park. People perform with the abandon that comes from being certain that they will never see one another again. Even those who attend karaoke closer to home on an occasional basis tend to regard it with a "touristic" attitude, as an out-of-the-ordinary lark rather than an ordinary routine. As a result, karaoke is not often seen as an activity connected to the everyday life of communities.

This sense of karaoke as isolated from everyday life is aggravated by its apparent faddishness. When it arrived Stateside in the early 1990s, karaoke was treated as another in a long line of sensational popular entertainments, from bear baiting to bungee jumping. It was hyped heavily in the media and adopted by countless bars, many of which did not have the proper conditions to sustain it. After an initial phase of oversupply and vicious competition among bars and karaoke services, many bars abandoned karaoke. Typical was a New York columnist's plaint as far back as 1991 that a local nightclub could "be forgiven its one faux pas: . . . it still has karaoke" (Musto 1991). In discussing my work with others, I've found that many people assume karaoke is no longer popular and some are unsure if it even exists anymore. (One academic advisor counseled against doing my dissertation on it, fearing it would be gone before I finished my research.)

In fact, karaoke has continued to thrive quietly in the interstices of U.S. nightlife. A survey of karaoke bars launched by the Jolt online karaoke forum in mid-1998 turned up more than 1,500 bars in fifty states ("U.S.A. Sings" 1998). Based on a volunteer sampling of karaoke enthusiasts who happen to be Internet denizens, this survey likely understates karaoke's prevalence. While fewer bars may feature karaoke than at the peak of its hype in the early 1990s, its position in the bars that continue to feature it is more stable.

A karaoke scene can take root only in a local culture of regular performers who have a clear sense of what makes for a good karaoke bar, some important factors being the sound system, song selection, physical space, and technical and social skills of the host. One emcee states that a few weeks after a bar adopts karaoke, "you start seeing this different clique that starts bonding together to do karaoke specifically." As a network evolves around karaoke, the social composition of the bar begins to change in ways that signal karaoke has "taken." "It starts weeding out the others who don't have an interest in it. You see a change in the clientele of the club, it's like this metamorphosis."

Performers who develop a penchant for karaoke may begin to attend and form new associations that are keyed from the start toward karaoke. When asked what draws them to karaoke, performers consistently make reference to the new relationships it has spawned among them: "I'm meeting new people every week, because everyone compliments each other after they sing. . . . It's like one big team." Regular performers become members of a talent pool that can lead to any number of associations: Cliques are formed and reformed, singing partners swapped, social and musical combinations tested. Often a particular performance or song provides the wellspring for a conversation or a relationship. After a mixed-sex pair of college students performs a duet on "Reunited," I ask how they met. The young man tells me: "I realized she was a good singer and she wanted to sing so I said, 'Hey, I'm there.' " I ask a chemist in his thirties how he met the retired laborer he's drinking with: "He bought me a drink because he liked my take on Sinatra's 'High Hopes.' . . . When I got done with it, there wasn't a very big reaction to it, and he says, 'What are they, all idiots?' "

Regular performers become accustomed to relating to their audiences, not as actual or potential acquaintances, but as a public—a group brought together by a common passion. Their performances become more generous, more sensitive to crowd and context. Some experienced performers can consistently stand before a roomful of strangers and bring them halfway to tears. What's extraordinary is not just that they're capable of doing so, but that they have the will to do so, for nothing in return but applause. One performer I met, a computer programmer in his late twenties named Michael, spent most of his Thursday and Saturday evenings at two neighborhood bars, sometimes taking the stage five times a night. Though he'd introduced some friends to karaoke, Michael was just as happy to arrive alone, since he was sure to run into other regulars. To hear him talk, in a quiet monotone with a slight stutter, I would never have taken him for a performer; yet whatever he sang and whatever he sounded like, he gave it his all. If it was "Rocky Top," he'd borrow a cowboy hat off the head of a spectator and quickstep around the stage, hollering in a Tennessee drawl. If it was "You've Lost That Lovin' Feelin', " he'd pull some poor woman on stage and wail to her from down on one knee as though he couldn't live without her.

Michael understood each performance as a kind of mandate in which every member of his audience had an equal stake: "I'm not actually singing for myself; I'm singing for the crowd." A good bar was one where the audience was willing to return the promise he offered them, where "people are into it, clapping, yelling, whistling. I hate going into a place where people just sit back and watch you." His pet peeve concerned the cliques who talked through most performances and paid attention only when one of their own took the stage: "It's like you're at home, singing to your friends." All regular performers share this craving to reach an audience beyond their friends at home, to conjure a group out of a roomful of strangers.

If it is true that public performance activities like karaoke offer freedoms and pleasures not available in private life, then women have a particular stake in them. Female performers seemed doubly transformed by the heady, vibrant atmosphere that prevailed among the neighborhood karaoke scenes. Carol, a regular performer at a neighborhood bar in rural Pennsylvania, not only sang several times a night but also served as a sort of facilitator on behalf of the emcees, whom she'd befriended. She coaxed patrons onstage, sang with them, and brought them together in new combinations. Her husband, one of the few people whom she couldn't persuade to sing, sometimes came in and watched with friends, yet she paid him and them no special attention.

Though Carol's manner was dynamic and engaging both onstage and offstage, she never allowed herself to get too mixed up with anyone. On one occasion, she was working through Bobby Vinton's "Blue on Blue," and a short, chubby stranger named Angelo sidled up to her for an unsolicited duet. Carol seemed a little disconcerted but stayed on course, mostly ignoring the trespasser. Afterward, the emcee politely asked Angelo if he'd like to put in a request himself. He declined, yet the moment Carol returned to the stage and began singing "You Don't Own Me," he was at her side again. This time, she gently tried to pull his mike away, but he held on tight. Angelo was a difficult lounge lizard to stave off, partly because he appeared to be a karaoke newcomer who was oblivious to the boundary between performer and audience. Yet when he joined Carol a third time for "These Boots Are Made for Walkin', " she'd had it; she summoned Joanne, a friend who was about twice her age, and asked her to take over, claiming the song was out of her own range. After this, Angelo finally stopped bothering Carol (though he did follow Joanne around for a while, begging her to do "The Impossible Dream" with him). Women who sing regularly thus become not just more confident and outgoing, but more skilled at heading off the ordinary troubles that can result.

The relationships thus formed among performers are not often very intimate, but neither are the relationships formed within most live-music scenes. Sara Cohen's description of interaction between amateur rock musicians in Liverpool could as easily describe regular karaoke performers: "They joked and gossiped together; debated the merits of other bands; passed on contacts, advice, technical and musical skills, information about gigs [and] venues" (1991, 34). Like these other musicians, karaoke performers relate to one another much in the manner of colleagues. They may know each other only by their stage pseudonyms. Although their bonds may occasionally extend beyond the bar, more often they remain spatially and temporally bound.

Yet while performers' interaction is circumscribed, it is also civil and dependable. As Ruth Finnegan notes in her study of local musicians in Milton Keynes, England: "People commonly did not know much about all their co-members in musical groups—but in the sense that mattered to them they knew *enough.*" No less than those of other musicians, karaoke performers' social links are "associated with an intense and deeply valued mode of activity," even if "not expressed through knowledge of names, ages, or social backgrounds" (1989, 303). Karaoke scenes thus provide their followers with known pathways through the social life of their cities and towns, "familiar and . . . taken-for-granted routes through what might otherwise [be] the impersonal wilderness of urban life" (306).

Competence and Commitment within Karaoke Scenes

We have seen that karaoke resembles other live-music scenes in the way it becomes a routine event within certain spaces, as well as within the lives and relationships of devotees. Another characteristic of music scenes is that they develop standards of commitment and competence, as well as status hierarchies that grow out of such standards. For instance, followers of rock scenes often adhere to classical beliefs in talent and commitment, according to which certain standout performers rise to the top, buoyed by their communities of fans. "The dynamic here is a push from below, the ruling ideology a Horatio-Alger type account of success being earned by hard work, determination, and skills honed in practice" (Frith 1988, 112). Rock fans often criticize sampling-based music genres like hip-hop and techno and their attendant scenes on the grounds that they de-skill popular music, bypassing the learning and effort that make music meaningful (Frith 1986; Scherman 2001). Even within dance- and style-based scenes, however, clear standards of competence are manifested in various forms of "hipness" or "subcultural capital," such as wearing fashionable haircuts, having the right record collections, using current slang, and knowing the latest dances (Thornton 1996).

In contrast, karaoke's promoters have always presented it as a form of music making that is open to all, regardless of competence. Much of the discourse around karaoke frames it as a kind of imaginary solution to restrictions on public communication that arise within a mass-mediated celebrity culture. "Karaoke is a natural for celebrity-obsessed Americans, since it gives everyone a chance to be a star," writes one reporter (Armstrong 1992); such comments were legion in early press coverage of karaoke. Karaoke emcees, too, are nearly unanimous in their agreement that all performers have something of value to offer and that every performer deserves attention and recognition. I could cite many comments by emcees to the effect that "this is not for professionals, it's just for everyday people," or "it doesn't matter how good or bad you are, there's always someone better or worse."

Yet karaoke's "anyone can do it" ethic is more complicated than either its devotees or its detractors tend to acknowledge. It's true that most karaoke bars will let almost anyone take the stage. Where there are restrictions, they are based less on vocal ability than on conventional criteria for admission to and conduct in bars (i.e., age limits, cover charges, and rules against drunkenness). However, a karaoke scene develops its own rites of passage and forms of subcultural capital to gauge the competence and commitment of its members and position them within its status hierarchy. No less than in other music scenes, becoming a karaoke insider can involve a considerable expenditure of time, money, and effort, as well as a seriousness and dedication to activities that many others regard as a lark.

Skill at karaoke is complex and multifaceted; in particular, it cannot be reduced to conventional standards of vocal skill. Karaoke performers are expected to walk onstage and sing on key to prerecorded background music. The many companies that produce karaoke music record each song in a particular key, and not always in the same key as the hit version of the song. Thus performers usually don't know what key a track is in until they perform it. "Like 'Waiting for a Girl Like You,' " says one singer, "I can sing it great on the radio, but karaoke's version of it is in a weird key, and I can't quite find it in my voice."

The result is that regular karaoke performers, even if they lack traditional voice training, have an advantage over trained singers who are inexperienced at karaoke. Trained singers know how their voices are classified in objective terms (soprano, mezzo-soprano, etc.), but without karaoke experience, they cannot know how their voices will jibe with karaoke's enigmatic backing tracks. Regular karaoke performers who are untrained may not know their objective range, but they build up a practical knowledge of their "range" of songs based on trial and error. Having a little repertoire of songs that they know they can sing lends regular performers a tactical advantage; they can open with them to establish their competence or fall back upon them when they've thrown it in doubt. In contrast, many trained singers are reluctant even to try karaoke, for fear of injuring either their voices or their egos.

Many karaoke machines include a "pitch control" function, which allows for further elaboration of karaoke competence and insider knowledge. Regular performers can sometimes be heard whispering something like "two notches down" to the emcee as they approach the stage, meaning that the key should be brought down two microtones from the backing track's default key. By experimenting with the same tracks at different levels week after week, singers can calibrate these tracks to their voices. Only experienced performers are aware of this feature and able to use it effectively. Perhaps the most foolproof step toward competence in karaoke, though, is acquiring a home karaoke system and music collection. This is an important expression of commitment to karaoke and a key form of capital among karaoke regulars. Increasingly, one finds performers arriving at karaoke bars carrying large, bound collections of karaoke CDs. These performers will dispense with the emcee's repertoire and simply sing along with music from their personal collections that they've already practiced at home.

Yet singing on key is only one of many determinants of success at karaoke. Some performers who sing well are nevertheless unpopular with audiences. They may violate karaoke etiquette by swearing onstage, blowing into the microphone, or talking to the audience at length. Or their onstage manner may be too formal or showy, which can itself constitute a rule violation, provoking comments like "This guy thinks he's auditioning for 'Star Search,' " or "Who does he think he is, Luciano Pavarotti?" Conversely, other performers endear themselves to audiences despite singing poorly by conventional standards. Often they do so by playing the clown; as one emcee states: "If you get up there and act like 'I'm being a clown and I want you to know it,' then they'll treat you like 'Hey, this guy's funny! He was wonderful that way!' " Often vocal ability is less important in karaoke than the ability to feel others out, laugh at oneself, and think on one's feet. The demands of karaoke can vary with the moment, and regular performers tend to be most successful not just because they sing better, but because they're more practiced at monitoring and fulfilling karaoke's changing demands.

Out of this complex of insider knowledge and practices arises a hierarchy. Every karaoke scene produces its own standout performers. At one bar I attended, a young man named Hector Rodriguez would take the stage decked in black leather and rant his way through rock classics, often sending the small crowd into hysteria. At another bar, a woman named Kathy Garson, whose only prior experience singing publicly was with her high school choir, became a crowd favorite for her soulful renditions of ballads. Such performers become something like celebrities within their venues. Others will attend just to hear them sing, and they'll receive requests to do particular songs and to stand in for duets (in the men's room at the bar Hector attended, the graffiti read, "Hector Rules, Ask For Him To Sing"). Often these performers have signature tunes that they are almost obligated to perform. At yet another bar the emcee tells me, "Joe and Jack couldn't come to Spender's without doing 'Sweet Emotion'—the crowd would kill them." (Compare Bennett's observation that on the British pub rock circuit, "even when the original recording artist was known, a song would often be associated primarily with the local band or singer" [1997, 101].)

Sometimes success within a particular karaoke scene can lead to further performance opportunities for individuals. For all the talk of fame in relation to karaoke, it is usually thought of as a very circumscribed kind of fame. Whereas "real" music scenes forge connections with larger regional and national music businesses (Olson 1998; Shank 1994), karaoke is understood as a mere fantasy of fame, yet for many performers karaoke is no more fanciful and no less consequential than any other musical activity. A few karaoke performers have enjoyed national success: country star Mindy McCready is said to have parlayed her karaoke tapes into a major-label contract, and pop singer Lina Santiago went from karaoke contests at Los Angeles restaurants to a top-ten national dance hit (Zimmerman 1996; Crowe 1996). Many more performers have drawn on karaoke for the confidence to join local bands or simply to sing publicly in other contexts for the first time (both Hector Rodriguez and Kathy Garson, mentioned earlier, obtained gigs singing for local bands as a result of their karaoke experience). As karaoke has taken root, its ties with local music scenes have multiplied: Bands sometimes use karaoke to scout out and audition vocal talent (Gonda 1993), while professional singers turn to karaoke to keep their voices supple between gigs.

Distinctiveness of Karaoke Scenes

"Scenes" are typically thought of as regions that produce original music that reflects the distinctiveness of a group and a locality. Some may doubt that a practice like karaoke can function in this way. Because it relies on backing tracks of national hits, karaoke is often viewed as a standardized form that has no local roots and bears no relation to local culture. As Johan Fornäs writes: "A conservative critic might see karaoke as yet another example of how . . . personal authenticity is removed and replaced by insipid copies of idols" (1994, 95). The same stigma often attaches to cover bands and tribute bands, which are "cast . . . as the 'low other' of the industry" and "seen as the worst examples of production to commercial order" (Homan 2002, 53; see also Weinstein 1998).

Such criticisms ignore the fact that most local bands hone their craft by copying national hits (Bennett 1980; Finnegan 1989) and that cover bands were the mainstay of popular music long predating the bebop jazz and classic rock cults of originality. Those who dismiss karaoke as mere consumption of national music overlook the fact that consumption itself can be a productive, identity-forming activity (Hebdige 1979). As Andy

Bennett notes: "While the popular culture industries may provide social actors with a common stock of cultural resources, the way such resources are subsequently re-worked as collective sensibilities will in every instance depend upon the conditions of locality" (1997, 98).

From an Anglo-American perspective, the localism of karaoke scenes may be most striking in accounts of karaoke among minority and immigrant populations. For instance, Vietnamese immigrants in Los Angeles karaoke bars sing tangos that evoke Vietnam's pre-communist past (Wong 1994), and Chinese immigrants in New York form singing clubs around karaoke versions of Cantonese opera songs (Lum 1995). Even among more mainstream U.S. bars, though, karaoke events vary with the character of the bar and region in subtle and complex ways. These variations are partly dictated by differences in the song repertoires available at bars. There are dozens of companies that produce karaoke discs, many of them specializing in particular pop-music genres. Karaoke services often purchase discs based on their sense of the clientele at the bars they serve, sometimes consulting performers themselves in their purchase decisions. As more venues have adopted karaoke and competition has increased among karaoke services, the latter have become savvier about marketing their repertoires to particular audiences. "Assuming your goal is to establish a for-profit karaoke service, the first thing to ask yourself is, 'Who am I going to charge for my service?' " advises one karaoke trade magazine.

Beyond this, karaoke bars vary widely according to the songs patrons choose to perform, the manner in which they perform these songs, and the audience's response to performances. Such details are not random but mirror the common experience of the bar's patrons and the region's inhabitants. For instance, early in my research I attended a college bar called Spanky's, whose owner had recently purchased a karaoke system with a small number of discs. As a result, patrons had only a few dozen songs to choose from. Many of these songs were oldies from before the college crowd's time, and in performing them the students would almost invariably make a joke of them. One young man did Elvis Presley's "Burnin' Love" and punctuated it with smart-alecky comments ("Help me, I'm flamin', must be a hundred and nine—excuse me, but anyone who's a hundred and nine degrees is technically dead!"). Another did Elton John's "Your Song" in a mawkish, exaggeratedly sincere manner and finally let go an enormous belch.

Things continued in this vein until a pair of boys took the stage for Prince's "When Doves Cry." The record was released in the mid-1980s, around the time that Spanky's audience was in their midteens and probably had flocked to *Purple Rain,* the Prince film that helped popularize the song. The boys faithfully reproduced the call-and-response of Prince's original vocal, one of them punctuating the other's singing with plaintive highlights. Spectators in the audience screamed and swayed and waved their arms in unison. A boy in the corner drummed frantically on a wall; a table of girls held up lighters in tribute. "That's the best song to sing," I heard one of the boys say as they descended from the stage to frenzied applause, and at this bar it certainly was. In the following weeks at Spanky's, it became a ritual that after several desultory recitals of oldies, someone took on "When Doves Cry" and worked the crowd to a fever pitch. The song became a crowd favorite, the sort of number that could prompt a roomful of strangers to suddenly sing and move and rejoice as one. Virtually every karaoke bar has such crowd favorites.

As a result of these variations in song repertoires and crowd preferences, karaoke scenes tend to distinguish themselves along lines of national music genres. There are bars and regions that lean toward country, hard rock, or rhythm and blues, depending on the demographics and the clientele. Two additional points should be made, though. First, as the Spanky's example illustrates, local variations in karaoke scenes are not a matter just of which genres are preferred, but of how multiple global genres are folded into the local music mix. Although they didn't have the same impact, the comical performances of moldy oldies at Spanky's defined the scene no less than did the reverential performances of the Prince song. It might be possible to map the tendencies toward serious versus parodic performances at different bars according to the geographic and social context of the bar. For instance, while the late-Elvis number "Burning Love" was an object of parody at Spanky's, it would likely be performed more seriously at bars with different clientele (where Prince might well be an object of parody). Again, this mixed local reception of different genres is evident in other sorts of music scenes. For instance, Homan (2002) observes that Australia's tribute band scene has polarized around serious tributes to classic rock bands like Midnight Oil and parodic tributes to pop bands like Abba and Spice Girls.

Finally, the distinctive musical mix of a karaoke bar does not simply reflect the music genres of the country but rather emerges from the actions and negotiations of individuals within the scene. It is easy enough to say, for instance, that the karaoke bar on the outskirts of a state university campus is home to a college rock scene or that the working-class karaoke bar in northeast Philadelphia harbors a hard rock scene, but things are rarely this simple. Sometimes, different genres vie for dominance due to factions within the crowd. Other times, a few individuals emboldened by one another's support may carve out brief or not-so-brief niches within the bar's generic mix. The diversity of karaoke song lists, the relative ease of performance, and the dynamism of karaoke sessions all invite this sort of conversation and conflict in the formation of karaoke scenes.

How Karaoke Differs from Other Scenes

Karaoke's ready-made accompaniment and "anyone can do it" philosophy create a context that distinguishes it from most other music scenes. Like the traditional sing-alongs of the 1960s folk revival (Rosenberg 1993) and early punk sensibilities two decades later (Laing 1985), karaoke allows great latitude for different levels and kinds of participation. While many performers are assiduous in their devotion to karaoke, others participate only casually. While many performers frequent only one or a few bars, others prefer a more diffuse and widespread mode of participation, and while for many performers, karaoke leads to new social and musical associations, for others it inspires little offstage social involvement. In all these ways, karaoke is easier and more accessible than perhaps any other contemporary form of public music making. To do it well takes skill and to do it at all takes nerve, yet beyond this there are few formal or informal barriers to participation.

All these traits dismay those who pine for more cohesive, committed music scenes, and who see karaoke as almost an invitation to dilettantism. In their gemeinschaft model of an organic community centered on music, advocates of more traditional scenes resemble those social critics who lament the supposed decline in civic involvement in the United States (Putnam 1995). Yet others have pointed out that, if older forms of civic involvement have declined, this is not the result of public apathy or disengagement but of changes in economic and social conditions. As Robert Wuthnow explains, older civic organizations were rooted in a society of stable bureaucratic institutions; such organizations "assumed an implicit link between service and belonging" (1998, 31). Yet such structures have become less relevant in a society of what Wuthnow calls "porous institutions." Due to economic instability and declining job security, people change jobs and careers more often than in the past. Family and friendship networks have become more attenuated. These changes, along with increased mobility, permit and sometimes demand more frequent travel and relocation. As a result, Wuthnow argues, people have not abandoned civic involvement but have opted for more short-term involvements with volunteer organizations, support groups, and hobby groups.

Karaoke is an excellent example of this casual public participation. Particularly in small towns and local neighborhoods that lack a viable infrastructure of well-equipped venues, bands, and paying audiences, karaoke thrives (Olson 1998). There are as many ads for karaoke nights in an average twelve-page issue of the Saginaw, Michigan, weekly *The Review* as in an average copy of the *Village Voice*. The ironic upshot is that karaoke finds itself perhaps the most ubiquitous form of public music making at the dawn of the new century. For all its devotees' talk of fantasy and wish fulfillment, karaoke may be more enmeshed in the daily lives of more people than any other musical practice. It allows music to happen in places that can't sustain more capital- and labor-intensive live-music scenes.

Like "virtual scenes," karaoke speaks to a society of asynchronous schedules, dynamic and sprawling communities, mediated and media-facilitated relationships. Even some skilled professional singers find guilty pleasure in karaoke for the simplest of reasons: It is always possible to perform. Karaoke requires no equipment, bookings, band mates, or rehearsals. Thousands of amateurs around the world can sing what they want, how they want, and when they want. There is today a no more immediate, accessible route to the gratifications of making music in public.

References

Armstrong, Larry. 1992. "What's That Noise in Aisle 5?" *Business Week,* 8 June, 38.

Bennett, Andrew. 1997. " 'Going Down the Pub!': The Pub Rock Scene as a Resource for the Consumption of Popular Music." *Popular Music* 16, 1: 97–108.

Bennett, H. Stith. 1980. *On Becoming a Rock Musician.* Amherst: University of Massachusetts Press.

Chaplin, Julia. 1998. "Once More, with Irony." *New York Times,* 5 July.

Cohen, Sara. 1991. *Rock Culture in Liverpool: Popular Music in the Making.* Oxford: Clarendon Press.

Crowe, Jerry. 1996. "The Teen Chart Queen." *Los Angeles Times,* 13 February.

Finnegan, Ruth. 1989. *The Hidden Musicians: Music-Making in an English Town.* New York: Cambridge University Press.

Fong-Torres, Ben. 1996. "Pass the Popcorn . . . and the Microphone." *Karaoke & DJ USA* 25:28–29.

Fornäs, Johan. 1994. "Karaoke: Subjectivity, Play, and Interactive Media." *Nordicom Review* 1: 87–103.

Frith, Simon. 1986. "Art versus Technology: The Strange Case of Popular Music." *Media, Culture, and Society* 8: 263–79.

————. 1988. "Video Pop: Picking Up the Pieces." In S. Frith, ed., *Facing the Music.* New York: Pantheon.

Gallagher, Maria. 1992. "You and Mike Are the Big Stars." *Philadelphia Daily News,* 10 March.

Gonda, Thomas A., Jr. 1993. "Cattle Call: Karaoke as Audition." In T. A. Gonda Jr., ed., *Karaoke: The Bible.* Oakland, Calif.: G-Man Publishers.

Hebdige, Dick. 1979. *Subculture: The Meaning of Style.* London: Methuen.

Homan, Shane. 2002. "Access All Eras: Careers, Creativity, and the Australian Tribute Band." *Perfect Beat* 5: 45–59.

Laing, Dave. 1985. *One Chord Wonders: Power and Meaning in Punk Rock.* Milton Keynes, U.K.: Open University Press.

Lum, Casey. 1995. *In Search of a Voice: Karaoke and the Construction of Identity in Chinese America.* Mahwah, N.J.: Lawrence Erlbaum.

Musto, Michael. 1991. "La dolce Musto." *Village Voice,* 27 August, 55.

Olson, Mark. 1998. " 'Everybody Loves Our Town': Scenes, Spatiality, Migrancy." In Thomas Swiss, John Sloop, and Andrew Herman, eds., *Mapping the Beat: Popular Music and Contemporary Theory.* Malden, Mass.: Blackwell.

Putnam, Robert D. 1995. "Bowling Alone: America's Declining Social Capital." *Journal of Democracy* 6: 65–78.

Ratliff, Ben. 1998. "Mixing with the Music in Downtown Clubs." *New York Times,* 20 November.

Rosenberg, Neil V., ed. 1993. *Transforming Tradition: Folk Music Revivals Examined.* Urbana: University of Illinois Press.

Scherman, Tony. 2001. "Strike the Band: Pop Music without Musicians." *New York Times,* 11 February.

Shank, Barry. 1994. *Dissonant Identities: The Rock 'n' Roll Scene in Austin, Texas.* Hanover, N.H.: Wesleyan University Press.

"Sizing Up Your Karaoke Library." 2000. *Karaoke Singer Magazine,* November, 25–26.

Stoute, Lenny. 1995. "Curtains for Clintons: Breeding Ground for New Talent Switches to Karaoke Format." *Toronto Star,* 7 December.

Straw, Will. 1991. "Systems of Articulation, Logics of Change: Communities and Scenes in Popular Music." *Cultural Studies* 5: 368–88.

Thornton, Sarah. 1996. *Club Cultures: Music, Media, and Subcultural Capital.* Hanover, N.H.: Wesleyan University Press.

"U.S.A. Sings." 1998, May 27. Retrieved 3 March 2000 from *jolt.karaoke.com/jolt?14 @^131126@.ee6c9e6*

Weinstein, Deena. 1998. "The History of Rock's Pasts through Rock Covers." In Thomas Swiss, John Sloop, and Andrew Herman, eds., *Mapping the Beat: Popular Music and Contemporary Theory.* Malden, Mass.: Blackwell.

Williams, Kevin M. 1998. "Karaoke Cool: Sing-Along Nights Find a Younger Audience." *Chicago Sun-Times*, 31 July.

Wong, Deborah. 1994. " 'I Want the Microphone': Mass Mediation and Agency in Asian-American Popular Music." *Drama Review* 38: 152–67.

Wuthnow, Robert. 1998. *Loose Connections: Joining Together in America's Fragmented Communities*. Cambridge: Harvard University Press.

Zimmerman, David. 1996. "Mindy McCready's One-Year Trek to Stardom." *USA Today*, 17 September, 7D.

4

"Tween" Scene: Resistance within the Mainstream

Melanie Lowe

The cover of the 14 February 2000 *People* reads: "Pop princess Britney Spears: Too sexy too soon? Little girls love her, but her image makes some moms nervous." The message is loud and clear: Mom, be nervous; be very, very nervous. And yet, as we shall discover in this ethnography of the "tween" scene, perhaps Mom doesn't need to be quite so apprehensive about the messages she assumes—or rather is told—her daughter is receiving from mainstream media. Much of the pleasure of participating in teen-pop culture resides in an invitation to resist subordination, objectification, and sexism in multiple manifestations, as "tweens," an advertising-industry term for girls between childhood and adolescence, exercise a surprising feminist consciousness.

The tween scene, as I shall call the cultural phenomenon that is centered around teen-pop fandom, exploded during the late 1990s as boy bands 'N Sync and the Backstreet Boys and "pop princess" Britney Spears ruled the top-forty airwaves. As global media, teen-pop music is slickly produced, studio manufactured, and multinational-corporation controlled. It most certainly transcends any particular geographic space. As the unavoidable soundscape of the United States (if not of much of the Western and a surprising amount of the Eastern world) around the turn of the millennium, its audience is simply enormous. According to the *Billboard* year-end charts, teen pop scored the three top-selling albums of 1999: The Backstreet Boys held the number-one position with *Millenium,* followed by Britney Spears's debut album, . . . *Baby One More Time,* at number two, and self-titled *'N Sync* close behind at number three. So, given its mainstream status, undeniable homogeneity, and global audience, how might we understand teen-pop culture as a "scene," and, more importantly, why would we want to?

Teen pop, as a subgenre of pop music, is marked by a clash of presumed innocence and overt sexuality, a conflict that mirrors the physical and emotional turmoil of its primary target audience and vital fan base: early-adolescent middle- and upper-middle-class suburban girls. Rather than occurring in a specific geographic location like a city, region, or even a particular nightclub, the social activity of teen-pop fandom is situated in arguably the "safest" place available to preteen girls—the domestic space of girls' bedrooms—doors closed, of course. Here, in the privacy of their own personal spaces, protected from threat of invasion by either boys or the more intimidating pop-music sound du jour, Korn and Limp Bizkit, tweens hang out, watch MTV's *Total Request Live,* plaster their walls with pictures of heartthrob Justin Timberlake of 'N Sync, giggle and drool over V-Jay Carson Daly, surf the Internet, complain about school, gossip about their "ex-friends" and other "sluts," read *Teen People,* and alternately adore, mock, and trash their favorite imagined playmate—Britney Spears. Joined by common tastes in everything from clothing to boys to television shows to music, as well as by such adolescent anxieties as their budding sexuality, changing bodies, and desire for more independence from their parents, early-adolescent girls negotiate such intensely personal issues through lively and often surprisingly intimate participation in the global mainstream culture that is teen pop. Moreover, as much of their engagement with teen pop involves an attempt to distance themselves from aspects of this culture they find morally questionable, tweens ironically find *in* the mainstream an opportunity to resist their perceived oppression *by* the mainstream.[1] In short, the tween scene is defined by politics.

Methodology

During the summer of 1999 I conducted focus-group sessions with groups of five to six early-adolescent middle-class girls.[2] Most focus groups met in private rooms at YMCA teen-center summer programs or summer camps, a very relaxed and casual atmosphere. Rather than conducting one-on-one interviews, I worked with focus groups in the hope of experiencing (or at least observing) teen-pop culture in action—that is, early-adolescent girls talking to each other rather than directly to me about music, pop stars, and any other topics that came up in conversations loosely centered on music.[3] I was also hoping to observe or participate in such afternoon activities as watching *TRL* and surfing the Internet. The rooms at the Ys were furnished with both televisions and computers.

Participation in the focus-group sessions was completely voluntary, and indeed a few girls, particularly those who seemed not as engaged with pop music, chose not to stay more than fifteen minutes or so. Those that remained, however, were quite excited to be able to just hang out together, leave the boys behind (for the moment), listen to music, and talk about anything they wanted to. I found the girls engaging, imaginative, informative, and refreshingly uninhibited.

Setting up these sessions required the usual formalities and meetings with center directors, but once I was on site with the girls I tried to be as casual as possible. As a young middle-class white woman who not only has listened to pop music since her own early adolescence but also still enjoys pop music and top-forty radio, I am reasonably well plugged in to their musical culture. Having worked for several years as the pre- and early-teen unit leader at a suburban summer camp, I also have much experience relating to early adolescents. Drawing on my genuine enjoyment of "their" music and my experience with preteens, I consciously strove to be seen not as a teacher or leader but more as an older sister or friend. Although I am around fifteen years older than the girls in the focus groups, I tried to dampen the sense of generational difference by dressing as they did (mostly cut-off shorts and T-shirts), wearing little or no makeup (even though, of course, most of the girls wear eyeliner, mascara, and lipstick or gloss), and remaining on their physical level at all times. Usually we all sat on the floor or lounged on gym mats. I avoided standing before the group and addressing them as a teacher or counselor might. By the end of the sessions, particularly in the two groups profiled here, I felt we had achieved a certain intimacy. The rapport we developed seemed to me something like friendship for the moment. I believe we had each other's confidence. But still, my position and power in relation to the girls inevitably influenced every aspect of the sessions, despite my attempts to minimize this power differential. In my reading of the relationships between these girls and teen-pop culture, I remain conscious of and attempt to relay how my presence, power, and position affected the discourse.

All focus-group sessions were audiotaped, and the transcriptions that follow are written as dramatic scripts. I have omitted no single word or phrase and have represented the significant pauses in their speech—pauses that occurred when they seemed to be searching for words, didn't want to finish a phrase, were looking to a friend for support, and so on—with an em dash (—). Most dialogue excerpts are unbroken, but, to avoid overly long excerpts and the risk of overwhelming the reader with detail unrelated to the main argument presented here, a few of the excerpts have been abbreviated. Omitted are only those bits of the conversation in which a girl got off the topic being considered, was distracted by something outside the group or room, or started up a private conversation on a different subject with another girl in the focus group. If a digression was significant itself or seemed an attempt to avoid or sidestep an issue, I left it in. An ellipsis (. . .) represents omitted material. Quite often more than one girl spoke at a time. The most significant cleaning up I did during the transcription process was to write out each girl's "lines" intact rather than to try to preserve the layered effect of the dialogue. In other words, I am privileging content over time in my representation of the conversations.

Profiles of Two Focus Groups

All dialogue excerpts are taken from transcripts of the audiotapes of my meetings with two focus groups. I met both groups of girls at suburban YMCA teen centers in the Nashville, Tennessee, area. Although the majority of the girls have lived in Nashville for most of their lives, I found their conversation, convictions, and aspirations not at all unlike those of girls I have met who grew up in other parts of the United States. I chose to center this discussion on the issues raised by these two focus groups because I was able to spend the most time with them. Moreover, as mentioned, the location of the tween scene is not a geographic one. The situation of this scene coexists in and migrates from one girl's bedroom to the next throughout Suburbia, U.S.A., and demographic boundaries are drawn mostly by gender and age, not by locale.

As evidenced by the contribution African American girls brought to our conversations, black and white girls both are consumers of teen pop and actively participate in the tween scene. Because there were no Latina, Asian American, or Native American girls in any of the focus-group sessions, I cannot speak for their engagement with teen pop. But, since I found those engaged in the tween scene to be mostly middle- to upper-middle-class girls, I would speculate that demographics would break down more by socioeconomic class than by race. Although the girls assured me they wouldn't mind if I used their real names, in the profiles of the two focus groups, I have nonetheless changed their names to conceal their identities.

Focus Group 1

Rachel, 14–10th grade
Jessica, 13–8th grade
Brenda, 13–8th grade
Wendy, 13–8th grade
Anne, 13–8th grade
Emily, 13–8th grade

Rachel, Jessica, Wendy, and Anne go to public schools; Emily and Brenda go to private schools.
Rachel, Jessica, Brenda, Anne, and Emily are white; Wendy is African American.
Jessica and Brenda have boyfriends.
Rachel and Brenda have cell phones.
All girls have lived in Nashville suburbs for most of their lives.

Focus Group 2

Allison, 12–6th grade
Catherine, 12–7th grade
Julie, 13–8th grade
Monique, 13–8th grade
Kara, 12–7th grade

Allison, Catherine, Julie, Monique go to public schools; Kara goes to a private school.
Allison, Julie, and Kara are white; Catherine and Monique are African American.
Allison, Monique, and Kara have lived in Nashville suburbs for most of their lives; Julie is a self-described "army brat" and has lived all over the United States, as well as in Latin America; Catherine is from Pasadena, California.

Each session started similarly. I introduced myself briefly, told the girls a little about what I was up to, and asked them if they were interested in music. I got the girls talking about music with a few questions about what radio stations they listen to, who their favorite artists are, what they like about these artists or their music, and so forth. Once the talking started I hoped the girls would take the conversation wherever they wanted to, and generally they did. I tried not to lead so much as to listen. The specific topics were entirely up to the girls, and they usually began by talking about music they enjoyed, bands they disliked, videos they found cool, and such. After only a few minutes, however, they settled into a conversation about the current teen pop.

The most striking early event in *every* session was an all-out attack on teenage pop sensation Britney Spears, *Rolling Stone*'s crowned "Teen Queen" (Daly 1999, 60). As soon as one girl mentioned her name, the others would jump into the conversation, and, with excited, raised voices, rip Britney to shreds:

> [Emily, who had left the room briefly, enters.]
> Anne: We're talking about Britney Spears.
> Emily: She's slutty!
>
> . . .
>
> Rachel [to Melanie]: Did you see the pictures in *Rolling Stone?* She looks
>   really trashy.
> Anne: Slore!
> Brenda: Slore!
> Anne and Brenda: Slore slore slore slore slore slore whore!
> Melanie: Is that a new word?
> Anne: Slut and whore together! [laughing]

"Slut," "whore," and "slore" (an elision of "slut" and "whore") were the first words out of their mouths. There was no such reaction to a mention of Christina Aguilera, another teenage pop star, or of Brandy, Monica, or Mya. Likewise, the hunks in the boy bands were neither here nor there.

At first, especially in light of my opening assertion that these tweens possess a feminist consciousness, we might argue that by calling Spears a "whore" the girls are enabling their own subordination. As Cowie and Lees (1981) first recognized, labels like "whore," "slut," and "slag" not only are applied to women and girls unfairly, but also, with the opposite constructs "virgin," "pris," and "drag," form a discursive dichotomy that is used to describe nearly all female behavior, sexual and otherwise. While the girls Cowie and Lees interviewed recognized such labels as degrading and unjust, they nevertheless used the words themselves in much the same way the boys did, thereby perpetuating the discursive process that controlled them. It is certainly possible to read the abject language hurled at Britney Spears by her female fans this way and to be disheartened by how little has changed in the twenty years since Cowie and Lees's study of working-class girls in London. But, as the conversation about Britney Spears progressed, what struck me most was not the girls' casual use of cruel and demeaning language, but the intensity of their emotion: They were *angry*. Although they may feel some discomfort with the no-win situation set up by the good-girl/bad-girl, slag/drag, or virgin/whore dichotomy that has plagued women for ages, what distresses them most is finding this good-girl/bad-girl combination in Spears herself. This confuses them: They struggle to reconcile their own feminist consciousness and conditioning with the allure and power of Spear's constant negotiation between youthful inhibition and unabashed sex appeal.

Young Feminists

To be sure, tweens would never label themselves "feminists," a term that to these girls, born in the mid- to late-1980s, conjures up images of angry lesbians and pushy, bitchy, ugly women. After all, they seem always to have known the insult "feminazi" and seem profoundly uncomfortable with the language of gender politics. And yet, when we listen to them speak, consider their conceptions of what constitutes fair social interaction and appropriate conversation, and learn of their personal and professional aspirations, today's tweens possess an undeniable feminist consciousness.

At one point during a meeting with Focus Group 2, the Offsprings' song "Why Don't You Get a Job?" came on the radio and, when the girls finally stopped singing along, they explained why they thought the song had a good message. Kara put it succinctly: "It's saying, 'Do it yourself, don't just rely on some guy.' "

Although the girls in the focus groups want nothing to do with the Spice Girls (who were the tween idols of two years earlier), they believe that the Spice Girls had a "good message" and that "Girl Power" is alive and well. For them, "Girl Power" is code for a certain type of feminism—girl solidarity, self-sufficiency, and equality. They believe that they should defend each other and stick together, they want careers so they don't have to "rely on some guy," and they expect girls and boys, women and men, to be treated equally in *all* situations.

Although the girls don't call it such, they also notice gender inequity all around them. And it gets them fired up, as revealed in their lengthy accounts of how girls and boys are treated differently in their schools. Nearly every conversation eventually turned to school at some point, and before long I was witnessing lively and animated girl gripe sessions that covered everything from the sexism they experience in physical education classes to the skimpy outfits they believe some cheerleaders are forced to wear.

From Focus Group 1

Emily: The guy teachers, like in PE, they treat you so much differently.
Rachel: They have, like, guy stuff and girl stuff.
Melanie: So you want to do the guy stuff too?
Brenda: I don't necessarily want to do the guy stuff, but I think they should treat us equally and not different.
Emily and Rachel: Yeah—
Emily: The guys think they're stronger and that's because the PE teachers let them do all the stronger stuff—so they get stronger and we just, like—'cause we never get to do any of the hard stuff, so we just, like—
Rachel: I mean, I don't want to do the hard stuff, but I just think—
Emily: They just give us the easy stuff.
. . .
Rachel: We'd rather do all the same thing.
Emily: So that's the reason we're not as strong as the guys are—we grew up thinking that we weren't as strong—so when we get to, like, middle school we're doing, like, the weaker stuff—so obviously we're not going to be stronger and the guys come at us with stuff like that.
Rachel: Yeah.

From Focus Group 2

Kara: The cheerleaders in my school, they get the skirts too big so that they will go down lower.
Catherine and Julie: Yeah.
Catherine: My grandmother, she sews a lot, and she has to sew them so that they come down further. They're too short and they don't like them—and then also when I was a cheerleader—they said that they bought the same size, every one was the same size, for everyone, and they were all small or whatever, so for some people they were eight inches too high or whatever and they did that on purpose—they bought a size too small for everyone because these skinny girls and—
Melanie: So, who was "they"?

Catherine: The coach, Coach Morantz, he is, oh god, such a jerk—like, on the softball team we said, "Why can't we go in the batting cage?" and he said, "You are girls, go get me some lemonade and cookies and come back and we'll talk"—and he was such a jerk—he's so sexist, it's not even funny, and he's the one who orders all this stuff, so we had to have someone come to our school and take out the skirts because they were so tight.

In these conversations the girls' complaints of gender inequity ring loud and clear.

The girls also voice concern about the "objectification" of women (although, again, they would never use that term for what they observe and experience). And here we can begin to see their personal politics interacting with the activity of teen-pop fandom. For example, they don't approve of the risqué outfits Britney Spears wears with increasing frequency, and they worry about the influence her attire might be having on younger girls, particularly their younger sisters. They condemned her performance at the *Kids' Choice Awards,* for instance, broadcast 1 May 1999 on Nickelodeon, as particularly inappropriate for kids. (Spears performed without a bra—or so it appeared—in a skin-tight and translucent, *very* highly cropped T-shirt, revealing not only the new shape and size that have resulted from her recent "growth spurt" but also much detail.)

Focus Group 2

Kara: She did this like little kids' tour thingy.
Julie: The *Kids' Choice Awards.*
Kara: And she wore this really skin-tight shirt and . . .
Julie: She doesn't wear a bra!
Kara: You could see everything.

But what disturbed the girls even more than Spears's revealing outfit was the reason they suspect she wore it:

Melanie: If you could see everything, why did she wear it?
Kara: To show off her boob job! Okay, guys see boobs, jugs, or whatever you call it in a little booty they see is tight, they just go—like their jaw falls and their eyes go "Wooooo."
Allison [laughing, jumping up and down]: Boing, boing, boing.

Focus Group 1

Brenda: Because she had that—surgery—breast enhancement. She
   should let them grow—you know—naturally.
Rachel: She's seventeen, so you know—she should just wait and see.
Anne: Most of her fans are guys, that's probably why she did it, to make
   her look sexier—and for the guys—to make them look at her more.
Brenda: All the guys, they like—[giggling and hesitation]
Rachel [laughing]: The bigger the better!

The girls explained that by "bouncing" around, showing off her "fake
boobs" and body, Britney Spears is sending a terrible message to the young
girls in the audience. In this short excerpt from Focus Group 2, Catherine
cuts right to the heart of the matter:

Julie: Her chest was sticking out, what a huge surprise—it's like.
Catherine: It's only your boobs and butt that matter.

And finally, Rachel, Wendy, and Jessica from Focus Group 1 articulate
clearly the impact they think other women's choices, celebrity or not, can
have on their lives. Here they're discussing the clothing choices of Brenda's
older sister, of whose behavior the girls obviously disapprove. (Brenda's
sister is eighteen years old and has three children by two fathers.)

Brenda: She [Britney Spears] dresses like my sister.
Melanie: How old is your sister?
Brenda: She's eighteen—she has three kids.
Rachel: Oh my god!
Brenda: And I think that's—that's crazy—she's getting married and I'm
   really happy about that, but—she should stop dressing like that.
Jessica [laughing]: What do you think she'll wear for her wedding?
Brenda: It makes her look loose.
Jessica: It makes her look like a slut!
Rachel: And it makes us—like—all women are sluts.
Wendy: The people who don't dress like that, it makes us look bad.
Jessica: Like a slut!

These girls are quite articulate when it comes to condemning patriarchal values. They complain about sexism, recognize the objectification of
women's bodies, and worry about the impact media images and messages

might be having on younger girls. They also fret about how other girls' attire and behavior might affect how they themselves are perceived and treated.

When the girls touched on issues like these, issues I found particularly significant, I occasionally asked direct questions, as the dialogue excerpts show. At these moments the girls spoke to me somewhat more formally and more seriously. During the review, transcription, and analysis of the audiotapes I listened carefully for how my direct address may have altered the group dynamic, affected their interactions with each other, or colored their responses. In general, I didn't hear their speech become more stilted, awkward, inhibited, or embarrassed at these moments. They didn't hesitate or clam up either. I'm quite confident that, for the most part, they weren't simply telling me what they thought I wanted to hear or what they thought I would consider legitimate. Although I took certain measures to dampen the sense of power differential during the focus-group sessions, as I have mentioned, my presence and role as an adult researcher may have invited such mature, thoughtful, sophisticated, "adult" comments.[4] Still, as I hear them, the girls—Catherine, Kara, and Rachel in particular—sound like young feminists.

Resistance

When they are confronted with images and messages that challenge their feminist consciousness, these tweens adopt an adult, protective, "Mom" persona, whether they are subjects in a sociological study or girls hanging out in their bedrooms. Just like their mothers, these girls are nervous. In addition to the conversations I heard, the private bedroom activities they revealed (and which I was of course unable to witness) demonstrate an active, if perhaps somewhat subconscious, resistance strategy. As we shall see, teen-pop fandom, a primary activity of the tween scene, is marked by a reconciliation of the conflict between tweens' enjoyment of popular musical culture and their disapproval of much of its content. In short, teen pop provides them with an opportunity to flex their nascent political muscles in the protected and safe space that—as they have learned, for better or worse—is ruled by women: the home.

As fans of teen pop, these girls struggle to reconcile their feminist consciousness with the contradictory meanings they find in the music and videos they consume, particularly those by female artists. During the summer of 1999, the tweens I got to know found Britney Spears particularly troubling. They read blatant contradictions in her lyrics, image, and career and struggled to make sense of her "message" (their word). By listening to them talk about two songs, the then-current hits from Spears's debut album, we can see how they actively employ reception strategies that separate disapproval from enjoyment. In other words, they have found strategies to take great pleasure in consuming music that in many ways disturbs them.

When we first started talking about particular songs, most of the girls said that "Sometimes," the second hit from Spears's debut album, was their favorite one. The lyrics to "Sometimes," sung by Spears as a direct address to a (presumably) male "you," seem to communicate quite clearly a girl's dismay that her boyfriend is moving too fast and her hope that he'll slow down and wait for her. She explains that she wants to be with him and wants to trust him, but she also wants him to know why she comes off as "shy" and "moves away" every time he comes too close. Although the sentiment of the chorus—that all she desires is to be with him constantly, to hold him, and to treat him right—might not sit entirely comfortably with many women, the song's "message" strikes me as reasonably palatable, particularly for teen pop. Once the girls in one group informed me that it was their favorite, I expected to hear them applaud the girl in the song's assertiveness for telling the guy to take things at her speed, not his.

But that's not at all what they hear in this song. Here's a short excerpt from Focus Group 1's discussion.

Melanie [to Emily]: So, what is your favorite song?
Emily: "Sometimes."
Wendy: Yeah, "Sometimes."
Melanie: Why that one?
Emily: I just like the concept—because she's like different at different times. She has a lot of different personalities.
Wendy: Yeah, she's different in that one.

I was surprised and confused by this response, but the conversation was moving on, so I let it go and the girls kept chatting. Later, while reviewing the session tapes, I came to understand what the girls meant. On the one hand, from watching them sing along nicely with the verses but *belt* out the chorus, it's clear that, for them, the song *is* the chorus. So forget the story. By the "concept" of the song, Emily seems to mean that, literally, sometimes "Britney" runs, sometimes "Britney" hides, and sometimes "Britney" is scared. In other words, as she sees it, Britney Spears's character in this song is different at different times, and she likes seeing her many sides. But

Wendy's follow-up comment, "Yeah, she's different in that one," is particularly interesting and suggests that there is another layer of interpretation, another possible meaning in play. For Wendy, like many of the other girls, Spears does not act or play a character external to herself when she sings. She is always Britney Spears, and it's Spears herself singing these words. So Wendy seems to mean that in "Sometimes," Spears shows a different side of *her* personality than she does *in her other songs*.

The music, perhaps even more than the words, invites Wendy's reading of the song. Musically, "Sometimes" is quite unlike Spears's other two then-current hits, " . . . Baby One More Time" and "(You Drive Me) Crazy." While all three are slickly produced pop tunes, the latter two have a pop rhythm-and-blues flavor, driving dance beats, and edgy synthesized instruments. Spears's voice is at times distant and hollow (likely run through a mid-pass filter).[5] "Sometimes," on the other hand, is pure romantic bubble-gum pop. It lacks rhythmic drive and the backing track is fuller, with smoother and rounder synthesized instruments. Here, Spears's voice sounds somewhat more natural. The positive message the girls find in "Sometimes" lies not so much in the song itself, but rather in its contrast—both lyrical and musical—with Spears's other songs. In the end, the girls celebrate the many sides of Britney and the idea, communicated musically, that she has different "personalities."

While the girls applaud the notion that Spears's personality has many different facets, they don't necessarily approve of each one. Even though they hardly pay attention to a song's "story" and become quite excited when *any* Britney Spears tune comes on the radio or television, they are nonetheless troubled by the singer's "I'll do anything to get my boyfriend back" tunes, particularly the title track, " . . . Baby One More Time." In the lyrics, we learn of a relationship gone bad and the girl's revelation that the reason she breathes is this boy. She confesses that there's nothing she wouldn't do for him and that she wants him to show her how he wants "it." Her loneliness is killing her, she explains, and because when she's not with him she loses her mind, she demands a sign—in short, the song's hook: "Hit me baby one more time."

Here, as in "Sometimes," Spears is singing to a male "you," only this time the message received is quite different. The girls don't like Britney throwing herself at some guy and are particularly concerned about the possible meanings of that one line: "Hit me baby one more time." We talked extensively in the focus group sessions about that line, and it's clear that some of the girls had talked about it before, either at home or with friends.

From Focus Group 1

Rachel: Hit me baby one more time—my mom says that.
Brenda: In the video she's like drooling over this guy—
Rachel: I think it's about an ex-boyfriend that she wants back.
Jessica: I think it's like—I don't really want to say this but—[laughing]—
Brenda: In the video, at the end, she's like drooling all over this basketball player.
Rachel: Not in the video he isn't, but in real life he's her cousin.
Wendy: I think Britney Spears should, like—like—I think she's really desperate and she needs, like—somebody to, like—to care for her and, like—and, like, take her around and everything.
Jessica: [still laughing] She wants more sex! Come on, baby, give me some more!

From Focus Group 2

Allison: Hit me so I can tell that you love me still, I don't know.
Julie: In the video, on the bleachers, it's her cousin she's looking at, it's her cousin!
Melanie: So what's the whole song about?
Allison, Julie, and Monique: Sex! [laughing]
Melanie: Does it have a story?
Allison, Julie, and Monique: No! [laughing]
Allison: Hit me again! Lay me, lay me, lay me!

Although they say the song has no story, the girls obviously have some sense of its narrative. " . . . Baby One More Time" is, to them, about lust. As they see it, Britney wants it, and wants it bad. She's desperate, and they're disappointed.

And yet, despite their frequent disapproval of teen pop's "message," tweens smile and laugh when they hear their favorite songs, dance and sing along nonetheless. At these moments, the social practice of being teen pop's target audience involves *not* reading or consuming a text individually but experiencing it together. The girls could be singing nonsense and still perform this communal activity. Together, in peer groups, they often choose to hear but not listen, to see but not read—a strategy that allows them to maintain strong, often feminist, convictions and still enjoy consuming music that does not jibe with their maturing politics.

Ultimately, however, the conflict at the heart of teen pop—this combination of presumed innocence and blatant sexual desire synthesized so brilliantly in the construction of Spears's image—drives the girls to practice active resistance to their own subordination in the safe space of their own bedrooms. Several girls described for me a favorite afternoon pastime: dressing up like Britney, watching *TRL*, lip-synching to their favorite songs while exaggerating her lustful sounds, mocking her gestures, and imitating her "slutty dancing." While I was, of course, unable to observe (or partici-pate in!) such play, I would argue that mocking and distorting Britney's revealing outfits (comfortably worn, as they informed me, over tank tops and tights) and exaggerating her sexual display provides tweens with an opportunity to explore their own budding sexuality while protected from "meaning it" by the guise of derision. Moreover, they label Britney a "slore," complain that she contributes to the objectification of women (my words, not theirs), and condemn nearly every aspect of her "Lolita" personality (again, my word) *at the same time* as they experiment with their own se-ductive gestures. Both inspired and incensed by teen-pop culture, these tweens test the waters of their own sexuality while beginning to flex their political muscles.

In the privacy of their own bedrooms and through the communal ac-tivity of the tween scene, the girls I got to know are finding the point at which they can feel attractive but confident, alluring but not objectified. They explore active ways to maintain their feminist consciousness and resist subordination while consuming and enjoying the products of a culture that many would maintain contributes to the degradation of girls and women. In short, mainstream teen-pop culture, full of images and messages that make Mom nervous, provides tweens with the opportunity to embrace their adolescence with surprising confidence, even if, for the moment, only in safe domestic spaces: The invitation to simultaneously imitate and attack that which may oppress them ironically offers liberation. To be sure, as Spears sings on her third and self-titled album, *Britney,* every tween I met would be the first to admit she's "not a girl, not yet a woman." But I have great confidence that, despite the "teen queen's" alleged "boob job," ever-shrinking outfits, provocative mock innocence, unabashed sexual display, and Mom's nerves, these girls will retain their sense of self as they endure the challenges of adolescence. Indeed, the tween scene is a site for empowerment: By participating in teen-pop culture, tweens experience the pleasure of resisting its patriarchal content.

Notes

1. The tween scene I describe in this ethnography bears striking similarities to girls' subcultures in Britain described by Angela McRobbie and Jenny Garber (1976) nearly thirty years ago. Like the teeny-bopper culture of the 1970s, the tween scene is situated primarily in the home and in the bedroom, is a "totally packaged" culture, is marketed to early-adolescent girls, and offers these girls a safe opportunity to participate in a "quasi-sexual ritual."

2. The meetings with these focus groups also provide the primary research data for my study of girls' readings of photographic images of Spears, particularly the photographs in the CD liner of her debut album, . . . *Baby One More Time,* and on the cover of and in the feature article in the 15 April 1999 *Rolling Stone.* See Lowe 2003.

3. As Barbara Bradby (1994) demonstrates in her study of preteen girls and Madonna, "the place to investigate the work women do in relation to texts of femininity," particularly resistance to patriarchy and dominant discourses of femininity, "is in the local, social organization of talk."

4. See David Buckingham (1991) for an analysis of how power and positionality affect children's responses to researchers' questions in sociological and media studies.

5. A mid-pass filter removes high and low frequencies of a sound. A voice put through a mid-pass filter sounds something like it would through a telephone.

References

Bradby, Barbara. 1994. "Freedom, Feeling, and Dancing: Madonna's Songs Traverse Girls' Talk." In Sara Mills, ed., *Gendering the Reader.* New York: Harvester Wheatsheaf.

Brown, Lyn Mikel. 1998. *Raising Their Voices: The Politics of Girls' Anger.* Cambridge: Harvard University Press.

Buckingham, David. 1991. "What Words Are Worth: Interpreting Children's Talk about Television." *Cultural Studies* 5, 2: 228–45.

Cowie, Celia, and Sue Lees. 1981. "Slags or Drags." *Feminist Review* 9 (autumn): 17–31.

Daly, Steven. 1999. "Britney Spears: Inside the Heart and Mind (and Bedroom) of America's New Teen Queen." *Rolling Stone,* 15 April, 60–65.

Lowe, Melanie. 2003. "Colliding Feminisms: Britney Spears, 'Tweens,' and the Politics of Reception." *Popular Music and Society* 26, 2: 123–40.

McRobbie, Angela, and Jenny Garber. 1976. "Girls and Subcultures: An Exploration." In Stuart Hall and Tony Jefferson, eds., *Resistance through Rituals: Youth Subcultures in Post-War Britain.* London: Hutchinson.

5

"Doin' It Right": Contested Authenticity in London's Salsa Scene

Norman Urquía

The past ten years have seen the emergence in London of nightclubs dedicated to set dances that can often be learnt in dance classes. These include jive, "le roc," line dancing, tango, and salsa. In the network of salsa clubs that makes up the scene examined here, the dance has become a vehicle for struggles over symbolic resources such as the authenticity and ownership of the genre and ultimately for the construction of boundaries in the salsa "scene" and on the dance floor.

"Salsa" is a marketing term that refers to a collection of Caribbean music genres that have interacted with each other (and North American music) over the last hundred years. The term is so imprecise that salsa musicians such as Ruben Blades insist that the music defies definition. Along with this ambiguity, the ownership of the music is also contested; however, the most common account is that salsa is Latin or Latin American in cases where the term has been applied to a popular music and dance since the 1960s (Manuel 1994; Padilla 1990). A great deal has been written about salsa, and the consensus is that the music plays an important role in constructing place, ethnic, and national identities for Latin Americans and people with a Latin American background. Singer, for example, highlights the role of salsa and other traditional Latin American music genres as ideological projects that are "consistent with aspects of Latino struggles for identity and self-determination" (1983, 186).

This view of salsa as Latin or Latino has dominated studies in the Americas, but there is, as Hosokawa (2000) notes, a shortage of work about how salsa is received outside these contexts. How would salsa be received in an entirely new and different setting—for example, in London's club scene—that has previously had little exposure to it?

The Dance

To pursue this question, I returned to the clubs that I used to dance in, to participate and attend dance classes as a dancing ethnographer. This required some adjustment, as the dance had changed during my eighteen-month absence from the clubs and many of my contemporaries had disappeared. Carrying out the fieldwork involved becoming briefly reintegrated into London's salsa network, making new contacts, learning new dance moves, and reflecting on my relationship with the scene.

The first impression on entering a salsa club is of a dance floor filled with couples performing an intricate dance from which very few seem to deviate. It is also striking that half the clientele are not dancing at all but sitting, drinking, chatting, or watching the dancers. There are usually pauses between songs, a distinct start and end, when some people who are watching try to find a partner, and the dancers either change partners or take a rest. Partners generally dance with each other for some three dances before changing partners, and experienced dancers tend to choose many partners and move around the club searching for dance partners. Some report that they search for their next partner even while dancing.

In basic dance-class salsa, dancers face each other: His left hand holds her right hand, his right hand is placed on her left shoulder blade or waist, and her left hand on his shoulder. He then leads her through various maneuvers, which may involve releasing the hands or pacing through the steps with hands still joined. The footwork appears counterintuitive and is not easily imitated without instruction. Salsa is a 4/4 music; a complete cycle of eight steps covers eight beats, or two bars. The basic step starts with a tap of the toes of, for example, the right foot on the spot on the first beat, followed by a step back with that foot for beat two. On the third beat the body's weight is rocked back to the other leg; the foot doesn't move, but the right leg is straightened, locking the knee and making the hip rock backward. Then the right foot is returned to the center for the fourth beat. The pattern is repeated, with the opposite foot tapping for beat five and repeating the sequence. The dancers mirror each other's steps. A number of variations and embellishments can be made to this basic style. For instance, some dancers replace the tap with a pause, and the backward step on the right leg (left for women) can be replaced by a forward step (imitating mambo) or by a side step in an abbreviated rumba step also known as the *cucaracha*. Experienced dancers accent different beats or break away from this template altogether. During the period of this fieldwork, this orthodoxy was being challenged by new styles that involved more complicated moves.

The Dancers

Salsa dancers at the London clubs I studied range in age from midtwenties to forties, and women just outnumber men. When there are more men than women, the extra men wait around for partners to become free. Alternatively, when women significantly outnumber men, they dance together in the traditional couple hold. Men more often dance together side by side, and almost never in the couple hold.[1] The club audiences appear ethnically mixed, aside from a lack of Latin Americans, and typical of London, with people who look and are referred to as African, Afro-Caribbean, Mediterranean, Northern European, Middle Eastern, South Asian, Oriental, and so on. There tend to be few Latin Americans in West End clubs, and English is the dominant language in these clubs, although staff spoke Spanish in two of them, Soneros and El Barco Latino. A few clubs, for example, Diamonds, have a largely black British clientele, and a larger proportion of black women than have most clubs.[2]

Dancers appear well groomed. Some women wear sequined, gold lamé, or diamanté evening gowns or specific dance-oriented clothing such as miniskirts that rise as the wearer turns—these are worn with short tops that expose the belly. Often women wear sweaters with dark trousers or leggings. Latin American women in these clubs generally wear more colorful clothes with bold printed designs, and larger Latin American women wear tight clothes that emphasize their bodies, while larger women of other backgrounds wear loose clothes that conceal their bodies. Men who dance wear small shoes and dark, solid-color shirts or tight dark T-shirts tucked into their trousers. It is hard to generalize about Latin American dress. One Cuban teacher wears a three-piece suit, another a bandanna, a bright jacket, and spats, while another young Cuban man with dreadlocks wears nothing but dungarees and boots.

Constructing Identity with Salsa

When speaking with dancers, while dancing or in interviews, it becomes clear that salsa is reconstrued by its consumers and that the Latin or Latin American view of salsa does not adequately describe that in London's salsa clubs. When informants describe the appeal of salsa, they emphasize the compatibility between themselves and what they perceive salsa to represent, and the characteristics that are important to them. It is therefore understandable that salsa was labeled "Latin," as this term united a group of salsa consumers in the Americas while distinguishing them from others. Informants also emphasize the elements they share with an imagined group of salsa producers or consumers, a phenomenon Lipsitz (1997) describes as "branching out." When asked what the appeal of salsa was, informants referred to groups who were thought to own salsa, in the sense that they had attempted to claim salsa by reconstruing it.

While salsa's Latin American connections are being reduced, ethnicity is not irrelevant to London's salsa consumers. Some informants emphasize their closeness to salsa's perceived ethnic or national associations; for example, one person of Jamaican origin noted: "There's an identification of similarity between the cultures; . . . Jamaica and Cuba are only ninety miles apart; . . . there are connections. And we all know we're not white, we all know we're not WASPs—initially we may not have that much kinship, . . . but it's not that huge a leap."

An informant with family from Guyana said his father "initiated" him into salsa, demonstrating his long familiarity with the music. He identifies salsa as Latin but then broadens this connection to create an ethnic link: "For me it's always going to be most definitely Latin, that's where it's from. Obviously you've got Afro-Caribbean mixes because we're all one and the same." This construction allows him to present salsa as "part of my heritage," which he clarifies by adding: "South Americans and Caribbeans, we're all the same people anyway." This symbolic connection extends the authority afforded Latin or South Americans to "Caribbeans," reinforcing his connection to salsa.

Such approaches assume that being Latin affords authority when dancing salsa, and the vagueness of the term "Latin" could also be useful, in particular the European usage of the term to refer to countries that use a romance language—in this way "Latin" becomes rephrased as "Mediterranean," broadening the availability of salsa. Other "cultural" links are also made, as when another informant drew a similar connection between herself and Colombians: "I feel more Latin than Greek, they are just so friendly and I get invited to parties; I feel as though I belong. They have very similar cultures—the men are similar to the Latin American men in many ways. The music is totally different. I prefer Latin American music too; it's more exciting, it's tradition, with Latin American music it's all over the world." Here feeling Latin is linked to friendliness and a feeling of belonging and the perceived similarities between Greek and Latin men. Locating the music "all over the world" removes its ties to specific locations and further facilitates the respondent's connection to salsa, which is eased by her presentation of the cultures as similar.

This technique is extended by other informants; for example, an Armenian informant felt salsa "got into me as well because of the cultural similarities, the hot bloodedness. We always had things to talk about, and friendships developed and relationships developed with Colombians." In this way salsa becomes a way to rally against negative stereotypes about the British.

Another strategy used by informants in explaining and justifying their connection to salsa was to focus purely on the dance. A number said that they had been dancing salsa for so long it had become a part of them and represents an expression of their true selves. Thus, one informant observed: "I was born dancing. I've danced all my life." Others simply described themselves as "dancers" or said they had rediscovered their love of dancing, for example: "I always saw myself as being a dancer, but I never did anything. I was always this fat. So I think it was just like a little thing you have inside. . . . I was very unsporty, but I found I was a good dancer so it gave me a little bit of, I don't know—I am good at something."

Marking Distance

While the sentiments expressed by informants so far might suggest that salsa can be all things to all people, dancers also construct devices to distinguish themselves from other consumers, often those they perceive to consume incorrectly. One informant noted that he disliked dancers motivated to socialize rather than to hear music. He saw their dance as inauthentic, not because it fails some notion of a classic style but because their socializing overrides their physical response to the music. Another described salsa as a mask that allows people unused to moving publicly to dance without embarrassment. Such distinctions are based on a dualism, dancing with the mind as opposed to dancing with the body, where the latter is seen as more honest.

Dance style was itself a source of difference. Dancing badly or incorrectly often meant not dancing at all. On several occasions I saw men left standing on the dance floor when their partners discovered that they couldn't dance correctly. But notions of correctness are a source of some disagreement. For those who value the Colombian dance, correctness was subtlety and restraint.

> Salsa, it's quite flexible in many ways . . . but you have to have the basics;
> . . . the steps . . . have to be small compact steps. . . . The other thing
> is the shoulders . . . have to be straight, not much movement, and the
> movements are in the knees and the hips. Once you have that, then
> you can express yourself in other ways, but when you start waving your
> arms around. . . .—I mean in Salsa Palladium sometimes when I watch
> the dance floor, it looks like the *Muppet Show,* . . . because everybody is
> . . .—no, no it's true—. . . yes, because [they] do this [he waves his arms
> about] . . . that's influenced with what they were dancing before. Maybe
> they were lambada students before and they think they can do this and it
> looks cool, and I can put my hand on my head and do this—and all that,
> it's not really salsa.

So there is a division between those dancing the "compact" Latin American style of salsa, which values subtlety, and those dancing the complicated spinning style. Despite such feelings, this spinning dance is common in clubs that were described as competitive and focused on constant dancing, that had a "gymnasium feeling, . . . clubs where people almost go in track suits to dance, dance the whole night away, you know, dance, dance, dance, dance. You can't have a conversation without it leading to the dance floor, the lady expecting you to take them on the dance floor and twist and turn them up to the ceiling."

Even accomplished dancers were criticized, as one informant noted:

> When they see teachers dancing, some of them [Colombians] say,
> "Are you sure that person is a teacher?" because for them it's a joke; . . .
> sometimes I play a romantic salsa and I'm dancing close with a nice
> lady and I get elbowed in the back and kneed in the back five or six
> times. And I turn around, and it's a teacher who's doing the fastest turns
> possible to a romantic salsa, which you're not really supposed to do.

Because informants complained that others turned excessively, I counted the number of turns dancers performed, defined here as maneuvers that involve the woman turning her back on the man. This includes "half turns" and "half nelsons," in which the woman turns her back on the man while he holds her hand behind her back. Women were turned about seventy times per song, while the men turned about thirty times. Multiple turns are sometimes performed in quick succession within a beat. The number of turns varied in different clubs; Colombians at El Unicornio, El Barco Latino, and Bar Salsa did not turn at all. Dancers at Salsa Palladium carried out the greatest number of turns. One of the staff in a Salsa Palladium T-shirt turned his partner, a slight woman in her twenties, thirty-one times, until she fell over; he helped her up and turned her another sixty-five times, until he was interrupted by someone asking for information. Above the dancers' heads, one sees a sea of raised arms gently swaying through continuous turns.

Contested Authenticity

There was thus some insistence that salsa conform to an "authentic" format, for example, Cuban or Colombian. But other informants challenged this; one dancer was affronted when another suggested his non-Cuban dancing was inauthentic. He distinguished between "original" and "authentic," undermining the value of the former and portraying the history of salsa as less relevant than the freedom in the interpretation of salsa: "[They said] I don't dance authentic salsa. Now what the hell is authentic salsa? Authentic salsa, is that the Cuban style maybe? I wouldn't say it was authentic, but I would say it's the origins, it started off in Cuba, but you dance salsa how you want."

This definition specifically detaches salsa from an established location, Cuba. The suggestion that any dance may be authentic implies that "authenticity" can be generated locally by dancers. So the focus of authenticity shifts from the production of salsa and its construction of ethnic identity to its consumption. By separating the meaning of salsa from its connection to the reproduction of the Cuban form of the dance, this informant implied a break with "branching out" or with ethnic or national consciousness as a connection between salsa and its consumers.

Rather than promote a free-form de-ethnicized dance, this serves to relocate salsa as North American rather than Latin American, as the same informant notes:

I prefer the style that I do. It is because it is the American style, and anything over in this country that is American is good. My personal style. I can dance with an American, I can dance with people from New York, L.A. It doesn't matter to me, but my style is still different to theirs because in London we generally have got a lot of moves, and everywhere you go everyone is just doing as many moves as they can in one dance, so that is the English style—lots of moves.

Portraying salsa as North American removes the need to pursue Latin American authenticity or the Latin American aesthetic described earlier. This eases the access to salsa for dancers from other backgrounds and other aesthetics that had been ridiculed by Latin American dancers. As a result, the "local" conventions that allow participation in the "local" scene are reinforced. The dominant aesthetic becomes demonstrating a repertoire of dance moves rather than resonating with the dance's ethnic associations.

As another informant noted: "When you dance with an English person or at least someone who has learnt in this country, you need to do a lot more movement and turns—otherwise they will think you can't dance."[3] This "local" salsa style is in many ways incompatible with Latin American salsa. The "compact" dance and continuity of tradition are rejected, and Latin Americans who "don't want to sweat too much" are caricatured. "Colombian" was in fact sometimes used as a disparaging term; for example, one informant described a Cuban band he didn't like as "so bad I think of them as Colombian." Interestingly, although Colombians were credited with bringing salsa clubs to London, Colombian dances are rare and not especially valued, and I was reprimanded for doing Colombian dance steps or for not turning enough.

Cultural Capitals and Social Capital

These observations can be understood using Bourdieu's (1986) model of noneconomic capital. Bourdieu suggests that certain knowledge bestows status on its possessors and allows entry into certain groups that exclude those without it. In order to participate, in this case, people need to perform compatible dances (displays of cultural capital) acquired in dance classes. This was expressed by a DJ who noted: "It's horrible people are getting snobby and dancing with certain people—there's the Miami thing which is in now, and people only dance with you if you know the Miami moves."

This knowledge becomes translated into social standing or social capital that is maintained by dancing with people at a similar or more advanced level and by avoiding beginners who, because of their limited ability, force their partners to dance at a less impressive level. In fact, some dancers I spoke with resented beginners and wouldn't pass on their expensive knowledge freely. One said she wasn't anybody's fairy godmother and went to clubs to enjoy herself, not to look after beginners.

Zoning

The segregation between dancers shows up in their use of space. Many clubs appear to be organized around distinct zones based on ethnicity, dance competence, and activities such as drinking. The most obvious and perhaps undisputed area is the bar, where people buy drinks, sit and chat, or just watch the dancing. Informants disagreed over whether these zones are segregated based on different levels of expertise or on competition for physical resources, such as a good dance surface, a breeze from a fan, proximity to the speakers, or distance from the seating area. But ethnicity can be an important dimension. In some clubs Latin Americans cluster near the DJ; for example, in Villa Stefano's, Cubans stood within four meters of the DJ. But as this is also the only area with a wooden floor, many non-Cuban dancers also congregate here to perform vigorous and flamboyant dancing.

In Bar Rumba and Bar Salsa, a group of Colombians also remained close to the DJ. They danced together, changing partners among some five couples, and did not mix with the rest of the club, although some danced around the fringes of this area. Their dances also contrasted with those of

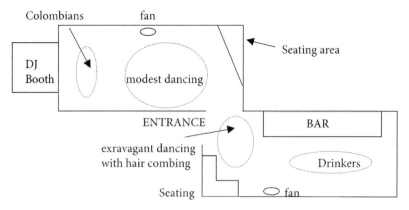

Bar Rumba

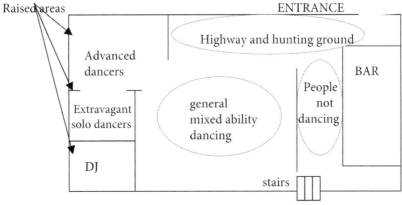

La Finca

others in the club and were fluid but less showy and featured no turns. At La Finca, Bar Rumba, and Villa Stefano's the spatial segregation appeared to be based on dance expertise, but in all clubs impromptu zones could arise, as cohorts of dance students and small groups of friends clustered together.

The most accomplished dancers stuck to specific areas and danced with a small number of other dancers, usually in prominent more brightly lit places, and even at the bar. They argue that the dance floor can be dangerous, and they keep away from beginners who might shove them or stamp on their feet. Occasionally, impromptu audiences formed around them and applauded when the dance was finished. Less accomplished dancers blended in and shoaled around each other in the middle of the dance floor, away from flamboyant dancers. There was a great deal of movement along the edges of the dance floor. People walked back and forth between the different dance areas or stood facing the dancing, either watching or dancing gently on the spot. These highways were the place, as one informant joked, to hunt for new partners who were waiting to be asked to dance.

Transferable Social Capital and Stigma

Social capital can be shared. One person noted that after a high-ranking teacher asked her to dance, her status was raised that night and she was subsequently asked to dance by other people for the rest of the evening. On the other hand, one can observe that beginners or those with very low status can effectively deplete the status of midranking people who dance

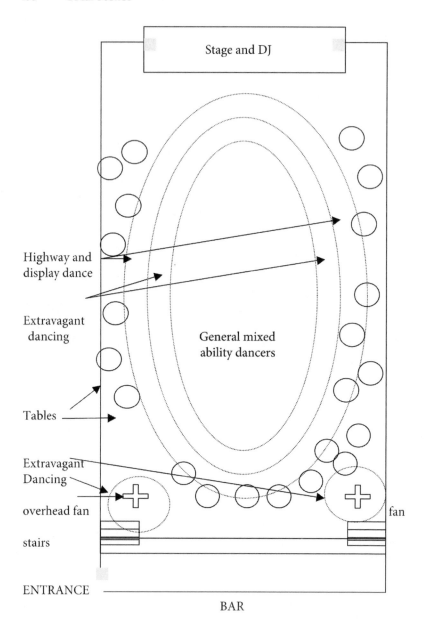

Salsafusion

with them. Dancers are only as good as what they can demonstrate, and beginners restrict one's opportunity to show off and make one dance like a beginner. Therefore, dancing with beginners for many can result in loss of social capital.

Social capital can be portable, as well. Dancers who are very well known because of their performance of the accepted dance style can move around the club and choose whom to dance with. Those who are less able dancers need to build up social capital in one zone and then rebuild this if they move to another zone, especially in a large club. The exception occurs where the person is well known enough as a good dancer to transport social capital to another zone and even to another club.

Solo and Display Dancing

There are several types of solo dancing in salsa clubs. Partners occasionally separate and perform fancy footwork before coming back together. Sometimes a group of dancers takes turns to demonstrate a particular step each has perfected. At La Finca, a spotlight was shone on them during such solos. When the solos are rehearsed and polished, they are called "shines" and are linked to the New York style.

Basic footwork was also performed solo at the edges of the dance floor. Women more often than men seemed to do this "display dance," which appeared to advertise their willingness to dance to those currently looking for a partner. These "display dancers" also appeared to be more conscious of what was going on around them and were always willing to dance when asked; people practicing shines were not.

Not Dancing Salsa

Not everyone in the clubs dances "basic salsa." Some perform a free-expression dance, as did a man with a German-sounding accent at Salsa Palladium, who walked into the middle of the dance floor and danced throwing each arm back alternately (as if preparing a tennis serve in slow motion), while rocking his torso in the direction of each rising arm. Every woman he subsequently approached refused to dance with him. The same evening, a well-known dance teacher danced by clapping his hands in front of him and flapping them behind his head while performing dainty little steps, which onlookers applauded. Those rich in social capital don't need to show off, and they receive praise even when they simply clown around.

Because of their cheap entry fees and late-opening bars, some Central London salsa clubs attract groups of people who do not dance salsa. Some of these dancers loosely imitate salsa, and the overall effect (with hip swinging and random taps) is a little confused. Others dance freestyle solo dances, or they dance among themselves as couples with little or no footwork, tracing alternate circles with their clasped hands (like pedaling a huge invisible cycle with their hands) and occasional turning. Often they disagreed about when to turn and stopped to laugh; in fact they seemed to laugh more than anyone else in the club. Sometimes they parodied the salsa dances of specific individuals and couples. They joked around, giggling and mocking the dance and dancers, who were absorbed in their dancing and not impressed by their clowning. Rarely did they approach salsa dancers, and they were usually turned down when they did, although a salsa dancer might agree to teach the very good looking among them.

There Goes the Neighborhood

Among dedicated salsa dancers, the dance became increasingly complex. In the older style of dance, single turns were the main embellishment, but as one informant noted, now "single turns are nothing." Such turns were more recently used only to introduce more complex maneuvers. This informant felt she needed to take more lessons just to keep up with the increasingly complicated dance. This kind of dance inflation maintains a distance for serious dancers from the mainstream, which has become familiar with salsa. Simply knowing how to dance basic salsa does not provide the distinction that it once did. This evokes McCracken's (1998) suggestion that fashion is spread by subordinates who want to imitate and appropriate the fashions of an elite and by the elite who want to differentiate themselves from their imitators. For the elite advanced dancers, basic salsa was becoming the epitome of the mainstream. By dancing in a complex way, they could achieve a symbolic distance between themselves and that mainstream. But dance lessons can narrow this distance. Another strategy was to specialize in a related but different dance that provides continuity with salsa but still differentiates dancers from the mainstream, such as contemporary Cuban timba and New York On 2.

Timba was described as free compared to the "straightjacket" of dance-class salsa. One teacher asked his students to " 'win' and grind their hips" to feel the music rather than follow regimented choreography.[4] One informant noted: "You know a Timba is playing because you can't dance to it with your old basic salsa steps." The music was described as free and "funky" and featured many musical changes. The overall effect was less precise and disciplined than salsa, but more spontaneous.

New York On 2 was described as a type of mambo; one teacher promoted it as a way to dance like Puerto Ricans without sweating, accomplished by "breaking" on a different beat and performing footwork flourishes—shines—and affected mannerisms called "stylings." For example, a woman being turned would extend the free arm quickly upward with fingers spread, then to the side, within the same beat. Another styling is called "hair combing": A woman places her fingertips on her forehead, elbow pointing upward, and gradually traces around the top and back of her head, finishing behind one ear. This move was usually carried out in combination with solo dancing.

Latin American informants remarked that this dance had few connections to Latin America. As one informant noted, "You'd never catch a Latin woman doing those moves." But the New York style was much in demand in salsa clubs, and some local informants attributed the popularity of such styles to the British fondness for following North American popular culture and fashion. New York On 2 appears to have moved the expertise away from Latin Americans, and this bolsters the authority of dancers from any other background. Instead of connecting themselves to Latin American dance authority, dancers seek the authority of the technical excellence they perceive in dance classes. Thus to an extent, New York salsa has allowed salsa to become locally owned and therefore British.

De-ethnicizing Salsa

Hosokawa (2000) suggests that outside Latin America, salsa could lose its ethnic associations, and it appears this is what has happened in London. It is startling that the Latin American style of dancing salsa should become among the least authoritative in London, especially as salsa has been such a well-established symbol of Latin American identity. It would be inconceivable that, for example, Jamaican styles of dancing to reggae would lose their authority.

Bourdieu's (1986) concept of cultural capital's theoretical tools helps in proposing a mechanism for how this situation may have arisen. In the early 1990s, being able to dance salsa functioned as a form of cultural capital in the salsa clubs and was implicitly linked to Latin Americans in general and Colombians in particular. Some Latin American salsa teachers even suggested that they held the essence of salsa by virtue of their ethnicity or nationality, and so they were the best people to learn from. The implication was that dancers from other backgrounds could never hope to rival their Latin American teachers, because dancing salsa was tied to knowledge of Spanish and experience of the Latin American culture in the broadest sense. At that time, Latin Americans dominated the club audiences, and theirs was the dominant dance style—which presents a leisure- based twist to Marx's proposition that the ideas of the ruling class are society's dominant ideas. Not only was the Latin American style the dominant way of dancing, but also it was considered the best way to dance salsa. To continue borrowing from Bourdieu's terminology, the dominant aesthetic provided the best rate of conversion of cultural capital into social and symbolic capital.

But this situation did not last. The clubs began to attract a local audience, and the old aesthetic discriminated against local dancers. Faced with a system of values that discriminated against them on apparently ethnic and racial grounds, these local dancers looked to an alternative aesthetic that avoided any deference to a Latin American aesthetic and authority. This alternative authority was available in the more cosmopolitan dance-class salsa and the New York style, shifting the privilege from Latin Americans to dance classes and dance teachers.

Superficially, this shift sets up a meritocracy that rewards effort or human capital rather than ethnicity or nationality. But success in salsa clubs has now become closely linked with taking dance lessons; good dancing has been redefined and reserved for dancers who pursue lessons. The widening popularity of salsa in London's clubs resulted in a shift of aesthetics that privileged the new dominant clientele, who had the time, money, and dedication to regularly attend dance classes.

Dance classes now shape the nature of the dance and the status associated with different dances, and this new authority has also shifted the aesthetics toward the dances in nonsalsa clubs. Instead of cultural knowledge and long-term familiarity with salsa, the key to success in London's clubs has become attending the right dance classes. They provide cultural capital in the form of the latest dance moves and conformity to the dominant style, and social capital by one's inclusion within a cohort of dance students. The dance classes have become more formal and offer examinations and certificates for different levels of skill. In short, dance classes now resemble an educational system.

Bourdieu suggests that an educational establishment reinforces itself by excluding those who do not possess the appropriate cultural capital

(Bourdieu and Passeron 1998). This pattern is certainly followed in London salsa clubs, as it is now ironically the Latin Americans (who tend not to attend classes) who are considered to be among the worst dancers and consequently marginalized in the very dance clubs where Latin American music is played. The new elite are the dance teachers, whose claim to authority is based on a notion of technical excellence rather than on cultural knowledge or claims of authenticity. In this cultural field, the skills and knowledge that function as cultural capital have themselves been replaced by new skills that benefit the new dominant audience. This presents cultural capital as temporally fragile, not because it loses its currency when it becomes abundant, but because it may privilege a particular group that is subsequently deposed. In this way, the clubs—at the same venues and playing the same music—now value entirely different forms of knowledge and skills as cultural capital because they suit the new audience.

Notes

1. In gay salsa events, the same-sex couple hold is common, but these events are uncommon.
2. The term "black" is used here as local informants use it.
3. "English" here, as often, means "British."
4. This Caribbean pronunciation of "wind" refers to a hip-gyrating dance that becomes "grinding" (sometimes pronounced with the d silent) when performed with a partner.

References

Bourdieu, Pierre. 1977. *Outline of a Theory of Practice*. New York: Cambridge University Press.

————. 1986. "The Forms of Capital." In J. G. Richardson, ed., *Handbook of Theory and Research for the Sociology of Education*. New York: Greenwood Press.

Bourdieu, Pierre, and Jean-Claude Passeron. 1998. "Academic Order and Social Order," preface to the 1990 edition. In P. Bourdieu and J. C. Passeron, eds., *Reproduction in Education, Society, and Culture*. London: Sage.

Duany, Jorge. 1984. "Popular Music in Puerto Rico: Towards an Anthropology of Salsa." *Latin American Music Review* 5, 2: 5.

Hosokawa, Shehei. 2000. "Salsa no tiene frontera: Orquesta de la luz and the Globalisation of Popular Music." Cultural Studies 13, 3: 509–34.

Lipsitz George. 1997. *Dangerous Crossroads: Popular Music, Postmodernism, and the Poetics of Place*. London: Verso.

Manuel, Peter. 1994. "Puerto Rican Music and Cultural Identity: Creative Appropriation of Cuban Sources from Danza to Salsa." *Ethnomusicology* 38: 249–350.

McCracken, Grant. 1998. *Culture and Consumption.* Bloomington: Indiana University Press.

Padilla, Felix M. 1990. "Salsa: Puerto Rican and Latino Music." *Journal of Popular Culture* 24: 87–104.

Quintero-Rivera, Angel G. 1999. "Ponce, the Danza, and the National Question: Notes towards a Sociology of Puerto Rican Music." In Vernon Boggs, ed., *Salsiology: Afro-Cuban Music and the Evolution of Salsa in New York City.* New York: Excelsior Music.

Roman-Velazquez, Patria. 1999. "The Embodiment of Salsa: Musicians, Instruments, and the Performance of a Latin Style and Identity." *Popular Music* 18.

Singer, Roberta. 1983. "Tradition and Innovation in Contemporary 'Latin' Popular Music in New York City." *Latin American Music Review* 4: 183–202.

Waxer, Lise. 1994. "Of Mambo Kings and Songs of Love: Music in Havana and New York from the 1930s to the 1950s." *Latin American Music Review* 15: 139–75.

PART II

Translocal Scenes

6

"Riot Grrrl Is . . .":
The Contestation over Meaning
in a Music Scene

Kristen Schilt

"We're Bikini Kill and we want revolution girl-style now."
—Bikini Kill

In 1992, Kill Rock Stars released a self-titled album by a new band called Bikini Kill, a feminist punk quartet from Olympia, Washington. Opening with the line quoted in the chapter epigraph, the album sounded a battle cry for girls across the country to move outside the "bedroom culture" (Frith 1983) of female fandom and into the realm of subcultural producer. The band, composed of three women and one man, was part of the burgeoning Riot Grrrl music scene, a local scene that emerged simultaneously from the punk and independent music communities of Olympia, Washington, and Washington, D.C. Riot Grrrl encouraged women and girls to take control of the means of cultural production and be a part of "revolution girl-style now" through producing music and zines (short for "fanzines," that is, fan magazines produced by fans themselves) that put their own personal experiences at the forefront.

While the majority of music and zines from the early Riot Grrrl scene had limited distribution, the infrastructure of record labels and fans necessary to sustain a music scene (Straw 1997) began to emerge in late 1992. Additionally, as more girls became involved in the production of zines, girl-run zine distribution networks emerged that allowed zines produced in Olympia and D.C. to travel beyond these local scenes to interested readers across the country. With this increase in informational access to a once local scene, Riot Grrrl became both translocal, as Riot Grrrl chapters related only in ideology to the Olympia and D.C. chapters sprang up across the country, and virtual, as discussions about the music and politics of Riot Grrrl began to travel across a complex zine network that spanned the United States and reached into Canada and the United Kingdom.

However, with this move outside the local communities of Olympia and D.C. came definitional battles both from within and outside the scene about the meaning of Riot Grrrl, with questions raised about the ways in which music scenes negotiate the countervailing pressures faced by many sites of musical activity (Straw 1997): the desire to remain true to the original, local form of the scene and the pressure to expand, grow, and become more inclusive in order to allow the scene to thrive with new participants. In this chapter, I focus on how this contestation played out in the Riot Grrrl scene between 1992 and 1995.

Methodology

This research was conducted through a combination of in-depth interviews with founders of the early Riot Grrrl music scene, analysis of Riot Grrrl–associated zines produced between 1992 and 1995, and archival research on news accounts of Riot Grrrl from both independent and corporate presses. I interviewed seven women who had been active in the D.C. and Olympia punk scenes in the late 1980s and early 1990s, both making music and publishing zines, who were frequently mentioned in newspaper articles about Riot Grrrl, making them among the most well known participants to people outside the scene. Interviewees included three members of Bikini Kill, Kathleen Hanna, Tobi Vail, and Kathi Wilcox; one member of Bratmobile, Molly Neuman; a zine maker and member of Suture, Sharon Cheslow; and two zine makers and founding members of Riot Grrrl D.C., Erika Reinstein and Nina Curzio (see Schilt 2000).

Background for the Early Riot Grrrl Music Scene

Riot Grrrl as a music scene merged the early punk ethos of Do It Yourself (DIY) with feminist politics that developed from the increasing dissatisfaction with punk gender dynamics felt by many women involved in the D.C. and Olympia punk scenes in the late 1980s. As Leblanc (1999) argues, women played a key role in the emergence of the early '77 British punk scene, and young U.S. women interested in challenging the norms of pa-triarchal society were drawn to punk, as it offered them a chance to reject mainstream ideas and to produce instead a culture on their own terms through music, zines, and clothing. However, women found increasingly less room for creative expression as U.S. punk scenes moved toward a new style of punk called "hardcore." Faster, louder, and more aggressive than the early British bands, hardcore shows became notorious for violence, particularly among male fans in the mosh pit (Azerrad 2001). As hardcore increasingly became an arena for male punks to assert their masculinity through aggressive behavior, female punks found themselves pushed out of active participation in the scene and moved into behind-the-scenes roles such as show organizers or band groupies.

About her dissatisfaction with the ascendance of hardcore and the ram-pant sexism she saw developing in the D.C. punk scene, Sharon Cheslow, a musician and zine maker, says:

I did a fanzine called *Now What*. There was this punk band called Scream. They were like this early Dischord records band. And you know, they were always talking about cumming on some bitch or something like that. I remember writing about it. I wrote a review of this record and said, "This is not acceptable." And of course, people got mad at me. Angry at this unchecked misogyny, Cheslow put her critique of the treatment of women in the punk scene in her zine in an attempt to open up a dialogue about sexism. Just as subcultural media such as flyers and fanzines brought interested parties together in the development of the U.K. dance-music scene (Thornton 1996), zines that carried feminist critiques such as Cheslow's would come to play a key role in the emergence of the Riot Grrrl scene, operating as "exploratory gestures" (Cohen 1955) that alerted women dissatisfied with their treatment in the punk scene that they were not alone in their discontent.

The Role of Zines in the Development of Riot Grrrl

Zines had become an important part of the punk scene in the late 1970s be-cause punks liked "producing a paper unhampered by corporate structure, cash and censorship" (Burchill and Parsons 1978, 37). Punk zines tended to contain show reviews, band interviews, and short personal rants. How-ever, women like Cheslow appropriated the medium as a forum in which to problematize the treatment of women in the punk scene. Through this use of zines as a format for discussing sexism, Cheslow was able to reach out to other women in the D.C. scene who were also feeling alienated by the sexist attitudes of their male scene mates.

Women who were involved in the Olympia punk scene also began to express their alienation from the scene through zines. Kathleen Hanna and Kathi Wilcox, members of Riot Grrrl–associated band Bikini Kill, both report being influenced by future band mate Tobi Vail's zine, *Jigsaw*. As Wilcox recalled in an online interview with the author:

> I met Tobi the summer before when we both worked at this shitty sandwich shoppe [sic] in Olympia and I knew her from her band Go-Team. I used to read her fanzine *Jigsaw* and was really impressed with her approach—she was the first person I ever met who unapologetically focused her attention on girls in bands, specifically. And made it an issue. Like in interviews she would ask girls how it felt to be a *girl* in a band, et cetera. It struck me as really unique because everyone in my college seminars was like, "You know, people are people, it's all the same. It doesn't matter if you are a boy or a girl." And she was acknowledging that there was a difference, especially if you are the girl in question.

In Juno's *Angry Women in Rock* (1996), Hanna describes why *Jigsaw* was so important to her. Like Wilcox, she was interested in Vail's focus on women in the music world. Hanna did a series of interviews with women in bands to see how they thought their gender affected their musical career. She sent these interviews to Vail, which led to collaboration and the beginning of their feminist band, Bikini Kill. Hanna and Vail realized how important punk music and zines, two cultural forms that do not place high value on expertise, were to giving a voice to their experiences, and they began to think about how to spread this kind of connection through subcultural media to a larger group of women and girls.

The link between the burgeoning feminist discontent in Olympia and D.C. was solidified in 1991 when Bikini Kill spent a summer in D.C. During that time, Hanna called together a group of women to discuss the possibility of starting a magazine dedicated to female musicians in the punk scene. She noted in our interview: "I've always wanted to start a magazine. A magazine that was about music and feminism. . . . So I invited people over to the house that I was staying at and we talked about it and ended up, we talked just a lot more about the scene and feminism than we did a magazine."

Hanna was not the only woman looking for a way to bring cohesion to the scene. Inspired by recent antiracist riots in D.C., Molly Neuman and Allison Wolfe, the founding members of Bratmobile, intended to start a "girl riot" against a society they felt offered no validation of women's experiences (White 1992). Together they started the zine *Riot Grrrl*, which reported on a series of all-girl meetings that were helping to spread the news about scene issues and articulate the *Riot Grrrl* ethos.

Subcultural Media and Feminist Politics

The bands most commonly associated with the Riot Grrrl music scene—Heavens to Betsy, Bratmobile, and Bikini Kill—appropriated punk musical style and shock performance tactics to express feminist viewpoints and to push women's experiences to the forefront.[1] For example, in the Bikini Kill song "Feels Blind," Kathleen Hanna addresses the way society teaches women to hate themselves. "As a woman I was taught to always be hungry / yeah women are well acquainted with thirst / we could eat just about anything / we could even eat your hate up like love" are lines that show how self-hatred can emerge in the form of an eating disorder, or in the tolerance of an abusive relationship.

Another Bikini Kill song, "Don't Need You," rejects stereotypical heterosexual relationship dynamics by proclaiming: "Don't need you to say we're cute / Don't need you to say we're all right / Don't need your protection / Don't need your kiss goodnight." Additionally, as Bikini Kill was invested in motivating young women to participate in Riot Grrrl's form of punk-rock feminism, several songs from the first album called upon girls to join in the feminist struggle. The song "Double Dare Ya" opens with these words: "Hey girlfriend / I got a proposition goes something like this / Dare ya to do what you want / Dare ya to be who you will." The song ends with Hanna screaming, "You do have rights."

As part of the DIY ethic, Riot Grrrl–associated bands also made themselves accessible to fans. They released their music on small record labels and often included their personal addresses and even personal phone numbers, so that fans could communicate directly with band members. Fans could also write to the bands in care of Kill Rock Stars, Chainsaw, and K Records, as the small record labels were quick to forward the mail to the appropriate band. This easy access aided in debunking the mythology of the unapproachable "rock star" and gave fans an active role in scene creation. The success of this tactic is still evident, as Kathleen Hanna notes that she today receives the same amount of mail from fans across the world as she did in the first year of Riot Grrrl. That the amount of mail has not decreased speaks to the fact that fans of Riot Grrrl–associated music were able to feel they had a strong investment in the music, rather than being merely passive consumers. Additionally, this accessibility helped build the Riot Grrrl community, as fans across the country wrote to invite bands to play shows in their cities and towns, helping to keep networked Riot Grrrl–associated bands and fans together.

Zines continued to play a key role in bringing scene participants together and in expanding the Riot Grrrl scene. Zine makers began to organize their own networks, establishing zine distribution services, such as Riot Grrrl Press, that photocopied zines from across the country and sold them for a few dollars each. These networks not only gave girls across the country access to zines coming out of Olympia and D.C., but also allowed alliances to form across state boundaries and gave individuals interested in Riot Grrrl a way to contact like-minded people in their immediate areas.

As these smaller Riot Grrrl communities outside of Olympia and D.C. began to grow, along with virtual zine communities, the idea for a Riot Grrrl convention developed. The first was held in Washington, D.C., in 1992 and drew several hundred girls from across the country, as the zine *Gunk* reported in 1992.[2] At the conventions, workshops dealt with a wide range of subjects, such as how to make zines, buy guitars, deal with eating disorders, and fight sexism in your community. As participants were able to meet other interested people in their area and trade zines with zine makers across the country, these conventions gave them a sense of community and allowed them to play an active role in the Riot Grrrl scene. Riot Grrrl chapters sprang up across the country, while zine networks gave a new virtual dimension to participation in Riot Grrrl, allowing zine makers to critique, analyze, and alter the Riot Grrrl scene to fit their lives.

Yet, while many women and girls took on the label "Riot Grrrls," they shied away from defining what exactly that identity meant, in an attempt to avoid allowing the media to co-opt the scene and create a static "Riot Grrrl" identity. What being a Riot Grrrl meant to a girl in Los Angeles could differ radically from what it meant to a girl in Louisville. This flexible self-definition was crucial to spreading the message of Riot Grrrl across the country; there was no manifesto or set of rules for participation. Girls had the autonomy to create their own branches of Riot Grrrl without worrying if they were "doing it right." While this lack of definition confused many reporters from the popular press who were looking for a quick sound-byte version of the Riot Grrrl scene, it was exactly what the women involved envisioned: a network that allowed each participant to create cultural products relevant to her life experience.

The Punk–White Privilege Scene

While one of Riot Grrrl's slogans was "Every girl is a Riot Grrrl," in practice, the group, like the punk scenes from which it emerged, was predominantly made up of white middle-class punk girls.[3] Critiques of Riot Grrrl as too white and too exclusive began to surface in chapter meetings and zines across the scene. One example appears in 1992 in *Gunk,* a zine written by Dasha, an African American punk girl. After attending a Riot Grrrl convention, Dasha writes: "I see Riot Grrrl growing very closed [*sic*] to a very chosen few i.e. white, middle-class punk girls. I constantly don't feel comfortable with this cuz I know so many girls that need to hear this shit, but weren't there because they don't look punk." Sisi, a Latina woman who made the zine *Housewife Turned Assassin,* says of Riot Grrrl:

> The reason I was disappointed by some of my experiences in Riot Grrrl was—everyone tried to create this utopia: "We should all love each other 'cuz we're girls. It doesn't matter what class, race or religious background we have, because we all share in common the fact that we are girls." I think that's a self-defeating, ignorant view to adopt, because it is just not true. There are disparities between us; there are differences. (Vale 1996, 54)

Denying the race issue led many nonwhite girls to feel that their experiences were devalued in the subculture. White feminists often expressed frustration at being regarded as second-class citizens and identified with their sisters of color as if race were irrelevant (de Alba 1995). Thus, while many young feminists of color initially felt very supportive of Riot Grrrl because it brought the sexism in the punk scene under close scrutiny, they quickly became frustrated by the white girls' failure to investigate their own whiteness or to move the discussion to how racism and classism often work in concert with sexism. Lauren, an Asian-American zine maker, sums up this feeling of alienation in 1997 in her zine *You Might As Well Live:* "Where's the riot, white girl? And yeah some of you say we are 'out to kill white boy mentality' but have you examined your own mentality? Your white upper-middle class girl mentality? What would you say if I said that I wanted to kill that mentality too?"

A second problem that emerged internally in the scene was the question of whether the Riot Grrrl scene was predominantly about music or about politics. The majority of women involved in the production of Riot Grrrl–associated music had a deep interest in supporting the punk-rock feminist cause of the scene. However, as musicians, they also wanted to make music. The separation between making music and talking politics began to blur as the scene attracted more and more young feminists who increasingly insisted on viewing Riot Grrrl as a political group rather than as a music scene. Discussions began to emerge about how much Riot Grrrl–associated bands needed to support female fans' personal causes while they were on tour. Some musicians balked at this demand, as it forced them to simply accept one side of a story and take a hard line that might or might not be warranted. In the local punk scenes where they performed, band members began to find themselves embroiled in issues for which they had no background. Talking about this problem, Kathi Wilcox noted in our interview:

> It got kind of weird and divisive. Like every personal cause of every individual in the group became a group cause by default and everybody's main priority and concern. . . . There were no real boundaries at times and things became sort of pedantic. And things kind of got applied to our band that were really issues of individual girls in the meetings. I was really resentful of being put in that position, as sort of a tool for personal politicking.

Thus, musicians involved in the scene began to see themselves as being asked to delineate themselves as feminists who supported all girls' individual issues, rather than as musicians who had a serious interest in making music, a choice that many participants were resentful at being expected to make.

Finally, the Riot Grrrl scene began to face the question of whether their bands were making music for ideology or for profit. This concern, which stems from the desire to spread the message behind political music while remaining in a subcultural location, is common to independent music scenes, which are characterized by controlling the means of production while eschewing mass fame (Gottlieb and Wald 1994). For example, Frith notes that the early British punk scene "articulated an explicitly anti-professional attitude to record-making, a concern for music as a mode of survival rather than as a means of profit" (1983, 156–57). Punk independents lived by the motto "Small is beautiful," which meant they released only a few hundred pressings of seven-inch records in an attempt to keep punk music authentic and out of the hands of the co-opting major labels (Frith 1983). Similarly, the Riot Grrrl scene retained tight control over their music production and put out music only on the independent labels associated with the scene.

As the Riot Grrrl scene began to attract attention outside of Olympia and D.C., bands such as Bikini Kill found themselves courted by major labels. It is common practice for major labels to use independent labels as "talent scouts," allowing the independents to test out new bands and then attempting to lure them away when they prove to have a potentially profitable audience base (Frith 1983). In 1993, major labels such as Geffen were turning more and more to the indie labels after the huge commercial success of Nirvana, a formerly underground Seattle punk band. While the lure of signing with major labels is evident, especially as most independent musicians are forced to maintain "day jobs" to support their art, independent music scenes tightly police their boundaries, expelling those who are seen as going too mainstream or "selling out." The specter of the "selling out" stigma haunts independent bands, and those who do choose to make the leap from indie to major find themselves with a loss of subcultural capital in the street-level music scene.

The members of Bikini Kill were painfully aware of the dangers of going major, in terms both of losing the ability to make political music and of being ostracized from the indie community for achieving mainstream, commercial success. Kathleen Hanna noted that the band had no intention of signing with the major labels, but they realized they could, in true punk fashion, appear to be interested and use the labels for free trips to New York and Los Angeles.

The Riot Grrrl music community proved to be critical of the band's use of label money, and in particular of Hanna's appearing in a Sonic Youth video. Defending herself against the attacks on her actions, Hanna argued:

I'm from a scene where I've done a fuck of a lot of shit work. I was a behind-the-scenes person for years and years; I've set up a lot of shows; I've done a lot of networking with women; I've just done a lot of work. And now, seven years later, I'm getting some notoriety, and I'm being resented for that. It's not like some businessman dreamed up the idea for Bikini Kill and we auditioned for the job and got it—we created this. (Juno 1996, 86)

Hanna also attacked the idea that to be independent, she must conform to the "suffering artist" image and deny the band trips that its members otherwise would not be able to afford. However, the specter of "going commercial" had begun to surround the Riot Grrrl scene, which became particularly problematic as Riot Grrrl music began to attract more attention from the mainstream press and the boundaries between independent music and pop music began to blur.

Defining a Riot Grrrl: The Media Steps In

Besides the internal debates about race, class, and the relationship between music and politics, bands associated with Riot Grrrl found themselves plagued by the popular press, who, having identified Riot Grrrl as the type of "spectacular subculture" (Hebdige 1979) that sells magazines, rushed to find out what exactly a "Riot Grrrl band" was all about. Familiar with the exploitative treatment of second-wave feminists in the popular press, the participants I interviewed were reluctant to discuss their scene or their politics with the mainstream media, even though the press offered a way to spread the word about Riot Grrrl's punk-rock feminism to girls outside of the subcultural scene. This apprehension stemmed from a fear of seeing the feminist message of Riot Grrrl diluted or ridiculed in the popular press. As Tobi Vail put it:

> I didn't see a need for mainstream press politically—I thought a political movement would grow with or without media coverage. . . . I thought it was good to not do interviews because it created a space for mythology to take place: sometimes what people imagined was happening was more exciting than what was really happening and that would evolve into myth.

Other participants noted that they did not want to be responsible for speaking for the ambiguous-by-design Riot Grrrl or for trying to explain their politics to journalists who were interested only in the spectacular aspects of the scene, such as the punk-inspired performance tactics of many of the Riot Grrrl–associated bands.

In an attempt to maintain the internal validity of the scene, Riot Grrrl participants issued a call, via zine networks, conventions, and the alternative press, for a mainstream media blackout. Faced with a dearth of participants willing to be interviewed, however, reporters themselves created a sound byte–friendly definition of the scene that was heavy on fashion and light on politics. The scene generated a great deal of media attention. From 1992 to 1995, articles appeared in popular magazines and newspapers, such as *Newsweek*, the *New York Times*, *Utne Reader*, and even *Playboy*.

Reporters expressed a wide variety of opinions about the scene, some positive and receptive to the scene and others negative, while most were sadly misinformed. For example, the *Washington Post* ran a story on Bikini Kill (without interviewing the band) and incorrectly reported that Hanna claimed her father raped her. Hanna had many relatives in D.C., and the article caused her a lot of embarrassment and hurt her family (Juno 1996, 85). Regardless of the stance they took toward the scene, identifying a Riot Grrrl "fashion" was a main theme of the majority of the articles. For example, Ann Japenga wrote: "Riot Grrrls have a distinct look, combining traditional fashions like round-collared, cinched waist dresses and incandescent red lipstick with harder touches: heavy black high-top boots and hacked off punk hair" (1992). Kim France described them as wearing "fishnet tights and midriff-baring tops" (1992, 26). Lorraine Ali, in contrast, said Riot Grrrls "adopted little-girl looks—from pigtails to lunch pails—as an ironic twist" (1993, 3).

Seduced by the lure of a defiant female music scene, reporters paid scant attention to the meaning behind the defiant style of some participants, and even less to the variation in style that existed in the scene. Instead, they represented Riot Grrrl as an "incorporated style" (Hebdige 1979) easily accessible as the latest fashion trend to those who chose to take on the media-constructed "uniform" of fishnets, baby-doll barrettes, lunch pails, and work boots. By presenting an article about fashion rather than about politics, reporters diffused the radical feminist message, just as the scene participants had feared.

In addition to reducing a political music scene to a fashion trend, reporters began to define any women who made punk or rock music as a "Riot Grrrl." Musicians such as Kim Gordon from Sonic Youth and Chrissie Hynde of the Pretenders suddenly were being called upon to discuss the Riot Grrrl movement, of which they had little knowledge. In response to this generic labeling, many female musicians attempted to distance themselves from Riot Grrrl. Kim Gordon said in *Rolling Stone:* "The problem now is that if you're a woman in a band, riot grrrl has become a yardstick by which you are measured. I don't have anything against it. But I've been doing it for ten years" (France 1993, 24). This focus divided Riot Grrrl–associated bands from other female musicians and led to a lot of Riot Grrrl bashing from women who probably would have otherwise been supportive of the scene.

Journalists also tried to pinpoint the "leader" of the Riot Grrrl scene, but this proved to be difficult, for several reasons. First, as part of an independent music scene, Riot Grrrl–associated bands shied away from anything that smacked of "celebrity," as the indie scene tends to see popular press attention as equivalent to "selling out." Second, as part of a feminist scene, participants attempted to create a scene that allowed each member to be equal. Ignoring this attempt to remain nonhierarchal, however, most mainstream accounts identify Kathleen Hanna as the head of the Riot Grrrl scene. For example, *Newsweek* called Hanna "the closest thing they [Riot Grrrl] have to a leader" (Chideya 1992, 85), while *Rolling Stone* reported that she embodies "the attitude of Riot Grrrl" (France 1993, 23). It was rare for any article not to mention Hanna by name or to refer to Bikini Kill as "her" band.

Participants attempted to counteract this celebrity focus, as it served only to further exacerbate the internal tensions raging in the scene. In the 1994 liner notes to the re-release of the first two Bikini Kill albums, for example, Tobi Vail inserted an article entitled "Bikini Kill Is Made Up of Four Individuals: Kathi, Tobi, Billy, and Kathleen," to try to take the focus off of Hanna. The celebrity treatment was also stressful for Hanna, who found herself undergoing press attention she did not want while being ostracized by the anticelebrity indie scene, as she explained in our interview in 1998:

> I didn't appreciate being made into a leader when I didn't feel like I was. . . . And it was frustrating that some people I felt really resented me for it. Because I was being written about and being called the leader. And it was like, I never said that. Not once did I say, "I'm the leader." Other people wrote that against my wishes; . . . it was really frustrating to have all these guys writing sexist shit about me . . . to have those kind of things going on and then to be resented for it was really frustrating.

This focus on Hanna began to alienate her from other women in the scene, and she found herself mistreated by the press with little sympathy from other participants, who saw her as being divisive. With the media hanging on their every word, Riot Grrrl–associated bands increasingly felt the pressure to put politics before music; at the same time, they tried to avoid being the "voice" for the entire scene.

Things Fall Apart and Endure

By 1994 the external pressures placed on the scene by the popular press, as well as the conflicts within the scene over race, class, and politics, began to take their toll on Riot Grrrl participants. As the image of Riot Grrrl seemed just a fashion trend with no real political message, young girls began to shy away from the scene. Additionally, as the boundaries between personal politics, musical production, and scene politics grew increasingly fuzzy, Riot Grrrl–associated groups began to disband so that participants could experiment with new forms of musical expression that were more relevant to their lives. Lacking new recruits and losing established participants, Riot Grrrl began to dwindle, and reporters began to refer to new feminist music as "post-Grrrl" in an attempt to signal the passing of the Riot Grrrl music scene (McDonnell 1994).

Articles of the period attempted to analyze whether Riot Grrrl was a success or a failure. For example, Gottlieb and Wald (1994) saw it as a failed feminist music scene, because participants did not transcend their subcultural location to reach out to girls in different scenes. In my observation, however, participants defined the success of the Riot Grrrl scene in a very different way from academics and reporters. Participants said Riot Grrrl would have a long-lasting impact on the women involved. As one commented: "Riot Grrrl is not something you grow out of; . . . I think we're going to be strong Riot Women" (Juno 1996, 181). The main goal of the scene when it emerged was to give girls a way to become "cultural producers" (Kearney 1998). If zine making and punk music were no longer modes of production relevant to the lives of participants, they were finding new ways to express their feminism. Thus, in the define-it-yourself spirit of Riot Grrrl, the dissolution of the scene was not a sign of death but rather evidence that women were continuing to find new ways to express their thoughts, emotions, and experiences.

The Riot Grrrl spirit has indeed lived on. The Riot Grrrl scene alerted white participants to the ravages of race, and the women of color who participated in the early Riot Grrrl scene said Riot Grrrl played a key role in introducing discussions about race and privilege into the larger punk scene (Vale 1996; Green and Taormino 1997). In addition, their Riot Grrrl experience acted as a stepping-stone for many women of color in the punk scene and encouraged them to come together and form their own feminist coalitions, as is shown in the compilation zines by zine makers of color, including *Evolution of a Race Riot* and *Yello Kitty*. These zines include articles by white women as well, illustrating that young white feminists were beginning to find more fruitful ways to discuss their privilege.

Finally, despite the media hype about the death of Riot Grrrl, the spirit of the Riot Grrrl scene lives on in the series of music festivals known as Ladyfest. Ladyfest began in August 2000 in Olympia, Washington, as a four-day music and activism event inspired by Riot Grrrl conventions. Taking the definitionless model of the early Riot Grrrl scene, the Ladyfests are unrelated except by name, organized by women from their local communities, and vary in content. The festivals are predominantly organized around four-day concerts with queer-positive and feminist bands, but they also include workshops about issues such as self-defense, sexual abuse, zine making, and music production. Since the Olympia festival, Ladyfests have occurred in Glasgow, Chicago, San Francisco, and Boston. The success of the Ladyfest conventions reveals that while scenes may shrink, shift, or break apart, they do not entirely disappear and, as in the case of Riot Grrrl, can inspire new local, translocal, and virtual communities.

Notes

1.   Because many of the bands involved in what came to be known as the Riot Grrrl scene shied away from using the label "Riot Grrrl" in reference to themselves (mainly as this label was constructed by the mainstream media), I chose to use the term "Riot Grrrl–associated bands" to signify participation in the scene without forcing a label on the bands that they may not have used in reference to themselves.

2.   As Riot Grrrl had no central headquarters, it is difficult to estimate how many conventions occurred and how high their attendance was. However, conventions were held between 1992 and 1995.

3.   The founders of the movement came from a mixture of middle-class, lower-middle-class, and working-class backgrounds; as the movement spread, however, participants were mainly middle class and white. The subhead phrase "the punk-white privilege scene" is taken from the Heavens to Betsy song "Axemen."

References

Ali, Lorraine. 1995. "The Grrls Are Fighting Back." *Los Angeles Times*, 27 July.

Azerrad, Michael. 2001. *Our Band Could Be Your Life*. New York: Little, Brown.

Bikini Kill. 1994. *Bikini Kill*. Kill Rock Stars.

Burchill, Julie, and Tony Parsons. 1978. *The Boy Looked at Johnny: The Obituary of Rock and Roll*. London: Pluto Press.

Chideya, Farai. 1992. "Revolution Girl-Style." *Newsweek*, 23 November, 84–86.

Cohen, Albert. 1955. *Delinquent Boys*. New York: Free Press.

De Alba, Alicia Gaspar. 1995. "The Alter-Native Grain: Theorizing Chicamola Popular Culture." In Antonia Darder, ed., *Culture and Difference: Critical Perspectives on the Bicultural Experience in the United States*. London: Bergin and Garvey.

France, Kim. 1992. "Angry Young Women." *Utne Reader*, September–October, 24–26

————. 1993. "Grrrls at War." *Rolling Stone*, 8 July, 23–24

Frith, Simon. 1983. *Sound Effects: Youth, Leisure, and the Politics of Rock 'n' Roll*. New York: Pantheon Books.

Gottlieb, Joanne, and Gayle Wald. 1994. "Smells Like Teen Spirit: Revolution and Women in Independent Rock." In Andrew Ross and Tricia Rose, eds., *Microphone Fiends: Youth Music and Youth Culture*. New York: Routledge.

Green, Karen, and Tristan Taormino. 1997. *A Girl's Guide to Taking Over the World: Writings from the Girl 'Zine Revolution*. New York: St. Martin's Griffin.

Hebdige, Dick. 1979. *Subculture: The Meaning of Style*. London: Routledge.

Japenga, Ann. 1992. "Punk's Girl Groups Are Putting the Self Back in Self-Esteem." *New York Times*, 26 November.

————. 1993. "Grunge R Us: Exploiting, Co-opting, and Neutralizing the Counter-Culture." *Los Angeles Times Magazine*, 14 November.

Juno, Andrea. 1996. *Angry Women in Rock*. New York: Juno Books.

Kearney, Mary Celeste. 1998. "Producing Girls: Rethinking the Study of Female Youth Culture." In Sherrie A. Inness, ed., *Delinquents and Debutantes: Twentieth Century American Girls' Cultures*. New York: New York University Press.

LeBlanc, Lauraine. 1999. *Pretty in Punk: Girls' Gender Resistance in a Boys' Subculture*. New Brunswick, N.J.: Rutgers University Press.

McDonnell, Evelyn. 1994. "Queer Punk Meets Womyn's Music." *Ms.*, November–December, 78–79.

Schilt, Kristen. 2000. "Not Just a Phase: Feminist Identity and Subcultural Movements." MA thesis, University of Texas at Austin.

Snead, Eleanor. 1992. "Feminist Riot Grrls Don't Just Wanna Have Fun." *USA Today*, 7 August, 5D.

Spencer, Lauren. 1993. "Grrrls Only." *Washington Post*, 3 January.

Straw, Will. 1997. "Communities and Scenes in Popular Music." In Ken Gelder and Sarah Thornton, eds., *The Subcultures Reader*. New York: Routledge. First published 1991 as "Systems of Articulation, Logistics of Change: Communities and Scenes in Popular Music," *Cultural Studies* 5: 368–88.

Thornton, Sarah. 1996. *Club Cultures: Music, Media, and Subcultural Capital.* Hanover, N.H.: Wesleyan University Press.

Vail, Tobi. 1994. "Bikini Kill Is Made Up of Four Individuals." Liner notes for *Bikini Kill,* by Bikini Kill. CD. Kill Rock Stars.

Vale, Vincent. 1996. *Zines: Volume One.* San Francisco: V Search Books.

White, Emily. 1992. "Revolution Grrrl-Style Now." *LA Weekly,* 10–16 July, 22.

7

Translocal Connections
in the Goth Scene

Paul Hodkinson

"Gothic" is a term currently used to describe a considerable variety of high- and popular-cultural phenomena, from ancient architecture to classic and recent novels to hit U.S. science-fiction television series. In referring to "the goth scene," however, I mean a more small-scale and particular music and fashion grouping, on which I recently conducted extensive ethnographic research.[1] Based around a particular blend of "dark" sounds and styles that emerged out of the remnants of punk, the goth scene's life began in the early 1980s. While diverse in some respects, the stylistic sounds and artifacts around which the scene revolved have been consistently united in their emphasis upon glamorous, and usually feminine, forms of the sombre, the sinister, and the macabre. Most obvious, perhaps, have been the emphases on black in clothing, hair color, album covers, and bedrooms, and the high-lighting of eyes, cheekbones, and lips with dark-colored elaborate makeup, often offset by a light foundation. Such visual references have cohered with a musical emphasis on lyrics, chords, rhythms, and bass lines with sinister or miserable overtones.

With the help, in the 1980s, of a record industry and music press in need of a new form of "alternative" music culture to market toward young people in search of a distinctive identity, the goth sound, style, and identity became transnationally popular among particular groups of young people from the mid-1980s to the early 1990s. Subsequently, a decline in large-scale media and commercial interest lowered the profile of the music, the fashion, and the lifestyle with which it had become associated. In the decade that followed, the goth scene survived and developed on a much smaller scale, often outside the realms of mass or even most niche media and commerce. Notably, however, while the overall size and presence of the grouping declined, it remained as widespread and as intimately connected as ever in terms of geographical scale. That such a small, distinctive music scene could transcend boundaries of place was a theme that dominated my research agenda, and it forms the particular focus of this chapter.

Background

My research on the goth scene focused on Britain and began in 1996. Broadly, its approach was ethnographic, revolving around a significant intensification of an existing personal involvement to gain as many useful contacts as possible and to observe and experience the goth scene across Britain from the position of a "critical insider" (Hodkinson 2002, 4–6). This participation, observation, and networking was complemented by more direct, interventionist forms of research, most notably the conducting of interviews with more than seventy individuals and the administering of a single part-quantitative, part-qualitative self-completion questionnaire. The apparently translocal form taken by the goth scene was a key theme investigated in interviews and during participant observation. In particular, I was concerned to assess the consistency of the goth scene from place to place and to establish the extent to which it was experienced as translocal by participants.

Although I visited goth events, shops, and individuals in a wide variety of places across Britain, I also specifically concentrated research on three differently placed British cities, in order to enable a comparative focus. The cities were the small and rather isolated port of Plymouth, located in the southwest of the country; the much larger northern city of Leeds in West Yorkshire, associated with several well-known 1980s goth bands, including the Sisters of Mercy and spin-off group The Mission; and the large and well-connected Midlands city of Birmingham, which was my home and base during the four-year project. In addition to this emphasis on the goth scene as physically manifest in different places, a deliberate focus was placed upon analysis of the networks of communication and commerce that linked goths based in different areas. The latter primarily took the form of qualitative analysis of specialist media texts, as well as interviews with the producers of such media and with specialist retailers of goth fashion and music.

Holly Kruse has suggested that what she terms the "alternative" music scene of the early 1990s, based primarily in Britain and the United States, can be regarded as translocal, in that its manifestations from place to place were connected "rather abstractly, though shared tastes . . . and quite concretely through social and economic networks" (1993, 33). While "translocal" is used by Kruse to imply the transcendence of national as well as town or city boundaries, such an international focus is, with some exceptions, a secondary matter for this chapter, which concerns itself primarily with translocal connections between manifestations of the goth scene in different British locations. Nevertheless, I report my findings on these connections here in a way that seeks to develop Kruse's distinction between "abstract" and "concrete" translocal connections. The first section focuses upon the former category, particularly in relation to the extent to which goths in different areas identified with one another and shared the same tastes and values. Subsequently, these somewhat "abstract" connections are explained by means of more "concrete" links. These are divided into those involving the physical movement of individuals and those created by specialist networks of consumer goods and media. Without wishing in any way to suggest that localities were of no importance to the goth scene, then, the chapter details translocal identities and tastes and seeks to understand them in relation to equally specialist networks of travel, commerce, and communication.

Abstract Connections: Identity

If one spends sufficient time around goths, the likelihood is that a strong sense of group identity will become apparent, alongside an equally strong sense of distinction from perceived outsiders (Hodkinson 2002). Furthermore, indications during my research were that this subjective perception of sameness and difference operated largely irrespective of the boundaries of place. While much of the argument of this chapter, as discussed earlier, relates to intranational connections, goths' sense of affinity with one another was a feature that clearly transcended national as well as local boundaries. This became most apparent when interview respondents were directly asked about their feelings toward goths based in different locations from them. A particular curiosity about and desire to meet goths from different countries came across in the following extract, from an interview with a couple based in Birmingham. They were asked what their feelings would be if they happened to see a group of goths of a nationality different from theirs while they were on holiday in a different country:

> Denise: I'd want to know these new people—especially from a different country because it could be interesting to find out what their country is like—"What's the scene like over here?"—that sort of thing.
> Brian: In some ways I think it's almost like a personal test in a way—because you're a goth and you like all these things . . . and you're dying to find out if somebody else likes them—so wherever you go—if there's that little link or whatever that you see—there's a chance they might.[2]

I did occasionally receive indications that some goths felt an affiliation to their locality or country. However, such attachments were usually expressed in the form of translocal comparisons *within* the goth scene, rather than, for example, expressions of solidarity with local nongoths. There were limited indications, for example, of distinctions and rivalries between "London goths" and "northern goths" in Britain. It was clear both from interviews and extensive ethnographic research, however, that such distinctions carried less overall significance than the shared translocal identification of both groups as goths of one kind or another. What was very clearly the case was—to adapt an observation made by Simon Reynolds (1990) about alternative music culture generally—that goths perceived that they had more in common with other goths hundreds or thousands of miles away than they did with most nonaffiliated members of their immediate locality.

Abstract Connections: Tastes

Linked to this translocal sense of collective identity was an overall consistency from place to place in the tastes exhibited by goths within Britain. There *were* subtle differences among my three case-study areas of Plymouth, Leeds, and Birmingham, often attributable to infrastructural factors such as the particular blend of music played by local DJs or the kinds of clothes or music shops available in the locality. However, such local distinctiveness was overshadowed by a remarkable degree of similarity in the overall range of tastes and values on show in each area, the details of which have been set out elsewhere (Hodkinson 2002). In addition to consistency of general stylistic themes, it was frequently the case that one could observe exactly the same makes and items of clothing or accessories worn by goths in different places, something even more applicable to the content of DJ set lists and individual collections of records and CDs.

There was equally little evidence of significant local differences in the status criteria by which participants judged and classified others in relation to the boundaries of their scene. To put this in another way, with reference to the work of Sarah Thornton (1995, 11), there was a considerable degree of agreement with respect to what characteristics, artifacts, knowledges, and modes of behavior would and would not bestow subcultural capital upon individuals in the context of the goth scene. Therefore, while there were some indications that certain sounds or looks held marginally more prominence in some places than others, there seemed no sense in which, for example, the same appearance would result in veneration in one area and total lack of it in another. This level of agreement on membership criteria is illustrated most effectively by the ease with which goths were able to identify one another, regardless of where they were. The following respondents, in two separate interviews, illustrated this by suggesting that they were easily and confidently able to identify goths from looking at them—sometimes even if they were not particularly dressed up:

> Tanya: You can just look at somebody and you can just tell they are just goth all over.
> Susan: Even if they dress down a bit for work or whatever.
> Joseph: You get to the stage where you can sort of pick out the off-duty goths. . . . I've seen them everywhere—most of the places I've been to.

I hope to have provided some clear indications, then, of the extent to which goths tended to identify with one another regardless of whereabouts and of the degree to which the tastes and norms that defined their grouping were similar from place to place within Britain. In the following sections I shall begin to identify the causes of this seemingly remarkable level of translocal consistency and identity in such a small grouping, by moving from abstract connections to more concrete ones.

Connections through Travel

Shared tastes and a sense of identity existed in something of a circular relationship with face-to-face translocal interactions, which were induced by the tendency for individuals and groups frequently to travel outside their locality to goth gigs, clubs, festivals, and shops. This day- and night-trip-ping (Hollows and Milestone 1995) occasionally took the form of organized minibus or coach trips, but more often involved carloads of goths setting forth for particular destinations in a more haphazard fashion. Sometimes people would travel to go shopping in different places, while on other oc-casions groups or individuals would turn up at regular events in neighbor-ing cities to sample crowds and DJs different from those they were used to. Brian, a respondent from Birmingham, explained that goth nights in that city tended to draw people from all around the Midlands of Britain: "[A lot] of people who actually club in Birmingham don't actually come from Birmingham definitely—I think they draw in from . . . surrounding counties."

The largest and most widespread translocal crowds, though, were at-tracted by unique and irregular events, notably live performances of high-profile goth bands and, even more notably, festivals. The latter usually encapsulated two or more evenings of live performances, together with discos featuring well-known goth DJs and stalls retailing specialist clothes and music. The most well-known and consistently well attended of these in late 1990s Britain was the Whitby Gothic Weekend, an event which twice a year attracted more than one thousand goths from all across Britain and a minority from Europe and the United States. For a number of goths I spoke to, this festival was the highlight of their social calendar and was anticipated months in advance.

Crucially, traveling to large and small events outside their locality tended to enter goths into a circular process whereby the motivation for further travel would be increased with each journey. This was primarily because traveling often resulted in the development of translocal friendship networks. Once established, such friendships created an extra incentive to make future trips. In the following example the respondent, Tanya, from Birmingham, describes the way in which the establishment of a translo-cal friendship was followed by a meet-up in her own city and then at the "neutral" location provided by the Whitby Gothic Weekend: "I know a few goths in different parts of the country. I know two in Carlisle. When I was in Carlisle I met them up there—and then they turned up at Whitby and then they turned up in Birmingham a couple of weeks back."

Meanwhile, the following questionnaire respondent explained that the primary motivation for his attendance at the Whitby Gothic Weekend was to create new translocal friendships and to sustain old ones.

Q: Please explain in your own words why have you come to Whitby.
Dave: We have been coming to Whitby for the past 3 years enjoying the
atmosphere, meeting old friends and making new ones.

The process of gradually getting to know more and more goths from
across Britain through traveling also inevitably enhanced a general sense
of taking part in and belonging to a movement which was translocal—as
opposed to merely feeling part of a tiny localized community. Furthermore,
in cities such as Leeds and Birmingham that were within easy reach of other
metropolitan centres, even goths who did not frequently travel outside
their locality were liable to come into regular contact with individuals or
groups who had traveled *to* their own area. However, this was less the case
for more isolated localities such as Plymouth, where few goths were liable
to visit from elsewhere.

The physical contact these networks of travel created between geographically separated goths also contributed to the overall translocal consistency of the style across the country. In a spontaneous, grassroots sense,
traveling individuals were potentially liable to influence and be influenced
by the music and fashion on display at the event to which they had traveled.
Meanwhile, key influential individuals such as DJs were equally liable to
pick up musical ideas and influences from attending events elsewhere, ideas
which may then be imported back into the set list of their local goth club.
Traveling, then, enhanced the perception that goths had of taking part in
a coherent translocal movement, and at the same time caused a continual
cross-fertilization of norms and tastes from area to area within Britain,
enhancing overall consistency.

Crucial though they were, however, the connections created by the
physical movement of goths between different areas were only a partial
factor in the overall translocal form taken by their grouping. Of equal or
perhaps even greater importance were specialist networks of commerce
and of communication, which functioned to create more constant links
between different areas. As we shall see, these networks played a role in
facilitating the kind of physical connections just described, as well as in
contributing to translocal consistency and identity in a more direct fashion—both for those who frequently experienced physical contact with
goths from elsewhere, and for those who did not.

Connections through Commerce

The distinctive forms of music, clothes, and accessories around which the goth scene revolved were sourced, by participants, from a variety of outlets. Some of these did not, in themselves, particularly emphasize or reinforce translocal connections. Nonspecialist local market stalls and main-street stores, for example, were often used by goths, who would sift through a variety of miscellaneous items and appropriate those they deemed consistent with their individual interpretation of the goth style. Although this was nearly always done with the current translocal range of goth tastes very much in mind, the practice, in itself, may come across as potentially more of a diversifier than a unifier. Individually selected external goods, though, accounted for only some of the consumption practices of goths, the remainder involving the purchase of rather more prepackaged specialist items, which were often standardized from one place to another.

I include in the latter category the purchase of CDs explicitly marketed at the goth scene, yet available in the majority of independent and chain record stores. During the 1990s, a number of compilation CDs were released, either of individual well-known goth bands from the past, or of goth music in general terms. Notable examples of the latter included *Nocturnal,* a compilation of mostly 1980s goth music (1998), and two volumes focused on more contemporary goth music entitled *Hex Files* (1997). Such general compilations played an extremely important role in the continual translocal standardization of goth as a musical style, with a potential direct and indirect influence upon general participants and key influential individuals such as DJs, producers of fanzines, and indeed new goth bands. Numerous respondents explained to me that they found such compilations to be an invaluable means of sampling a variety of goth bands, some of whose back catalogues would be sought out proactively afterward. Geoff, when asked about how he discovered new music, explained that although they had certain disadvantages, compilations were extremely useful to him both as a participant and as a local DJ: "Compilation albums are probably the easiest way of doing it [finding out about new music]; . . . you end up with an album with a couple of tracks you do like and a lot of tracks you don't like, but I just find them useful for taking to the club [to DJ] because you get such a variety of music."

Potentially even more significant in terms of the translocal construction of a consistent style, though, were specialist retailers of music and clothing.

These took the form of localized goth-oriented shops and mail-order retailers. In different ways, both of these contributed to the translocal consistency of the goth style. In the case of specialist local stores, while the precise range of items stocked by each would vary somewhat, they often shared the same suppliers and as a result frequently stocked similar or sometimes the same items. This was partly because the proprietors of such stores tended actively to gain ideas from one another. If a new line of clothing or accessories sold successfully in one goth-oriented store, then it tended soon to appear in others across the country. Such influences were particularly direct in the case of those stores from across Britain that came together every now and again to form specialist markets at high-profile goth festivals such as the Whitby Gothic Weekend. Proprietors from one store would often seek to find out what was being sold by others, and this information would be taken into account in decisions over future stock back in their locality. Of course, the presence of so many local retailers at translocal events such as this also had the effect of combining their respective assortments of goods for direct purchase by participants from across the country, who would then take various influences back to their own towns and cities.

In the case of specialist goth mail-order CD retailers, the translocal construction of the goth scene in musical terms was even more direct, bypassing any local intermediaries. Such stores very explicitly defined themselves as catering for the specialist tastes of goths and operated via catalogues, usually available in both web site and printed form. These catalogues, which included CDs from numerous countries around the world, provided goths from across and beyond Britain with the chance to easily purchase virtually whatever goth music they were looking for. Furthermore, such retailers, by virtue of their decisions about what to include and recommend in their catalogues, played an important gate-keeping role in the construction of translocal stylistic boundaries. An indication of the importance of such mail-order companies to the consumption practices of goths—particularly for music—was provided in a number of questionnaire responses to the question "How easy/difficult is it for you to find goth music and clothes to buy?" Some examples are given here:

Jessica: Music is easy—especially with the growing number of specialist mail order companies.
Stephen: Music is impossible if were not for mail-order.
Jason: Reasonably easy by mail order—much harder from shops.

Goth flyers (S. L. Hodkinson).

Connections through Media

Important though they were in their own right, shared identity, consistency of tastes, traveling to events, and networks of commerce in the goth scene were each interlinked with what might be referred to as "virtual" connections, in the form of a variety of interconnected media forms. As I have set out elsewhere, niche and mass media were extremely important to the initial construction and subsequent transnational marketing of goth music and the style which accompanied it (Hodkinson 2002). Although there were occasional references to the goth scene in such external media during the late 1990s, participants by this time had become more reliant upon small and highly specialist media produced by and for goths. Such internal media took the form of printed flyers and fanzines, and online resources such as web sites and discussion groups.

Although this chapter is primarily about translocal connections, it is important to emphasize that some of these media functioned to facilitate and construct the goth scene on a local scale. Flyers, for example, were used primarily to advertise local events to predominantly local goth crowds. Consequently their distribution was often centered on spaces such a shops, pubs, and clubs within the area concerned. Goth online discussion groups—which may at the outset evoke images of globalized virtual community (Wellman and Gulia 1999, 169)—were also sometimes used for socialization and information transfer between goths based in particular cities or regions of Britain. Some respondents specifically indicated that they valued these localized forms of communication because of their value as a resource for everyday local participation in the goth scene. Mary, for example, explains the value of local e-mail lists, compared with their national equivalent, for initiating meet ups with other subscribers: "If I want to just arrange to meet some people in the pub, I'm not going to do it through UPG [*uk.people.gothic*, a national discussion group], but that's what we used to do before TARTS [a London e-mail list]."

In these respects, then, media might be said to have played some role in ensuring that place continued to matter, whether practically or symbolically. However, the most significant function of media in the goth scene was the provision of vital translocal connections between goths, in the form of information, influence, and direct "virtual" socialization.

Practical translocal information provided by such media included details of forthcoming events, CD releases, and sources of music and clothing. While flyers have been presented here primarily as a localized form of media, promoters were also increasingly using them to attract a more widespread clientele, either by swapping batches with promoters in other areas, by asking fanzines to include them in the envelopes they sent out to subscribers, or by compiling and utilizing their own mailing lists. Meanwhile, goth fanzines, most of which were distributed across Britain at the very least, usually contained sections that detailed a range of forthcoming events throughout and sometimes beyond the country. They also provided information and reviews focused on new goth music—as well as, in some cases, direct ads from specialist businesses or promoters. The significance of printed media such as fanzines and flyers in informing goths about consumables, gigs, and events was illustrated in a number of interviews when respondents were asked how they found out about such things. Richard's response is an example: "Word of mouth, often from fanzine advertizing, you know, you find out the address of a fanzine. . . . They're good at trying to keep as current as possible and advertize up-and-coming events; . . . I guess, yeah, flyers, fanzines, word of mouth."

Toward the end of my research in the year 2000, the Internet was rapidly becoming the most efficient and significant means by which translocal information was communicated within the goth scene. Significantly, whereas fanzines tended to be published only every few months, and hence to include only events planned well in advance, information sources on the Internet were regularly updated, reliable, and inclusive. In spite of their geographical designations, local e-mail lists frequently involved contributions from external subscribers. Meanwhile, national discussion groups constituted a more extensive translocal resource. While sometimes direct announcements were made by key individuals, information came up just as frequently in the general course of discussion. This online form of "word of mouth" enabled subscribers to keep up with the translocal goth scene with minimum proactive effort. However, there were also more organized Internet resources—notably in the form of web sites specifically devoted to collating and displaying translocal information useful for goths, from regularly updated event listings to details of bands, shops, or publications.

Through channeling suitable information to relevant audiences, specialist media acted as an important facilitator of the translocal networks of commerce and travel already described. In this respect, "virtual" connections were indirectly responsible for the aforementioned effects of "physical" connections on stylistic consistency and strength of identity. In addition to this, however, media played a direct gate-keeping role in the continual translocal construction of the goth scenes' distinctive tastes and values. Through their decisions about inclusion and exclusion, they contributed to the establishment of different sounds, looks, artifacts, and even forms of behavior as either consistent or inconsistent with being a goth. Of course, it was not the case that all flyers, fanzines, and web sites were entirely consistent with one another in their editorial policy with regard to style and taste. Furthermore, one could argue that consistency must surely have been undermined by the range of viewpoints and voices one might encounter on goth Internet discussion forums. However, because so many of these media forms were translocal, they contributed to a similar *range* of different interpretations of goth from place to place. In other words, while diverse interpretations of goth were constructed through different media forms, these points of difference crosscut geographical boundaries.

The final key role played by media connections concerns online discussion groups only and consisted of a direct form of translocal socialization. While I have for the most part presented media here as facilitators for other activities, online discussion groups also provided goths with the chance directly to converse with large numbers of other goths electronically. Among other things, this meant that they were able to maintain continual contact with translocal friends they had made through previous traveling and to establish new acquaintances online.

I asked Vicky whether she felt the Internet made her less localized. "Yes, you know people from London, you know people that go to Slimelight [London goth club], you know people from Edinburgh, you know people from Glasgow, you've talked to them."

Crucially, rather than removing the need for physical travel, the tendency was for such virtual interactions to encourage goths to want to see their friends in face-to-face circumstances. More generally, it meant that more people became more able to attend events across the country with the confidence that they would come across people whom they knew.

While specialist media enhanced intranational socialization between cities, the desire to utilize virtual connections to facilitate "real life" activities rather than as an end in themselves established limits to respondents' interest in non-British Internet content. In spite of a strong sense of identification with goths around the world, the tendency was for individuals to focus on seeking information and contacts that related to places within a feasible traveling distance—and this usually meant within their own country. Therefore, although international media links offered the potential of a globalized virtual scene, in practice such connections were utilized rather less intensively than communications networks within Britain.

Discussion

In much theoretical and empirically based work on popular-music scenes, there has been a tendency to focus on geographical place as the primary basis for small-scale distinctiveness and substance in the midst of a world otherwise dominated by global media and commerce, which are regarded as catalysts for either cultural fluidity or homogenization. The most -impressive and rich ethnographic description of localized music-related identities, practices, and infrastructures has been provided by the likes of Finnegan (1989), Cohen (1991), Shank (1994), and Bennett (2000), whose work is referred to in the introduction to this book. There can be little doubt as to the significance of the contribution they make, both as a direct attack on overgeneralized descriptions of a placeless, meaningless, or homogenized world and in terms of the levels of detail they each provide on the kinds of cultural processes involved in the everyday functioning of local music scenes.

However, the geographically specific focus of such studies, alongside their accentuation of local music processes—sometimes to contest academic descriptions of globalized meaninglessness—has tended to allow only a relatively limited emphasis on small, distinctive groupings that are *not* reliant upon, organized around, or confined within any particular town or city. The highly specialized "abstract" and "concrete" connections that operate within such translocal groupings may comprise just as significant a challenge to theories of globalized meaninglessness or homogenization as their local equivalents, yet until recently, they appear rather to have been overlooked. Their study has been valuably pioneered by a recent body of work focused on "virtual communities" on the Internet (for example, Jones 1997, 1999, 2000), together with a number of emerging studies which have sought to understand the relationship between the local and translocal processes in relation to geographically dispersed formations, including alternative or "college" music (Kruse 1993), Riot Grrrl (Leonard 1998), and extreme metal (Harris 2000).

This chapter has sought to ask similar questions in relation to the goth scene—with a particular focus on the nature of the translocal connections involved in Britain. What I hope is relatively clear is that this example, rather than consisting of a series of highly separate, distinctive, and clearly bounded local scenes, comes across more as a singular and relatively coherent movement whose translocal connections were of greater significance than its local differences. While locality remained highly important to

Dancing Goths (S. L. Hodkinson).

everyday participation, the identities, practices, values, and infrastructural elements of the goth scene usually operated beyond the bounds of particular towns or cities. Furthermore, we have begun to see that abstract, physical, commercial, and media connections were interlinked, in the sense that each induced and was induced by the others. The picture, then, is of a complex translocal network of "concrete" connections which functioned to construct and support the strength of subjective identity and the consistent and distinctive tastes around which the British goth scene revolved.

Whether or not such coherence and connections are equally intense from nation to nation seems rather less clear, however. As part of our largely intranational explorations in this chapter, I have emphasized an undoubtedly international sense of identity as well as significant flows of specialist music between countries. However, I have also noted the apparent reluctance of many goths to spend significant amounts of time engaging with media whose content seemed somewhat removed from the physical confines of Britain. While more in-depth internationally focused research would be valuable in coming to more confident conclusions here, my limited evidence on this issue suggests, at the very least, that "concrete" or practical connections tended to be rather less intense at the transnational level than they were from city to city within Britain. Perhaps this tentative finding might suggest an interesting twist to the academic consensus that nations are increasingly bypassed by simultaneous processes of globalization and localization.

Notes

1. Elsewhere (Hodkinson 2002) I have sought to emphasize the continued value of the notion of subculture as an analytical tool to conceptualize groupings such as the goth scene. I have suggested that this term might be used to emphasize the relatively substantive, bounded form taken by certain elective groupings, something which contrasts with an emphasis on fluidity and multiplicity elsewhere (for example, Muggleton 1997, Bennett 1999). However, in order to emphasize the primary concern here with considerations of place and to avoid inconsistency in the context of this book, I do not reemphasize that particular argument here and hence refer to the grouping with which I am concerned only as the goth *scene*. By doing this, I do not intend to imply any particular support for the notion of "scene" as an interpretive device, but merely regard it as the nonacademic way in which goths themselves referred to the grouping in which they participated.

2. Readers of my book *Goth: Identity Style and Subculture* (Hodkinson 2002) may

be interested in why I used codes to refer to interviewees and questionnaire respondents in that text, while pseudonyms are used here. In both cases the decision was complex, but the relatively small number of respondents referred to here and the lack of any well known individuals was deemed to make pseudonyms a more preferable option. In my book, there were clear problems with changing the names of high-profile individuals and hence with deciding precisely who counted as a high-profile individual and who did not among the large number of respondents referred to. In addition, some respondents were specifically unhappy about being given a different name to their own in a book that was likely to receive considerable publicity within the goth scene itself.

References

Bennett, Andy. 1999. "Subcultures or Neo-Tribes? Rethinking the Relationship between Youth, Style, and Musical Taste." *Sociology* 33, 3: 599–617.

———. 2000. *Popular Music and Youth Culture: Music, Identity, and Place.* Basingstoke, U.K.: Macmillan.

Cohen, Sara. 1991. *Rock Culture in Liverpool: Popular Music in the Making.* Oxford: Clarendon.

Finnegan, Ruth. 1989. *The Hidden Musicians: Music-Making in an English Town.* Cambridge: Cambridge University Press.

Harris, Keith. 2000. " 'Roots'? The Relationship between the Global and the Local within the Extreme Metal Scene." *Popular Music* 19, 1: 13–30.

Hodkinson, Paul. 2002. *Goth: Identity, Style, and Subculture.* Oxford and New York: Berg.

Hollows, Joanne, and Katie Milestone. 1995. "Inter City Soul: Transient Communities and Regional Identity in an Underground Urban Club Culture." Paper presented at "Contested Cities," British Sociological Association Annual Conference, University of Leicester, U.K., 13–15 April.

Jones, Steve, ed. 1997. *Virtual Culture: Identity and Communication in Cybersociety.* London: Sage.

———. 1999. *Doing Internet Research: Critical Issues and Methods for Examining the Net.* London: Sage.

———. 2000. *Cybersociety 2.0.* London: Sage.

Kruse, Holly. 1993. "Subcultural Identity in Alternative Music Culture." *Popular Music* 12, 1: 31–43.

Leonard, Marion. 1998. "Paper Planes: Travelling the New Grrrl Geographies." In Tracy Skelton and Gill Valentine, eds., *Cool Places: Geographies of Youth Cultures.* London: Routledge.

Muggleton, David. 1997. "The Post-Subculturalist." In Steve Redhead, Derek Wynne, and Justin O'Connor, eds., *The Club Cultures Reader: Readings in Popular Cultural Studies.* Oxford: Blackwell.

Reynolds, Simon. 1990. *Blissed Out.* London: Serpent's Tail.

Shank, Barry. 1994. *Dissonant Identities: The Rock 'n' Roll Scene in Austin, Texas.* Hanover, N.H.: University Press of New England.

Thornton, Sarah. 1995. *Club Cultures: Music, Media, and Subcultural Capital.* Cambridge: Polity Press.

Wellman, Barry, and Milena Gulia. 1999. "Virtual Communities as Communities." In Marc Smith and Peter Kollock, eds., *Communities in Cyberspace.* London: Routledge.

Discography

Hex Files Vol. 1. 1997. Credo Records.

Hex Files Vol. 2. 1997. Credo Records.

Nocturnal. 1998. Procreate.

8

Music Festivals as Scenes: Examples from Serious Music, Womyn's Music, and SkatePunk

Timothy J. Dowd, Kathleen Liddle, and Jenna Nelson

Music festivals exist for numerous and diverse music genres. Festivals resemble local scenes, as they occur in a delimited space, offering a collective opportunity for performers and fans to experience music and other lifestyle elements. However, festivals are also components of broader music scenes that simultaneously exist on local, translocal, and virtual levels. This chapter highlights three characteristics of music festivals that, taken together, enhance the scenes perspective.

First, while music festivals occur more rarely than do events that constitute local scenes, the intensity of a festival compensates for its infrequency. Drawn together from geographically dispersed locations and away from the expectations of everyday life, fans and performers can immerse themselves in a particular culture and experiment with different identities. This intensity can have several consequences. For instance, the complexity of festival logistics leads those in charge to adopt formal organizational structures. It also demands commitment from attendees, as they must be willing to immerse themselves in festival culture, as well as make arrangements for travel, vacation time, and attendance fees. If we draw a religious analogy, comparing the events of a local music scene to a weekly church service, then the festival—with the challenges involved in participation—more closely resembles a pilgrimage destination. Also, as with a pilgrimage, the experience of being temporarily immersed in festival culture can profoundly transform attendees.

Second, music festivals face time constraints that demand deliberate boundary work on the part of organizers. While the regularly occurring events of a local scene allow boundaries to emerge organically, festival organizers must make explicit decisions regarding the appropriate music for inclusion or the characteristics of acceptable participants (Santoro 2002). The resulting boundaries shape how a given festival relates to local, translocal, and virtual scenes. Finally, music festivals often create change beyond their own borders. This catalytic potential stems from the intensity of such events. Festivals can provide a forum for creating, mobilizing, and rejuvenating both performers and audience, as when they helped revive the bluegrass genre (Peterson 1997). They can also facilitate changes that may not be viewed as positive, such as their contribution to the commercialization of popular music (Seiler 2000).

To illustrate these characteristics of intensity, boundary work, and impact, we focus on three recurrent festivals that span both disparate genres and time. We begin with the Yaddo Music Festival (1932–1952), a gathering for "serious" composers in the United States that helped expand the range of "high culture" music in America. Next, we turn to the Michigan Womyn's Music Festival (1976–present), an annual women-only festival that celebrates women's music and feminist ideology. Finally, we discuss the Vans Warped Tour (1994–present), an annual touring festival that features alternative, punk, and hardcore bands, which taps into the current resurgence of skateboarding culture. In offering these three cases, we draw on primary (for example, press releases, organizational documents) and secondary sources (for example, histories, biographies), supplemented by interviews with participants in a particular festival or scene.

Yaddo Music Festival

The Yaddo Festival emerged amidst the musical flux of the early to mid-1900s. Classical music thrived as never before in the United States (DiMaggio 1991; Dowd et al. 2002), through an exploding number of symphony orchestras, an expanding presence in university curricula, and the products of emergent recording and radio industries. Despite this increased availability of musical "high culture," the emphasis on works of deceased European composers hindered the attempts of living U.S. composers to disseminate their music (Dowd et al. 2002; Zuck 1980). Consequently, these avant-garde composers founded organizations (for example, the League of Composers) that championed "serious music"—a label used by some composers to distinguish contemporary, dissonant music from the "classical music" of Beethoven and others. Milton Babbitt, an eminent composer and Pulitzer Prize recipient, noted in a 1994 interview that these organizations "made it possible for [serious composers] to hear live performances of these things that they would not otherwise hear. It gave them some sense of what had been going on. . . . And made it possible for them to hear their own music. There's nothing more important than that."[1]

The Yaddo Music Festival resulted from the impetus of Aaron Copland—a premier U.S. composer. In 1930, he was invited to spend a summer at Yaddo, an estate and nonprofit corporation in New York that serves as a retreat for artists. Copland proposed that Yaddo host a festival of contemporary music. After receiving financial support from Yaddo's board of directors, the festival commenced in 1932 and occurred sporadically until 1952 (Copland 1968; Copland and Perlis 1984; Shackleford 1974).

Intensity

The festival provided an intensity of experience not often found in the world of serious music. It brought together composers with a similar aesthetic agenda: They sought to advance music beyond the accomplishments of classical composers, pushing the musical envelope regarding such elements as harmony and rhythm. While at Yaddo, they organized forums and informal conversations devoted to the challenges that composers confront (Copland 1968; Copland and Perlis 1984). The description offered by composer George Antheil illustrates:

> In Yaddo, this last September, a number of outstanding young composers discussed the danger of not cultivating their public, the fact that foreign conductors do not play enough American music, and ways and means of remedying this appalling lack of audience and appreciation. Most were agreed that we should take part in some active educational movement, should develop some kind of association with an understanding of the public, or at least cultivate a public. (1934, 93)

Although such discussions were not limited to Yaddo, the festival facilitated a probing dialogue not possible when composers were geographically scattered.

The festival also fostered intensity by offering a multiday event that featured multiple compositions. The first festival featured the music of eighteen composers. This was notable, given that music groups rarely performed *any* avant-garde compositions. The earliest festivals relied on only a few performers (for example, pianists, vocalists, and string quartets), but in later years the number of musicians grew to include entire chamber orchestras. This growth expanded the range of music that could be performed, as when the festival presented Charles Ives's Third Symphony (Shackleford 1978).

Finally, the festival's intensity was marked by an audience that was receptive and knowledgeable—a far cry from the negative outbursts (for example, booing) that avant-garde music inspired elsewhere. Copland wrote to a colleague: "At Yaddo, for the first time I had the impression that the audience was 'getting it' " (Norman and Shrifte 1979, 402). In later years, technology augmented this audience. Recordings were made of select performances from 1936 onward, while radio broadcasts from Yaddo occurred in 1938, 1940, and 1952. Given the limited attendance and media coverage at early festivals, these were welcome developments (Howard 1941; Shackleford 1978).

Boundary Work

While organizers of the Yaddo Festival were clear on what did *not* constitute "serious" music (for example, popular music and classical music), a lower consensus existed regarding what best represented serious music and merited performance. Consequently, boundary work regarding the selection and evaluation of compositions became important.

Selection initially proved contentious and eventually spawned a bureaucratic response. At the first festival, in 1932, Copland simply invited composers he admired to submit works of their choosing. Critic Paul Rosenfeld accused Copland of favoring friends while snubbing the "ultramodern" composers who were not part of Copland's circle, such as Carl Ruggles and Henry Cowell: "It was plain that with a certain pardonable cocksureness Copland . . . had placed on his programs only what conformed to his own taste" (Rosenfeld 1972, 355). Copland responded by chairing a selection committee for the 1933 festival; not surprisingly, Ruggles and Cowell were among those whose works were featured that year. Following that festival,

Copland suggested to the Yaddo board of directors that others be in charge of the festival; they agreed. Beginning in 1936, a committee of experts oversaw the selection process. Moreover, the selection process in subsequent festivals entailed a review process. In 1937 and 1938, more than a hundred compositions were submitted for consideration, yet fewer than forty were featured in the festivals. Thus, the selection of music went from an ad hoc to a formalized process (Copland and Perlis 1984; Shackleford 1978).

A good deal of the boundary work occurred during festivals, as composers and others evaluated performances and argued over which works successfully pushed the musical envelope. Their discussion could be highly critical, as when composer Lou Harrison lamented: "It was quite clear from the series of six concerts presented by the Music Group of Yaddo this September, that the young are marching together in an almost solid phalanx of technical reaction and are conducting the battle on a low level of competence" (1946, 296). Still, their discussion sometimes celebrated works and composers, as with the "discovery" of Charles Ives. An early composer of serious music, Ives encountered little interest in his discordant works, and his compositions were rarely performed. Composer Bernard Herman encouraged Copland to include Ives's music at the first Yaddo Festival (Copland and Perlis 1984). Composer Wallingford Reigger wrote to Ives about the warm response that his music generated in 1932:

> Your beautiful songs that were given at Yaddo aroused not only
> enthusiasm and wide-spread interest on the part of the audience (of about
> 200 discriminating music-lovers) but keen appreciation in the numerous
> composers present. About 16 of these remained a few days after the festival
> and your songs were a constantly recurring subject. (Rossiter 1975, 239)

The music of Ives would be included in subsequent Yaddo festivals—and would become a major touchstone for serious composers as they returned to their local scenes (Cowell and Cowell 1955; Copland and Perlis 1984).

Impact

The Yaddo Festival had an impact on U.S. musical life. It brought attention to serious composers such as Ives who were once neglected in the United States. Hence, John Howard could write that, "while no New York newspapers were represented at the first Yaddo Festival, held in that autumn of 1932, it is nowadays self-understood that Yaddo events must be commented upon in detail in the columns of these journals" (1941, 333). It also had an impact on local scenes of serious music, as it was one of many composer-founded organizations that helped spawn additional organizations like the American Music Center, which distributes the published music of contemporary composers (Copland and Perlis 1984).

The festival also helped expand the range of musical high culture. Among "the first significant gathering[s] of the clan of younger American composers" (Zuck 1980, 273), it brought together knowledgeable critics, patrons, and a core audience—thereby mobilizing resources and awareness. Many composers who participated in Yaddo would later be featured in the performances of major symphony orchestras, the curricula of higher education institutions, and recordings (Dowd et al. 2002; Mueller 1973). Indeed, academic positions awaited these and subsequent composers. As composer Milton Babbitt recounted in our interview: "[S]uddenly every university felt it had to have a music department that had to teach composition. . . . The explosion took place so that it wasn't a question of could you [a serious composer] get a job, but *where* would you get a job." Thus, the "high culture" organizations such as symphony orchestras and universities that traditionally championed only classical music began to acknowledge and disseminate serious music. Although serious music never replaced the classical music of Beethoven and others, it ceased being completely eclipsed.

Michigan Womyn's Music Festival

Each August since 1976, as many as ten thousand women—most of them lesbians—descend upon a site in northern Michigan, toting equipment for a six-day camping trip. Their destination is the Michigan Womyn's Music Festival—the oldest, largest, and best known of its kind (Morris 1999). At the heart of this gathering beat the rhythms of "women's music," a genre that emerged in the early 1970s to express "the anger of women who reject male supremacy and the joy of women who are coming together to fight for equality and justice" (Women's Songbook Project 1978, iii). Many of these songs openly celebrated lesbian relationships, giving voice to a community ignored by the popular culture of the time (Morris 1999). The genre currently exists as a kaleidoscope of musical styles with a common denominator of gender and feminist consciousness.

Intensity

"Michigan"—as it is known in shorthand—provides space for musical performances in an intense temporary living environment. Crews of volunteers arrive several weeks early to assemble tents, build performance stages, and unfurl strips of carpeting that render woodland paths wheelchair-friendly. By the time "festiegoers" arrive, the transformed forest offers hot showers, shuttles, shopping, community centers, first aid, child care, services for disabled women, and vegetarian meals (Morris 1999).

Living temporarily in a separatist women's community fosters intensity and invites culture shock. The festival cultivates an environment where all women are celebrated, not only those who conform to mainstream media ideals. Morris describes attendees as

> women who are sexy in wheelchairs, women who are sexy at 260 pounds, women who are sexy at age 70, long-term interracial romances, young women in charge of complex light and sound technology, poor women who speak with eloquent brilliance—and all the rest of womankind that television will not show us or will tell us does not count. And it can be a shock, a shock so profound that it may take the entire festival for some women to adjust. (1999, 67)

Certain practices assist with such adjustment. "Festievirgins"—women attending for the first time—receive a special "Tips for First Timers" sheet in advance. On an Internet bulletin board, seasoned festiegoers dispense advice on everything from pitching tents to coping with open-air showers. At the festival, peer counseling is available at The Oasis.

A sense of community permeates Michigan and contributes to its appeal. As part of a collectively run village, each festiegoer completes two four-hour work shifts, chosen from many possibilities. One attendee recalls:

> I did kitchen prep with dozens of women shucking bushels of corn into plastic wading pools. When they were overflowing, someone would drag them away and bring us new ones. It was astounding to see the amount of food we needed. Other conferences are sterile, you pay and the food magically appears. This was a real communal experience.

An additional unpaid work force of about six hundred women creates, maintains, and dismantles the village. This logistical work helps build a sense of community. As one woman put it, "It wasn't until I began volunteering to work that I really began to have fun and to make fast, fast friends."

The shared values of those in attendance further contribute to the festival's intensity. In stark contrast to life outside the festival, safety and acceptance are taken for granted. One woman describes it as:

> the one place on the planet where for one week out of the year, I can live without fear and in my body in complete safety. Where I can dance naked in the open air or walk through the woods at night surrounded by respect, trust, joy. Where I can share a public kiss with my partner of fifteen years and have our relationship be recognized fully, with no need to gauge the people around me for how they are reacting to us.

Despite the commitment of time, energy, and money that the Michigan festival demands, it draws thousands of women back each year. "The expense is tough," one festiegoer admits, "but I really feel it's worth it. For one week of absolute sanity in a place that's absolutely safe, I will do just about anything." Of course, battling capricious weather and relying on "porta-janes" can dampen the idyllic setting. Still, this combination of experiences bonds the community together, creating a culture with its own legends, language, and customs, which often become part of the larger "lesbian code" (Morris 1999).

Boundary Work

In addition to managing logistics, Michigan organizers grapple with boundary work in two realms: choosing performers and determining appropriate attendees. They seek performers who represent "women's music"—an elusive genre that focuses to varying degrees on lyrical content, musical style, and the gender of composers and performers. Pianist and songwriter Margie Adam points to this diversity of artists, which includes "women of color, working class women, disabled, straight, old women who play and sing jazz, folk pop, rock and roll, classical, punk, international, new age, gospel music" (Post 1997, 143).

Rather than being wedded to particular stylistic conventions, organizers turn to music whose creators, performers, and subjects are women. They also consider other factors when reviewing performer applications. Morris notes: "Many artists, including emcees, are women whose performances are considered 'too feminist' or 'too lesbian' for mainstream commercial venues. . . . Ironically, it is only in festival culture that some hopefuls go unhired because they are not lesbian enough" (1999, 9).

In essence, as performer Sue Fink asserts, what we really have is a women's music audience, rather than a strictly bounded genre (Armstrong 1991). Selections from the 2002 lineup provide evidence that this is the case: feminist-punk band Le Tigre, acoustic singer-songwriter Cheryl Wheeler, African-drum artist Ubaka Hill, Afro-Celt-funkabilly artist Laura Love, and women's music legend Holly Near. While some performers have eventually entered the mainstream market (for example, Melissa Etheridge, Tracy Chapman, and Michelle Shocked), most who appear at Michigan are associated with independent recording studios, feminist distributors, locally produced concerts, and the annual circuit of women's music festivals (Lont 1992).

In addition to determining appropriate performers, Michigan organizers wrestle with questions regarding appropriate attendees. The festival strives to be inclusive, demonstrating "the world that feminists are trying to build and proof that it can be done if everyone involved is committed to making it work." Sliding-scale entrance fees and other subsidies acknowledge economic inequalities. Separate campgrounds are designated as quiet, nondrinking, fragrance free, over fifty, or for families with children. Outdoor concert seating similarly designates areas as nonsmoking and nondrinking. Services for disabled women include sign-language interpretation, assistance with carrying equipment, and handicapped-accessible shuttles.

More controversial are efforts to define and create a women-only space. Those hoping to attend as a family are sometimes restricted by current policies. Girls of all ages are welcome to attend, but boys over ten years old are not permitted. Younger boys are required to stay with their families in a special camping area and participate in separate child-care programs.

The festival's "womyn-born-womyn" policy, which excludes male-to-female transsexuals, is a perennial controversy. While festival organizers and many attendees defend their definition of a woman, activists organize "Camp Trans" in protest outside the festival gates (Vanasco 2001) arguing that their gender identity should be the determining factor for admission (Gamson 1997). Festival organizers make a commitment that "no woman's gender will be questioned on the land." Press releases reiterate their support of the trans community, asserting that a one-week gathering excluding these individuals is not a contradiction. Rather, they acknowledge the benefits of separate space along with the importance of coming together "in broader alliances to fight prejudice that affects all of us."

Impact

This temporary village—envisioned, created, and inhabited solely by women—provides both a performance venue and an experimental enactment of certain lesbian-feminist principles: separatism, primacy of relationships between women, feminist ritual, and adherence to a set of values that includes egalitarianism, pacifism, collectivism, and experiential knowledge (Taylor and Rupp 1993). While the musical content reflects such characteristics, the festival as a whole consciously incorporates these principles into its organization and activities. In the words of activist Urvashi Vaid, these music festivals "are the bedrock on which a lesbian political consciousness was founded" (1995, 65).

In addition to seeking out entertainment and community, women attend to experience a touchstone that provides them with inspiration to sustain them throughout the rest of the year (Morris 1999). "A petri-dish in which the popular discussions of the lesbian community are incubated," Michigan spurs conversations that follow women back home (Michigan Womyn's Music Festival 2000). The festival becomes a place, one attendee said, "where I can immerse myself in this amazing creation we rebuild each year, and return to my daily life knowing that the way I wish the world could be is possible and actual."

As such, the annual reconstruction of the Michigan festival constitutes a temporary musical scene that exists within the context of the larger lesbian-feminist and women's music communities.

Vans Warped Tour

The Vans Warped Tour is a self-described "punk rock summer camp on wheels." Founded in 1994, the tour travels for seven weeks each summer, performing at outdoor venues to a predominantly young male audience. It features SkatePunk music from emerging and established bands, as well as extreme-sports exhibitions and carnivalesque activities that invite active participation by festivalgoers. This effective combination of performance and participation facilitates interaction among local, regional, and national levels of the SkatePunk scene. However, the tour is sponsored primarily by Vans Inc., a shoe and apparel company that has strong ties to skateboarding. This infusion of commercial interests into SkatePunk through corporate sponsorship of the festival exacerbates tensions within the scene and threatens its core values.

SkatePunk originated in the early 1980s as a distinctly U.S. scene. Punk bands wrote songs about skateboarding, and kids across the country skateboarded to the sounds of punk music. *Thrasher*—a skateboarding magazine—distributed seven compilation tapes featuring SkatePunk bands (see Brooke 1999; Heckler Magazine 2001; Maikels 2001). Independent record labels, such as BYO and SST, soon produced touring packages that played dozens of shows, bringing California-based punk bands to the East Coast. Similarly, Sunday afternoon Hardcore Festivals sent punk bands on regional tours. These prototypes for today's touring festivals underscore the unparalleled significance of festival-like events for the growing scene. The tours circulated bands while keeping production costs low and created an opportunity for SkatePunks to come together.

Intensity

The Warped Tour emerged as a combination music-sports event that mirrors earlier Hardcore Festivals but operates on a much larger scale. Bands, equipment, exhibitors, athletes, and sponsors make a grueling trek in a caravan of buses to more than forty shows. The tour currently averages ten thousand attendees per day with an average ticket price of twenty-five dollars. In 2001, the tour grossed more than $6 million (Waddell 2002). Bands can be paid for their performances or can play in exchange for lodging, meals, and transportation. The *Tour Book* provided to performers for the 2002 tour indicates that athletes, sponsors, and regional bands tend to travel with the tour, while larger acts elect to sign on for cash. The tip jars prominently displayed at every T-shirt booth indicate that while the tour makes money, many people working on the tour barely break even.

The inclusion of nationally recognized acts alongside new artists speaks to the relative equity among performers at the Warped Tour. Typically, a few bands play all tour dates, while others sign on for a couple of weeks or for the "locals" stage in a particular city. The bands perform on a rotating schedule and adhere to thirty-minute sets, keeping everyone on a relatively equal footing with no headliners or supporting acts. The festival centers on two main stages that operate in tandem, creating a nonstop flow of music throughout the venue. While the lineup of bands and athletes remains consistent in style, the Warped Tour deliberately adds new names and changes the sideshow elements from year to year. The "Plug and Play" framework, whereby bands require minimal setup for playing short sets on one of several stages, lends itself to an easy replacement of bands in the lineup, allowing the tour to maintain continuity while keeping each experience fresh. Past bands performing on the tour include Bad Religion, Blink 182, the Mighty Mighty Bosstones, No Doubt, and Quarashi. The range of music offered either resonates with the historical roots of SkatePunk or is calculated to appeal to SkatePunks and other teens.

The tour lives up to its "summer camp" reputation with a high level of audience participation. Skateboarding, BMX, and Moto-X exhibitions are central events, featuring impressive performances by respected athletes (for example, Steve Caballero, Mike Frazier, Mike Mancuso, and Jeremy "Twitch" Steinberg).[2] Skating and moshing by audience members are encouraged. Sports contests, scavenger hunts, "DJ School," and an oversized slip 'n' slide keep festivalgoers actively engaged. To its credit, the tour also promotes several causes, ranging from breast cancer research to the Pennywise Food Drive.[3]

Tour founder Kevin Lyman observes: "You look over at the ramps and these kids with their boards, and then you look at the stage, and you see the connection. Punk and skate crowds just gravitate toward each other" (Scribner 1997). In this sense, the tour reflects the basic elements of the SkatePunk scene. Catering to a concentrated range of interests, this festival gives SkatePunks an opportunity to see performances that probably would not happen without the tour. At the same time, it offers immersion in only the most basic elements of the SkatePunk scene. Attendees can use this festival as an access point to the SkatePunk scene, an affirmation of their membership, or as a good time without any commitment to SkatePunk required.

Boundary Work

Decidedly commercial from the outset, the Warped Tour began as a barebones operation designed to provide affordable entertainment to teenagers. Yet even with its modest beginnings, the tour's scale carried weighty costs. To bankroll operations, Kevin Lyman turned to sponsorship and would do so aggressively in years to come. He reconciles the infusion of millions of corporate dollars into a punk festival as a means to an end: "I've got an even more amazing skateboard ramp, the climbing wall, the Epitaph Records video room. . . . I say, 'Let's use our corporate dollars and have a great day' " (Scribner 1997). Simply put, tour organizers draw on existing boundaries about appropriate performers and desirable audiences, but violate SkatePunk ideals by relying on corporate sponsorship. Backstage, there is an unsettling fusion of punk-rock ideals and corporate interests. Lyman insists that the tour is for the kids, but as this commercialized version of SkatePunk grows, it threatens to overtake the scene.

Each year, twenty to thirty sponsors travel with the Warped Tour, passing out information and product samples to the audience. Chief among the sponsors is Vans Inc., a leading manufacturer of clothing and shoes. Vans's longstanding relationship with skateboarding enables it to capitalize on the festival. According to Gary H. Schoenfeld, Vans president and CEO: "Our goal (through The Warped Tour) is to further the leadership position of our brand and leverage our unique 35-year heritage through a combination of leading edge product and unparalleled experiences" ("Vans, Inc." 2001). Vans Inc. employs marketing strategies (for example, innovative web design, e-marketing, streaming radio, and live-concert webcasts) to engage participants in highly commercialized activities. Moreover, Vans recently produced the skateboarding documentary *Dogtown and Z-Boys* and launched a record label that features punk and hardcore artists. Sponsorship of the tour, then, provides Vans Inc. with a perfect opportunity to secure both brand loyalty and increased sales.

Many tour sponsors have a tenuous association to SkatePunk and rely on their sponsorship to gain valuable credibility. In 2001, for example, Yoo-Hoo became a sponsor as part of a strategy to connect their brand of chocolate drink with kids. Yoo-Hoo encourages participating bands to wear Yoo-Hoo T-shirts while on stage. At the Yoo-Hoo booth, kids are offered a "Shoe-hoo"—Yoo-Hoo served in the festivalgoer's shoe. "They're all looking for their Jackass moment," comments Yoo-Hoo's marketing director, proudly describing the brand's innovative strategy for immersing itself in the festival (Hein 2001). Similar language is present in most of the sponsors' public discussion of the Warped Tour—including that of Target, Sony Playstation, and Yahoo. The commercialization of the tour further escalated with the designation of Label Networks as its official market research firm. Label Networks collects information from festivalgoers for the tour's owners and for a number of other companies. The founders claim that the tour is "the ideal Petri dish for studying youth culture nationwide" (Label Networks 2002). Kevin Lyman attributes the success of the Warped Tour to knowing his market (Waddell 2002); however, it seems unlikely that the audience is fully aware of just how closely Lyman, and others, are paying attention.

Impact

As corporate sponsorship becomes more entrenched, the festival risks alienating its core audience and the scene from which it emerged. While some companies affiliated with the tour are core contributors to the Skate-Punk lifestyle, many sponsors focus on the SkatePunk scene as a market to be exploited. Some SkatePunks question the integrity of the tour, adamantly opposing it as a commercialized "sellout." One attendee recalls his experience in an interview in August 2002: "It was a fun day of music and meeting people, but it seemed like the fast-food version of punk rock. All the bands are on short sets. It's all very efficient. Eighteen years ago you had to seek this stuff out. Now it's served up in a to-go bag. It was fun but it wasn't genuine."[4]

Ambivalence over the tour's commercialization extends to the press and performers. Tour sponsors *Transworld Skateboarding, Spin Magazine,* and *Alternative Press* give the tour extensive, favorable coverage. By contrast, many punk zines treat the Warped Tour with disdain (see Cross 1991; Laughter 1999; Sinker 1999). Mixed reviews are also common among the bands. Several young bands can attribute their mainstream success to exposure they received from the tour, and many return year after year. Established bands appear unsettled by the tour even as they participate. Henry Rollins, former vocalist with the U.S. punk band Black Flag, comments on the 2001 tour:

> I was kind of conned into playing Vans Warped Tour . . . I don't think [mall punk bands know me]. They might remember their older brother had a Black Flag record when they were four. They've never heard it. . . . By-and-large they have their own little world and they're all selling more records than I am to other people their age. (Mernagh 2001, bracketed material in original)

The broadening appeal of the tour likely contributes to this ambivalence. Unlike earlier Hardcore Festivals, for instance, the Warped Tour is increasingly a family event (for example, Reverse Daycare offers an air-conditioned area where kids can drop off their parents to enjoy the quiet company of other parents).

As a festival, and as a scene in its own right, the Warped Tour is increasingly a pale imitation of the SkatePunk scene that continues to fuel it. Peppered with authentic SkatePunk elements, the Warped Tour presents a compelling illusion of authenticity that seems to satisfy some—but not all—participants. Through the participation of respected bands and athletes, the tour gains credibility among certain SkatePunks and claims a high degree of affiliation with local scenes. However, the DIY integrity of the earlier Hardcore Festivals has been replaced with a corporate structure and lucrative sponsorships, infusing the SkatePunk scene with commercial interests that are antithetical to its original values.

Conclusion

Our focus on these particular festivals offers important advantages. First, it shows that the characteristics that we identify—intensity, boundary work, and impact—are salient for festivals that span disparate genres (for example, serious music versus SkatePunk) and time periods (for example, the 1930s versus the present). Second, it shows that the pilgrimage-like nature of music festivals has the *potential* to transform participants, as when festiegoers at Michigan return home empowered both by the music itself and by the experience of being surrounded by thousands of lesbians. Finally, our focus shows that the link between a music festival and a given scene can grow tenuous when commercialization is prominent, as in the case of the Vans Warped Tour.

While any scene faces the challenge of securing resources for operation, this chapter shows that music festivals face particular logistical challenges. Anticipating and meeting the needs of performers, technicians, and audience is further complicated by the time-bound nature of festivals. Their brief and infrequent occurrence places additional pressures on organizers, as poor handling of these logistical challenges can cause the demise of festivals.

This chapter also draws attention to the varying degrees of commitment displayed by festival attendees and expected by festival organizers. Teenagers at the Warped Tour need only the price of a ticket, a single day off work, and ten dollars for the T-shirt that proves they were there. In contrast, Yaddo participants had to make advance arrangements for travel, vacation time, and expenses; Michigan festiegoers also dedicate themselves to living at the festival site and actively contributing to the functioning of the temporary community. These experiences, while reflecting different levels of engagement, are equally valid manifestations of scenes.

Logistical challenges are joined by the challenges of boundary work which, following DiMaggio's (1987, 1991) theoretical work on classification, we suggest is shaped by the goals of those who organize festivals. For example, when commercial success is the primary goal of festival organizers, they are likely to downplay aesthetic and political concerns when putting the festival together. In contrast, when organizers are driven by philanthropic or ideological concerns, they intentionally elevate the substantive (for example, noncommercial) values of the scene. This helps explain why Yaddo could focus on experimental music that was unpopular and why the Michigan festival is able to create an environment that melds politics with entertainment. It also underscores why the Warped Tour can effectively transform SkatePunk into a marketable lifestyle.

The boundary work found in music festivals is a contested process (Santoro 2002). While festival organizers create boundaries regarding music and participants, such decisions are open to debate. We have seen that Rosenfeld criticizes the lack of ultramodern composers at the first Yaddo festival. Competing groups in the womyn's music scene argue about gender politics and the acceptability of admitting male-to-female transsexuals to the festival. Finally, the Warped Tour increasingly distances itself from the SkatePunk scene that was its inspiration

The festivals we consider exist respectively as part of the serious music, womyn's music, and SkatePunk scenes. Moreover, they serve as catalysts that affect the trajectories of these scenes and their associated cultural elements. The Yaddo Festival allowed controversial music to be heard by appreciative audiences, fueling a network of composers whose work was eventually admitted to the symphonic repertoire. The Michigan Womyn's Music Festival provides women with renewed energy, an alternative model of community, and exposure to new performers. These experiences fuel action back at home and further disseminate music. Similarly, the Warped Tour extends the reach of SkatePunk to new audiences, but regrettably undercuts the substance of the scene in the process.

Our findings suggest further directions for research on festivals as scenes. First, our cases are necessarily limited by their reliance on historical data. In-depth ethnographic studies of various festivals would provide a basis for assessing the validity of our claims and exploring subtler nuances of the scenes in question. While directly observing the Yaddo Festival is no longer feasible, examinations of other "high culture" festivals (for example, Tanglewood) would provide interesting fodder for cross-genre comparisons. Second, we call for further attention to the issue of participant commitment and organizer expectations, both of which exist along a continuum. Comparative ethnographic work may shed further light on these variations. For example, while the intensity of festivals may appeal to committed fans, it may also offer a total-immersion training ground for potential scene members. Finally, this chapter shows that music festivals can both constitute scenes and be embedded within existing scenes. Future explorations of festivals may reveal that, at times, neither is the case. In other words, we leave open the possibility that a festival could simply be a gathering of disparate individuals whose only commonality is the purchase of a ticket.

Notes

We thank Pete Peterson and Andy Bennett for their editorial guidance, Cathy Johnson for her feedback, and interviewees for their responses.

1. Milton Babbitt, interview by Timothy J. Dowd, 19 July 1994, Princeton, N.J. Unless otherwise noted, quotations are drawn from our interviews or from electronic bulletin-board postings.
2. Moto-X is a competitive sport in which athletes ride motorcycles up steep ramps or dirt inclines, launching themselves into a variety of "tricks" that include several release moves and, lately, complete back flips on the bike followed by (they hope) a graceful landing. BMX is a competitive sport similarly concerned with tricks and daring, but it occurs on bicycles.
3. A "slip 'n' slide" is a common children's toy that involves a sheet of thick plastic hooked up to a hose to create a water slide.
4. Clarence A. Brooks (pseudonym), interview by author, August 2002, Atlanta, Georgia.

References

Antheil, George. 1934. "Opera—A Way Out." *Modern Music* 11:89–94.
Armstrong, Toni. 1991. "True Life Adventures of Women's Music." *Hot Wire* 7:2.
Brooke, Michael. 1999. *The Concrete Wave.* Toronto: Warwick.
Copland, Aaron. 1968. *The New Music.* New York: Norton.
Copland, Aaron, and Vivian Perlis. 1984. *Copland.* New York: St. Martin's Press.
Cowell, Henry, and Sidney Cowell. 1955. *Charles Ives and His Music.* New York: Oxford University Press.
Cross, Charles. 1991. "What's Warped about This Picture?" *Punk Planet* November–December, 77–78.
DiMaggio, Paul. 1987. "Classification in Art." *American Sociological Review* 52: 440–55.
———. 1991. "Social Structure, Institutions, and Cultural Goods." In Pierre Bourdieu and James S. Coleman, eds., *Social Theory for a Changing World.* Boulder, Colo.: Westview.

Dowd, Timothy J., Kathleen Liddle, Kim Lupo, and Anne Borden. 2002. "Organizing the Musical Canon." *Poetics* 30:35–61.

Gamson, Joshua. 1997. "Messages of Exclusion." *Gender and Society* 11: 178–99.

Harrison, Lou. 1946. "Reflections at a Spa." *Modern Music* 23: 296–98.

Heckler Magazine. 2001. *Declaration of Independents.* San Francisco, Calif.: Chronicle Books.

Hein, Kenneth. 2001. "Here's Chocolate in Your Eye." *Brandweek,* 12 November. Lexis-Nexis, retrieved July 2002.

Howard, John Tasker. 1941. *Our Contemporary Composers.* New York: Crowell.

Label Networks. 2002. "Label Networks Named Official Market Research Firm for the 2002 Vans Warped Tour." Press release, 2 May. Retrieved July. *www.labelnetworks.com/warped2002_5_3_02.html.*

Laughter, Tristin. 1999. "Warped and Woodstock." *Punk Planet,* November–December, 78–80.

Lont, Cynthia M. 1992. "Women's Music." In Reebee Garofalo, ed., *Rockin' the Boat.* Boston: South End Press.

Maikels, Terence. 2001. *Thrasher.* New York: Universe.

Mernagh, Matt. 2001. "Henry Rollins." Retrieved July 2002, *www.chartattack.com/damn/2001/07/3004.cfm.*

Michigan Womyn's Music Festival. 2000. "Michigan Womyn's Music Festival Affirms Womyn-Born Womyn Space." Press release, July 24

Morris, Bonnie J. 1999. *Eden Built by Eves.* Los Angeles: Alyson Publications.

Mueller, Kate Hevner. 1973. *Twenty-Seven Major American Symphony Orchestras: A History and Analysis of Their Repertoires, Seasons 1842–43 through 1969–70.* Bloomington: Indiana University Press.

Norman, Gertrude, and Miriam Lubell Shrifte. 1979. *Letters of Composers.* Westport, Conn.: Greenwood Press.

Peterson, Richard A. 1997. *Creating Country Music.* Chicago: University of Chicago Press.

Post, Laura. 1997. *Backstage Pass.* Norwich, Vt.: New Victoria Publishers.

Rosenfeld, Paul. 1972. *Discoveries of a Music Critic.* New York: Vienna House.

Rossiter, Frank R. 1975. *Charles Ives and His Music.* New York: Liveright.

Santoro, Marco. 2002. "What Is a 'Cantautore?' " *Poetics* 30, 111–32.

Scribner, Sara. 1997. "Warped Tour Hooks the Skate Crowd." *Los Angeles Times,* 3 July.

Seiler, Cotton. 2000. "The Commodification of Rebellion." In Mark Gottdiener, ed., *New Forms of Consumption.* Lanham, Md.: Rowman and Littlefield.

Shackleford, Rudy. 1978. "The Yaddo Festivals of American Music, 1932–1952." *Perspectives of New Music* 17:92–123.

Sinker, Daniel. 1999. "Extreme Exploitation." *Punk Planet,* November–December, 72–77.

Taylor, Verta, and Leila J. Rupp. 1993. "Women's Culture and Lesbian Feminist Activism." *Signs* 19:32–61.

Vaid, Urvashi. 1995. *Virtual Equality.* New York: Anchor Books.

Vanasco, Jennifer. 2001. "A Tale of Two Festivals." *The Advocate,* 9 October, 68–69.

"Vans, Inc. Acquires Control of the Warped Tour for $4.1 Million." 2001. *Business Wire,* 29 June. Lexis-Nexis, retrieved July 2002.

Waddell, Ray. 2002. "Warped Still Going Strong." *Billboard,* 30 March, 25.

Women's Songbook Project. 1978. *Out Loud!* Oakland, Calif.: Inkworks.

Zuck, Barbara A. 1980. *A History of Musical Americanism.* Ann Arbor: University of Michigan Research Press.

9

"Not For Sale": The Underground Network of Anarcho-Punk

Tim Gosling

From the Sex Pistols to pictures of punks on postcards, many commentators see punk as a phase of music and fashion that burst onto the scene in the late 1970s, only to burn itself out in a festival of spit and safety pins. This of course is the reflection of how it was viewed in the popular media at the time. In actual fact, behind the media glitz, "punk" saw itself as having an attitude that was counterposed both to established society and to the theatrical rock it had generated. The media stars of the mainstream movement were reviled and heckled for their betrayal of the cause by placing themselves in the hands of the industry. As the countercultural group Crass asserted on *The Feeding of the 5000* (1998) on the track "Punk Is Dead": "CBS promote The Clash, / It ain't for revolution it's just for cash." Thus, to a large extent the development of the underground punk scene was a reaction of disappointment with "mainstream" punk.

The established record companies were unwilling to support the underground punk scene and so, for both practical and ideological reasons, these underground bands could not depend at all on the mainstream industry. Instead they survived by transforming the "anyone can play guitar" idea into an ethos that stressed self-reliance ("Do It Yourself" or DIY). In the process a system evolved that united fans, bands, record labels, distributors, promoters, and media—often with one individual performing several or all of these roles at the same time—in a loosely affiliated support network that operated behind the scenes. This network developed between the late 1970s and the mid 1980s and came to stretch across much of North America and Europe. This underground punk scene was distinctively characterized by the sociopolitical nature of its lyrics, artwork, and commercial activities. To narrow our inquiry, the focus here is what I will term "anarcho-punk."

We can identify two camps in the anarcho-punk scene; one in the United Kingdom, and one mainly centered on the West Coast of the United States. Although these two factions can be seen as part of a whole in many respects, especially in the sound they produced or in the content of their lyrics and artwork, there are important differences between them. For the purpose of this chapter, the most important divergence is between the long-term operation and success of the commercial enterprises run by the U.S. bands in contrast to those from the United Kingdom, whose operations remained small and were short-lived.

Three U.S. companies that evolved as record labels early in the anarcho-punk scene will be examined: SST, set up by Black Flag, a hardcore punk band from Southern California that existed from 1978 to 1985; Alternative Tentacles, the record label and publishing house set up by Dead Kennedys, a San Francisco band of the same period; and Dischord, the label operated by Ian McKaye, previously of Washington, D.C., band Minor Threat, the original "straight-edge" band, and now of Fugazi, described as "the arche-typical political punk band."[1] Their U.K. counterparts, for the purpose of this chapter, are Crass, Flux of Pink Indians, and the Subhumans; their respective record labels are Crass, Spiderleg, and Bluurgh. The selection of the British examples, with the exception of Crass, is a little trickier than the U.S. examples, as a number of U.K. bands from this period can be seen to have a similar profile.

The development and operations of these companies are deliberated from a production-of-culture perspective, acting in contrast with and as a consequence of the political economy of the mainstream music industry.

Ethos and Imagery

The anarcho-punk scene developed around late 1977. It built upon the momentum surrounding the mainstream punk scene while at the same time reacting against the direction the mainstream was taking in its rela-tionship with establishment society. The anarcho-punks viewed safety pins and Mohicans as little more than ineffectual fashion posturing stimulated by the mainstream media and industry. The subservience of mainstream artists is satirized in "Pull My Strings" by the Dead Kennedys: "Give me a toot, / I'll sell you my soul. / Pull my strings and I'll go far" (*Give Me Convenience*, 1988).

Artistic integrity, social and political commentary and actions, and personal responsibility became the scene's central points, marking the anarcho-punks (as they would assert) as the opposite of what had come before under the name of punk. Whereas the Sex Pistols would proudly display bad manners and opportunism in their dealings with "the establishment," the anarcho-punks kept clear of "the establishment" altogether, working in opposition to it instead, as will be shown.

The outward character of the anarcho-punk scene did nevertheless build upon the roots of the mainstream punk that it was reacting to. The extreme rock 'n' roll of earlier punk bands such as the Damned and the Buzzcocks was taken to new heights. The anarcho-punks played faster and more chaotically than had been heard before. Production values were reduced to the lowest levels, a reflection of the budgets available under the DIY system, as well as a reaction against the values of commercial music. The sound was trashy, discordant, and very angry. Reflecting their outlook on the societies to which they objected, there was no respite, no chance to catch the breath, only a sense of imminent destruction, fear, anger, and desperation.

Lyrically, the anarcho-punks were informed by political and social commentary, often presenting a somewhat naïve understanding of issues such as poverty, war, or prejudice. The content of the songs presented allegories drawn from underground media and conspiracy theories or lampooned political and social mores. At times, the songs displayed a certain philosophical and sociological awareness, thus far rare in the world of rock but having antecedents in folk and protest songs.[2]

Live performances broke with many of the norms of conventional rock. Concert billings were shared between many bands, as well as other performers such as poets, with the hierarchy between headliners and support acts either limited or completely scrapped. Often films were shown, and there would normally be some form of political or educational material distributed among, or by, the audience. "Promoters" tended to be anyone who arranged a space and got in touch with the bands to ask them to play. Hence a lot of gigs were played in garages, at parties, in community centers, and at free festivals. When gigs took place in "normal" venues, there was a huge amount of derision poured upon the principles and operations of the "professional" music world. This often took the form of vitriol against, or even pitched battles with, the bouncers or the management. Performances were loud and chaotic, often marred by technical problems, politically and "tribe"-motivated violence, and closures by the police. Overall, unity was primary, with as few of the trappings of showbiz as was possible (see Rollins 1997).

Organization and Ideology of Record Labels

The companies that were set up by the anarcho-punk bands need to be understood within the context of the major record industry. The ways in which music is produced directly influences the form of that music. Therefore, if a few large companies control the market, then the range of music on offer will be constrained. The underlying fact of the "production of culture" perspective is the recognition that the mainstream music industry is a business that has profit as its central purpose (Peterson 1994). Thus "product" is sought out that will sell the most units, while product that is uncommercial remains ignored and undeveloped. The leaders of the industry are explicit about what they do, that is, they maintain the "ability to control" the industry by maintaining the "barriers to getting into [the] business." The main tactic of control has been that of vertical integration, meaning control not only of production but also of marketing and distribution: "If there was anything the [major] record companies had it was a distribution network" ("Record Industry" 2000).[3]

It should be noted that it is not purely the size of a company that is essential for the purposes of its authenticity, but also the philosophy and mode of operating because the history of small-scale independent production of music goes back a long way. In the United States and the United Kingdom, the independents had been in operation for decades before the 1970s. What sets most of the punk independents apart was the ideology that lay behind them. The earlier U.S. independents, such as Chess Records in Chicago or Atlantic, were really little more than small-scale versions of the majors, and they are often described as being even more ruthless toward their "product," taking advantage of black or southern artists that could not gain access to the business via the mainstream channels. In other words, they still had at their core the profit motive, the "hit-parade philosophy" (Laing 1985, 10).

Dischord, SST, and Alternative Tentacles were all set up so that the bands behind them could get their music produced and distributed without having to compromise themselves to adhere to the majors' priorities of commercial appeal via a homogenized sound and limited lyrical content.[4] All three were prompted and funded by revenues from live performances (see Larkin 1998, 48).[5] All three labels quickly expanded their operations to work with other artists they shared shows with.[6]

Many of the notable independent U.K. labels from the same decade have not managed to survive independently. For instance, Stiff dropped by the wayside reasonably quickly, while the majors swallowed up Factory. In the vital area of distribution, many were not as independent as they may have been and conceded it was inevitable that they hand over their records to the majors for distribution. Rough Trade was an exception to both of these trends in a way. Although, according to commentators after its demise, the company "grew too fast" for its own good with its "blend of idealism and alternative business opportunism," it did provide, from the late 1970s onward, an organized distribution network for the underground. Named at first the Cartel, it was a model of the form of network that the anarcho-punks were developing at the same time—namely, one based on informal networks and small localized units. The Cartel lasted until the early 1990s, when its expansion into a multimillion-pound business was undermined by an inefficient structure (Bassett 1991).

Without an impetus to satisfy mainstream commercial traits, the anarcho-punk labels were able to make huge savings on production. Studio facilities and time could be reduced to a bare minimum. Artists were not paid to get them under contract. In fact, to this day, Alternative Tentacles operates without contracts, artists being free to decide whether to work with the label or not on each project they undertake.[7] Distribution was vital to the success of the anarcho-punk labels, as to "feed original material into [mainstream systems] was to surrender it to the definitions of the 'cultural repertoire,' the hit parade and the hard sell" (Laing 1985, 21). With the anarcho-punk labels, distribution grew from the retail end of the industry. Shops that took an active interest in the scene joined with small local distributors to form networks that were capable of national and eventually international distribution. In this we can see the importance of a collective DIY ethic and the authenticity of the bands. The members of the networks worked hard, not with financial motivations but with a common belief in the integrity of the networks and a common opposition to the mainstream industry. With the retailers taking an active part in the distribution of the records, this also meant that small-scale marketing was provided at the point of sale. The other marketing tool operating was the many fanzines that inevitably developed within a scene that put such emphasis on unity, active participation, and DIY attitudes. Thus record labels would advertise their mail-order services in fanzines, both to individual customers and to shops, often via certain retailers designated as distributors in a particular area or country.

The U.S. anarcho-punk companies Alternative Tentacles, Dischord, and SST all saw great success, went on to work with a large range of successful bands, and expanded their operations into such areas as publishing. They all survive to this day. In contrast, the U.K. companies—Crass Records, Spiderleg, and Bluurgh—although running for a few years and achieving good sales figures, remained known essentially for the records of the bands that started them and had little or no success in working with other bands. Their operations did not expand into other areas, although Crass did operate a branch that published a few books. Either they folded pretty much immediately after the demise of the bands that ran them, or they essentially ceased to operate except to sell back catalogues of those bands. The differing fortunes of these companies are remarkable because they had such strong similarities in both their motivations for being established and the ways in which they operated.

How Have the Counter-capitalists Survived?

How then were these differences between U.S. and U.K. companies produced? The bands that set up these companies had a lot in common. They all maintained deep commitment to a DIY spirit, an antiauthoritarian stance, and a belief in authenticity. All were popular on an international level and suffered from a similar amount of trouble at the hands of the establishment for the content of their material and the nature of their live performances.[8] Perhaps part of the reason lies within the realm of authenticity and the differences to be found in the definitions of authenticity in the United Kingdom and the United States? To be more specific, at the point where the DIY ethic and authenticity of punk and alternative rock consciousness meets dominant U.S. ideology. It is because of the U.S. companies' position at this "crossroads" that we shall label them the "counter-capitalists."

Punk, like mainstream rock music, has always relied heavily upon authenticity as a form of legitimization. However, the punk version has a heightened regard for ideological adherence to the expected norms of commitment to the scene and of avoiding at all costs contact with "establishment" society. Linda Andes, in her study of punk subculture, assesses the large part that authenticity plays in it. She identifies stages through which, she maintains, members of a subculture pass. The final stage, "transcendence," she identifies as involving an "internalization" of the core values of "personal integrity, honesty and individualism." She correlates the stages with age, regarding this final stage as occurring in the midtwenties and finding that the end result was the leaving of the scene or "participation at a creative or organizational level" (1998, 223).

The interviewees represented in Andes' book may provide us with examples of the authenticity requirements that the counter-capitalists satisfy for their audience. She notes the way that, while earlier "stages" ("rebellion" and "affiliation") in the "punk career" have at their core acceptance by the group, the final stage involves instead the definition of "punk as a system of values and beliefs, and thus become concerned with expressing an ideological commitment to the subculture." As one interviewee replies to her question of what "punk" means: "Punk is not a rip in your jeans, it's a rip in your mind!" (Andes 1998, 226–27). This insistence on the "real" punk being situated in ideology, values, and action as opposed to fashion is a common theme of all of the originating bands of the labels.[9] It can be seen to lead core values of authenticity within punk, for both the artists and the audience: "The glorification of self-expression serves as an aesthetic rationale for the authenticity and superiority of punk cultural artefacts relative to those produced by the culture industries" (226).

All the bands and organizations considered here can be seen to have adhered to the requirements that authenticity requires within punk. They actively stress this mode of operations symbolically; for instance, Dischord Records does not have barcodes on the sleeves of the records it releases, rebelling against not only the world of commerce but also that of Big Brother. Alternative Tentacles insistently plays upon an image of the enemy within, manipulating the original scare stories about the insidious destruction of moral values that came with punk in the late '70s—the name of the label being a prime example. All of these aspects are manifestations of the "desire for a break with commercial culture and a disavowal of the commodity status of rock" (Pfeil 1994, 75).[10]

In addition, more classic rock 'n' roll authenticity has also been vigorously applied in the case of at least two of the bands, that of earning respect by live performance. Pfeil details "the through-line" of Bruce Springsteen as "a mythologised biography dwelling on, and so reinforcing, a pre-given set of associations in rock culture; the white working class kid who . . . pays his dues by playing year after year in his own area, building a following among kids like him, playing the joints and developing a name" (ibid., 78). Fugazi are noted to "concentrate their efforts more on live shows than in the studio" (Larkin 1998, 178). Their shows, which they play for extremely low prices, are taken to unlikely locales, such as Chile and Malaysia, and described as "unrivalled for showmanship and crazed, soulful catharsis."[11] However, it is Henry Rollins, detailing his time with Black Flag, who most tangibly exposes the extent to which these bands work on this element of authenticity:

> During the next five years, I was to learn what hard work was all about. Black Flag/SST was on a work ethic that I had never experienced and have never seen since. . . . They went into whatever it was that we had to do without questioning the time it took, the lack of sleep or food. . . . No one had any time for anyone else's complaining. If you ever made a noise about anything, Mugger would just start laughing and say something like, "This isn't Van Halen! Get it happening!" (1997, 11)

Land of Opportunity versus Land of Class Conflict

Why is it that the U.K. anarcho-punk companies failed to expand their operations and extend their horizons beyond their immediate instinct to enable the originating bands to put out records, while the U.S. companies were for many years successful in these terms, continuing to provide vital energy to the scene? While anarcho-punk in both countries defined itself as a rebellion against the mainstream, it seems that, ironically, this resistance took differing forms rooted in the distinctive values of the two societies.

A prime pillar of the belief system in the United States is the "rebel." One need only think of the Pilgrims who first colonized the country in search of religious freedom, of Marlon Brando, James Dean, or countless western heroes in order to understand this.[12] This "hero is free from dependence on the will of others and he is essentially the proprietor of his own person and capacities, for which he owes nothing to society" (Wright 1975, 138). The values of mainstream society in the United States are based upon an idealized form of rebellion—a freedom that is possible only through re-sponsibility, the Protestant work ethic, and the bourgeois values that this inspires (see Emerson 1994).[13] This places the individual and the potential metamorphic powers of that individual above all. In other words, at the core of U.S. thinking and belief lies a faith in the abilities of man (it is a strongly gendered ideology) to control his destiny via the "simple bourgeois formula of honesty, sobriety and industry," which are "cornerstones of the original examples of the fictional American hero" (Hoffman 1961, 37).

I would suggest that the hegemony of such a U.S. ideology informs the counter-capitalists. Their extensive and extended use of the commercial system is very different from that of their British peers, and suggests that they feel optimistic insofar as the opportunities it offers them in their "underground" aims. Both individually and collectively they appear to be socialized to expect to be able to exploit opportunities within the commercial world to advance their own distinctive goals. This is hardly surprising; the U.S. "market" and the "individual" are as concepts irreversibly intertwined under the ideology that "what makes a man human is freedom from dependence on the will of others." The individual "provides a philosophical underpinning for the market"; in other words, in the general theory of free-market capitalism, the individual is the central point around which all revolves (Wright 1975, 136).

The U.S. anarcho-punk record companies were able to operate in an entrepreneurial manner to survive. In fact, further than that, with the particular sense of freedom and opportunity that is associated in general with commerce, the U.S. scene can positively partake in these ventures without endangering its sense of authenticity. Instead, operating independent business ventures appears to be a rallying point. The U.S. companies (and therefore the bands) are seen to be expressing the central points of the scene: working hard to achieve independence via self-reliance and self-direction. The whole scene then can associate itself in this sense with the core values by taking part in the scene, supporting the bands and companies who in turn perpetuate the scene via their independent operations.

The list of notable bands on the U.S. labels is extensive. SST put out records by the Minutemen and Husker Du, among others. In 1981, the bassist of Black Flag left the band to concentrate his efforts on running the label (Friedman 1996). The Dead Kennedys initially set up Alternative Tentacles to operate in Europe only, with the idea of gaining exposure for U.S. bands. A compilation album, *"Let Them Eat Jellybeans,"* and a few singles by bands such as D.O.A., Bad Brains, and Black Flag were the immediate results. However, the album proved itself to be popular in the United States on import also. The label then went on to become fully operational, going on to release albums by Nomeansno, TSOL, and the Butthole Surfers.

The scene in the United Kingdom operated within a very different atmosphere as regards commercial operations. Europe, and perhaps particularly the United Kingdom, has for centuries understood society as divided into distinct social classes, and the members of each class are expected to be loyal to their own class. Because the anarcho-punk scene in the United Kingdom grew around the image, if not the reality, of being working class, all commerce and business was understood as the activity of the class enemy, the establishment, against which they were rebelling. For the U.K. scene, operating commercial companies was at best a necessary evil, to be engaged in only because it was impossible or even more objectionable to work with the established industry.

In practice, then, to operate a company was an awkward if not impossible position. How could a scene that understood "business" to be a central point of mistrust and an ultimate enemy engage in commerce? The authenticity demanded within the scene would not stand it; in the tradition of the British working class, business represented one of the cornerstones of the establishment, meaning exploitation and hierarchy. It seemed that the scene was being taken for a ride by the very people that screamed against the bosses. Out of the conflict between the need to find a way of getting out records and the horror of becoming a part of the establishment, the only pragmatic course was to run record labels purely as a vehicle to get out records, to sell them as cheaply as possible, to restrict the price of concert tickets, and not to expand the scene on a commercial level. Hence, as noted, the U.K. labels remained very much centered on the bands that began them and folded very soon after the bands themselves did.

J. J. Ratter (a.k.a Penny Rimbaud, the drummer from Crass) illustrates the conundrum in his memories of conversations among the members of Crass:

[When it was] suggested that [Crass] should establish [Crass Records] as a legitimate company, most of the . . . members of the band objected.

"I don't want to become a bloody capitalist," Pete exploded.

"For fuck's sake, why let someone else have the money when we could use it to expand our operations," I countered.

"Because that's playing into the hands of the system," interjected Phil.

But nonetheless I argued that Crass records was the only way forwards for us, and eventually, realising there wasn't any viable alternative, the rest of the band reluctantly agreed. (Ratter 1998, 114–15)

Ratter notes that at a later stage members of the band were "embarrassed by our mounting wealth." From these accounts, at least, Crass was hardly having a guitar-shaped pool built in the back garden of the commune they all shared: "We found ourselves to be substantially wealthy. . . . I replaced my battered drum-kit . . . and we each awarded ourselves a brand new pair of Doc Martens" (115).

Fan Perspectives?

Further evidence for the importance of authenticity and antibusiness attitudes can readily be seen in the continuing discussions among U.S. and British fans of anarcho-punk. It is of course tricky to investigate the reactions of those who count themselves fans of a scene that reached its zenith two decades ago, but, it is interesting to see that fans make the same distinctions between U.S. and U.K. bands.

The British reaction is given via a written interview in November 2001 with Gil, a thirty- four-year-old living in London, as well as via some samples from an Internet discussion board dedicated to Crass. In explaining what these specific bands meant to him, Gil's lengthy replies all recognized and stressed the difference between the British and U.S. bands. He stressed the feeling of "realness" of the British bands and the way in which this connected with his own feelings and thoughts at the time. He says in part that

> these bands weren't about being cool; they were about revolution/
> change. Not status, not icons. No pretensions, not about money (cheap
> records on independent labels), they were about education, criticism,
> socio-political defiance; . . . they didn't sell out by signing to major
> corrupt labels. They didn't compromise their message or sound. Yank
> bands (apart from [Dead Kennedys]) never seemed to go into so much
> detail as the Brits, but added weight to the fears of the Americanisation
> of the world.

It is also notable that Gil appears to equate the U.S. bands with commerce. The "Americanisation" that he speaks of is another way of referencing the expansion of free-market capitalism on a global scale, the realm that is considered to be represented by Coca-Cola and McDonald's. Thus, for him, the U.S. bands' commercial operations do appear, to some extent, to undermine the authenticity he demands from them.

Comments from the Crass discussion board reinforce the importance that members of the U.K. scene place upon an absence of normal commercial operations by the British bands. The subject of the discussion is recent U.S. punk bands that have become popular in the mainstream. Most of the discussion revolves around why they are not "punk"; in other words, why they lack authenticity. Two of the British postings (details of users are available on the Web site) contrast the commercialism of Kill Rock Stars, a contemporary U.S. label, with the "authenticity" of Crass: "Kill rock stars, [is] like young punk bands which only wants [sic] to have a piece of the cake. . . . [In contrast] Crass hardly made money; . . . they act out of true convictions." This announcement is replied to by another British contributor: "Crass DID make money—lots of it, (even with the 'pay no more than' stickers & one pound entrance to gigs—which shows just what a rip off most other bands, record promoters, etc are/were). Thing is they gave it all away—nearly all their gigs were benefits. [14]

The U.S. perspectives come from a Web site, Friends of Incentive, that centers on Nomeansno, a Canadian band that records on Alternative Tentacles and could be considered a direct descendent of anarcho-punk in many respects. It is noticeable that it is the Dead Kennedys that are the subject of these discussions among U.S. fans—the Dead Kennedys being the one exception that Gil makes in his reactions against U.S. bands. It appears that the reasons behind Gil's approval of the band (a specific and upfront political edge) are a cause of concern for those from the United States:

Jello [Biafra, lead singer of the Dead Kennedys] used to be a punk, but over the last little while I've found his brand of punk to be not much more than attempts at trying to be shocking. . . . Jello has too many political affiliations. There's a fine line between trying to make people open their eyes to new ways of thought and just forcing your weird opinions on people.[15]

Other U.S. contributors stress Biafra's commercial activities in his defense: "Jello is the only reason we had Nomeansno in the U.S. for many years. . . . He always tried to sign bands that didn't quite fit the mould."[16]

So, for the U.K. fans here, the primacy of political matters is a central, positive point that elevates the U.K. bands and the Dead Kennedys. In contrast, fans from the United States suggest that political posturing could actually corrupt the authenticity of bands. The answer to the original criticism of Jello Biafra suggests in fact that, for these members of the scene from the United States, the ex-singer of the *Dead Kennedys* retains his authenticity via his commercial activities, despite his political involvement—the provision of consumer choice, and commercial opportunity for other bands, perhaps rescuing him in their eyes?

The anarcho-punk scene was rooted in a radical break from the capitalist logics of the major record companies. However, this ethos has played itself out quite differently in the United Kingdom and the United States, the demands of authenticity apparently requiring that the scene adapt itself somewhat to the ideologies pertinent in the societies in which they operate. Does this mean that the commodity status of music is inescapable? Perhaps to an extent, but at the same time the U.S. labels demonstrate that it is possible to establish strong and long-lasting record companies that are genuinely independent—just as long as the cultural stories within the larger society allow them to remain authentic while doing so.

Notes

1. The cultural and commercial success of these companies is referenced in Larkin 1998: Regarding "Fugazi, . . . each of their albums has gone on to sell more than 100,000 copies, produced entirely independently within their own Dischord Records framework" (178); "Alternative Tentacles . . . [has] gone on to be a staple of the US alternative record scene" (119); "SST . . . [is a] prolific outlet, . . . one of America's leading and most influential independents" (48).

2. This connection was made concrete by bands such as Chumbawamba—a direct descendent of the anarcho-punk scene. See the EP *English Rebel Songs, 1391–1914* (Agit-Prop, 1988).

3. Quoted are Dick Parsons, president of Time Warner, and Roger Ames, chair of Warner Music, at a press conference to announce the merger of the two Industry giants.

4. Black Flag was originally scheduled to release its first album on MCA, but the company withdrew, citing "outrageous content."

5. Rollins 1997; www.sxmedia.com, accessed 16 November 1999; and www.alternativetentacles.com, accessed 6 February 2000 all detail the process by which live performance is the vital element underpinning both the direct financing to set up the respective labels and the customer base for their records.

6. Dischord has a less high-profile roster of artists, apart from Fugazi, Mckaye's own band, than the other two. Alternative Tentacles has been the label for such bands as the Butthole Surfers, D.O.A, and Nomeansno, as well as the Dead Kennedys. SST released records by Husker Du, the Minutemen, Bad Brains, and others.

7. *www.alternativetentacles.com,* accessed 24 January 2002.

8. Cloonan 1996, Ratter 1998, Rollins 1997, and *www.alternativetentacles.com* all

provide details of numerous run-ins with the police and the courts over the various bands' activities.

9. There are many examples of this insistence in the lyrics of all the bands, as well as in Rollins's tour diaries: "They were much too cool to acknowledge us at all. I looked out at them with their punk rock clothes and the haircuts two feet above their heads. I knew they were just a bunch of weak punkers and I shouldn't take them seriously" (1997, 27). The most explicit, however, are the Dead Kennedys; for example: "Punk ain't no religious cult, / Punk means thinking for yourself, / You ain't hardcore coz you spike yer hair, / when a jock still lives inside your head, / Nazi Punks Fuck Off" (*In God We Trust*, 1982).

10. On the front of the cover of every record issued by the British labels was a large sign detailing the price that the label wanted the record to go out at. Most of the U.S. releases had no such advice on the front cover. Again, the focus of the Crass operation is summed up by Ratter: "[D]espite Crass Record's budget price policy, we continued to fund a diverse range of organisations and individuals, from Peace News to single sheet fanzines, from Rape Crisis Centres to direct action groups. It didn't seem to matter how much money we gave away with one hand, there always seemed to be more dropping into the other" (1998, 114–15).

11. *www.sxmedia.com*, accessed 16 November 1999.

12. Will Wright says in *Six Guns and Society*: "The Western, like any myth, stands between human consciousness and society. If a myth is popular, it must somehow appeal to or reinforce the individuals who view it by communicating a symbolic meaning to them; . . . thus a myth must tell its viewers about themselves and their society" (1975, 2).

13. A reading of various authors from the eighteenth and nineteenth centuries reveals the deep-rooted nature of the bourgeois ethics and optimism inherent in U.S. ideology. Of course, not all subscribed to this. For instance, Emerson's preachings of frugal "self-reliance" and optimism at its results were satirized by Melville, who presented him "in 'The Confidence Man' as a great American philosophical con man" (Emerson 1994, 989).

14. *www.audiogalaxy.com*, accessed 6 June 2002.

15. Some quick references to Biafra's political activities can be found in Larkin 1998, 23; *Fuck Facts*, the first issue of the newsletter of the "No More Censorship Defence Fund," distributed with the Dead Kennedys *Bedtime for Democracy* CD; and Biafra, *No More Cocoons*, a spoken-word album. In 1979 Biafra ran for mayor of San Francisco and came in fourth. His most prominent political battle started in 1986, when Alternative Tentacles was prosecuted, with help from the Parents Music Resource Center, for "distribution of harmful matter to minors" over artwork distributed with the Dead Kennedys' *Frankenchrist*.

16. *incentive.plik.net*, accessed 14 November 2000.

References

Andes, Linda. 1998. "Growing Up Punk: Meaning and Commitment Careers in a Contemporary Youth Culture." In Jonathon S. Epstein, ed., *Youth Culture: Identity in a Postmodern World*. Malden, Mass.: Blackwell.

Bassett, Philip. 1991. "Like Punk Never Happened," *The Guardian*, 20 July.

Cloonan, Martin. 1996. *Banned*. Aldershot: Ashgate.

Emerson, Ralph Waldo. 1994. "Poor Richard's Almanac." In Nina Baym, ed., *The Norton Anthology of American Literature*. New York: W. W. Norton.

Friedman, Glen. 1996. *Fuck You Heroes*. Los Angeles: Burning Flags Press.

Halasa, Malu. 1996. "So, Did We Do It Their Way?" *The Guardian*, 6 September.

Harker, Dave. 1980. *One for the Money: Politics and Popular Song*. London: Hutchinson.

Hoffman, Daniel. 1961. *Form and Fable in American Fiction*. Charlottesville: University Press of Virginia.

Laing, Dave. 1985. *One Chord Wonders: Power and Meaning in Punk Rock*. Milton Keynes, U.K.: Open University Press.

Larkin, Colin. 1998. *The Virgin Encyclopaedia of Indie and New Wave*. London: Virgin Publishing.

Nehring, Neil. 1997. *Popular Music, Gender, and Post-Modernism: Anger Is an Energy*. Thousand Oaks, Calif.: Sage.

Peterson, Richard A. 1994. "Culture Studies through the Production Perspective." In Diana Crane, ed., *Emerging Theoretical Perspectives in the Sociology of Culture*. London: Blackwell.

Pfeil, Fred. 1994. "Rock Incorporated." In Laurence Goldstein, ed., *The Male Body*. Ann Arbor: University of Michigan Press.

Ratter, J. J. 1998. *Shibboleth: My Revolting Life*. Edinburgh: AK Pr. Distribution.

"The Record Industry Takes Fright." 2000. *The Economist*, 29 January, 87–88.

Rollins, Henry. 1997. *Get in the Van: On the Road with Black Flag*. Los Angeles: 2-13-61.

Savage, Jon. 1996. *Time Travel: From the Sex Pistols to Nirvana: Pop, Media, and Sexuality, 1977–96*. London: Vintage Books.

Tsitsos, William. 1999. "Rules of Rebellion: Slamdancing, Moshing, and the American Alternative Scene." *Popular Music* 18, 3: 397–414.

Willis, Susan. 1993–1994. "Hardcore; Subcultural American Style." *Critical Enquiry* 19: 365–83.

Wright, Will. 1975. *Six Guns and Society: A Structural Study of the Western*. Berkeley: University of California Press.

Discography

Black Flag. *Damaged.* SST, 1981.

————. *The First Four Years.* SST, 1983.

Crass. *Stations of the Crass.* Crass Records, 1979.

————. *The Feeding of the 5000.* Small Wonder, 1977.

Dead Kennedys. *Bedtime for Democracy.* Alternative Tentacles, 1986.

————. *Frankenchrist.* Alternative Tentacles, 1985.

————. *Give Me Convenience or Give Me Death.* Alternative Tentacles, 1988.

————. *In God We Trust.* Alternative Tentacles, 1982.

Flux of Pink Indians. *Strive to Survive.* Spiderleg, 1982.

————. *The Fucking Cunts Treat Us Like Pricks.* Spiderleg, 1984.

Fugazi. *Fugazi.* Dischord, 1988.

————. *Margin Walker.* Dischord, 1989.

Jello Biafra. *No More Cocoons.* Alternative Tentacles, 1989.

Minor Threat. *Out of Step.* Dischord, 1984.

Subhumans. *From the Cradle to the Grave.* Bluurgh, 1984.

————. *The Day the Country Died.* Spiderleg, 1981.

PART III

Virtual Scenes

10

Internet-based Virtual Music Scenes: The Case of P2 in Alt.Country Music

Steve S. Lee and Richard A. Peterson

The commonly held understanding is that a music scene involves intense face-to-face interaction among music makers and fans with a shared enthusiasm for a particular music and its associated lifestyle (see Peterson and Bennett in this volume). If this is true, how can there be a scene that is formed and thrives on the Internet? To begin to answer this question, we here seek out the scenelike characteristics of the interaction generated by a listserve dedicated to a specific genre of music. In the process we show that Web-based interaction generates characteristics that are in may ways like those of local scenes and in some ways quite distinct. Our second research question derives from the fact that music scenes can play a large role in the process of genre formation (see Laing 1985; Escott 1991; Lee 1995; Thornton 1995; DeVeaux 1997). We explore the ways that virtual interaction can be the source of music genre formation. The case study used in this exploration is the listserv Postcard Two (P2), the leading listserv devoted to alternative country music, a genre of music that has coalesced since the mid-1990s in scattered places around the United States., Canada, and Europe. The music's indebtedness to Internet communication is widely recognized (Smith and Kollock 1999). In fact, it is often called alt.country (Goodman 1999).

Alternative Country Music Defined

It is fashionable to say that alternative country music is difficult to define. In fact, the leading magazine devoted to the genre, *No Depression,* commonly tops its first page with the slogan "The Bimonthly Journal of Alt-Country Music, Whatever That Is." This equivocation is understandable because, as with any other new genre, there is much debate about what sorts of music to include and what sorts to exclude from the designation. In addition, numerous other words are used to designate the music, most notably "Americana" (Peterson and Beal 2001), but we will use alternative country because it is the term of choice used by the Internet group being studied. Its statement of purpose gives a good sense of the range of music included within the purview of alt.country:

> Postcard2 (usually called P2) began as an offshoot of Postcard, the Uncle Tupelo mailing list, and was created for people who wanted to discuss a wider range of music, including but not limited to alt.country, country rock, hard country, bluegrass, insurgent country, roots rock, and hillbilly music, and a wider range of topics, including but not limited to the music's forerunners and historical background, the sociology of the music and its listeners, and the contemporary business practices that make the music possible.
>
> Artists discussed on P2 include those bands that followed Uncle Tupelo by mixing indie-rock aggression with country twang. These bands include Tupelo offshoots Son Volt and Wilco, along with others such as the Bottle Rockets, Old 97s, Whiskeytown, and the Waco Brothers. The list also generates a healthy amount of discussion of earlier practitioners of country mixed with attitude, like Johnny Cash, Buck Owens, Gram Parsons, the Flatlanders, and Steve Earle, as well as current renegade country and roots-rock types, such as Alejandro Escovedo, Kelly Willis, Dale Watson, Robert Earl Keen, Big Sandy & His Fly-Rite Boys, Iris DeMent, Gillian Welch, Ralph Stanley, Rhonda Vincent, Robbie Fulks, Junior Brown, Lucinda Williams, Waye Hancock, Neko Case, Kelly Hogan, Ryan Adams, and others deemed too country and/or too adventurous for regular mainstream country airplay, and even a few of today's mainstream country singers like Alan Jackson, Vince Gill, and Brad Paisley.
>
> People on P2 are happy to discuss what alternative country is or isn't and who's playing it now, and to range over all kinds of roots music (including blues, r&b, and roots-rock as well as alt-country in all its varieties), all kinds of classic country music (including bluegrass,

honky tonk, western swing, rockabilly, gospel, western, old-timey, and country-pop), alternative rock, Nashville's [corporate music industry] wickedness and virtues, and retail, radio, and record-label practices, along with anything else that relates to their passion for hearing honest and innovative music that has some connection, however farfetched, with twang (Laura Levy and Nina Melechen).[1]

Photo by Richard A. Peterson

It is clear from the characterization of alt.country that it grows out of punk sensibilities that embrace the traditional country music instrumentation and a number of loosely affiliated forms such as rockabilly and bluegrass that historically were set off against each other (Rosenberg 1985). It is also clear that alt.country is not a single style of music comparable to jazz, house, bluegrass, or acid rock, whose development is largely in the hands of performers. Rather it is more a collage of quite different sorts of music that *fans* find sound well together and that expresses much the same range of sensibilities for them. In effect, alternative country music is a prime example of an emergent class of musical genres not based in an aesthetic of music production but in an aesthetic shared by consumers. Thus alternative country music can be any music, irrespective of its source, that has the following characteristics: It seems homemade and heartfelt (rootsy, authentic), and it uses one or more styles of country or (white) folk music, be it rockabilly, bluegrass, or singer-songwriter. Songs commonly have lyrical themes that fit the backward-looking alternative country zeitgeist, but acceptance among alt. country fans does not require an artist to be rural, poor, and living in the past. Rather, artists need to create such an image and stay within its bounds.[2]

P2, an Alt.country Listserv

There are numerous forms of groups on the Internet. Many, like the common chat rooms that use the World Wide Web, allow for anonymity, which seems to encourage short statements that generate identity role playing and heated name calling (Markham 1998). In contrast, a listserv operates on the Internet with messages sent to a single e-mail address and thence out to all members, as in *mailto:postcard2@u.washington.edu*. Since each message contains the sender's e-mail address and often the sender's personalized "signature" as well (Smith and Kollock 1999), there is much less frivolous or aggressive communication than in anonymous Web environments.

Postcard2 is the most active listserv devoted to alternative country music as a whole.[3] It was established in 1995, and in mid-2002 there were, according to the list administrator, something over seven hundred members. In August 2002, P2 changed servers and it is not yet clear what this portends for P2, but we will return to this question. The description that follows refers to P2 as it was between 1998 and early 2002. In busy seasons, the traffic involved something over a hundred messages each weekday and somewhat fewer on weekends. The strategy commonly used by members to deal with this flood was to read only those with an interesting subject line, called a "thread." Most threads are very short, but occasionally a thread will pile up more than two hundred messages in the several days it is active. The list administrator does not prescreen postings.

Study Method

Several research techniques were used in this study. First, we observed the group by joining the list and reading messages (Peterson for about twenty-four months between 1998 and 2002, and Lee for thirteen months between 2000 and 2003). Second, we participated in the group by posting messages. This was done sparingly and only to ask questions or give information—not to offer opinions or debate those of others. Third, messages that seemed interesting for our study were printed out and archived for use in our work. Fourth, the list administrator keeps an archive of all messages ever sent, and we accessed the archives several times. Fifth, occasionally we communicated off-list with other members about questions relating to P2. Sixth, we occasionally talked with other list members at performances and other public events. Seventh, in 2001 and 2002 one or both of us attended Twangfest, the annual event where P2ers meet for a weekend to party and listen to alternative country music bands. Eighth, we analyzed the data from a self-survey of group members we made in 2001 (217 respondents). The results of the study are interspersed throughout the discussion as appropriate. Finally, we sent the manuscript to several members of the list and posted the manuscript on P2 for comment.

The Sceneness of a Virtual Scene

To suggest the ways in which a virtual music scene is like and unlike local scenes, we will now compare the general characteristics of local scenes with those of the virtual scene P2. The characterizations of local scenes are necessarily brief and do not fully cover their range and nuances.

The Nature of Interaction

Interaction at local scenes is face-to-face, complexly textured, and not readily visible to the researcher. Interaction on the Internet is flat, in that it consists of words on paper and the images they can conjure. Although it is readily available to the researcher both in real time and from archived messages, understanding the nuances imbedded in the discussion takes long exposure in either kind of scene. P2 list members are conscious of these nuances, as evidenced by the comment of a longtime member that a newbie "doesn't understand" what a discussion is about, and by the claim of seniority voiced in the assertion, "I have been on the list for four years and . . ."

Recruitment to local scenes begins within a small circle, but if the scene becomes well known, draws participants from a greater distance. Recruitment to Internet-based scenes is open to the entire world that writes in the language used and regularly uses computer-based communication resources. As in other virtual scenes, membership in P2 is not bound by geography. The 2001 study shows that it has members in the United States, Canada, Great Britain, New Zealand, Australia, South Africa, France, Germany, Norway, and Sweden. Not all members have P2 as their sole Internet-based music group, and in fact 72 percent report belonging to other such groups.

Most local communities are limited to a narrow age range, body type, sexual orientation, recreational drug use, and worldview. But, as with other virtual scenes (Smith and Kollock 1999), the demographic composition of P2 is much broader. As shown in the 2001 survey, one percent are teenagers and an equal number are over sixty. Fifteen percent are in their twenties, 42 percent their thirties, 29 percent their forties, and 14 percent their fifties. Seventy-two percent are male, 36 percent never married, and 51 percent are married or partnered. Members have the option of maintaining anonymity by using a pseudonym and a generic Internet provider, but interaction in long-thriving Internet groups usually takes place between people who reveal their identities (Jones and Jones 1997). Almost all active P2 members use their real names, and their address line often includes their place of employment.

Local scenes generally involve intense interaction for a few hours a week, but as with other virtual scenes (Parks and Floyd 1996), active P2 members interact intensively for several hours each day. Three percent of P2ers report being on P2 for more than fifteen hours a week, while 20 percent report being on for six or more hours a week. At the other extreme, 11 percent report being on for less than an hour. At the same time, fully 45 percent report posting no messages; these are pure "lurkers," people who observe the interaction but do not themselves communicate. According to our count, in the first week of October 1998, 772 messages were sent by 332 members, and the top 20 percent of these posters accounted for 55 percent of all messages, suggesting that a small number of people are responsible for most of the communication on P2.

Lurkers who filled out the survey do not differ notably from frequent message senders except that they are more often female and they are less likely to hold music-related jobs. In addition, there is anecdotal evidence that at least some lurkers are not as interested in interacting on P2 as they are in fulfilling a professional interest in knowing what is going on. For example, the second author once sent a sarcastic message about a *New York Times* writer, and as it turns out, he was a lurking member of P2 and immediately rose to the bait with a clarification. Also, when an esoteric topic comes up, such as the best earplugs or bass speakers, or the death of an obscure older music person, members are drawn out who are rarely heard from otherwise.

The biggest difference among participants in a local scene is between the core members who fully live the life of the scene, and participants who take on the roles dictated by the norms of the scene but shed them to play quite different roles. As David Grazian suggests elsewhere in this book, participants can be arrayed like the rings of an onion, from the fully committed core to the casual tourist. For virtual scenes too, the implicit but well-recognized differences between the core, who post often and on a broad range of topics, and the rest of the members is the most clear line of demarcation. In proposing that the list work up a FAQ (a list of frequently asked questions), one member said, with a characteristic mix of strong assertion and self-deprecation: "To become a member of the inner circle of P2 all you have to do is contribute. Just jump right in. Don't worry, there is no way you can make a bigger fool out of yourself that I have repeatedly made of myself" (Jiff Stone, 3 April 2001).[4] This may be true but there is a significant correlation between length of membership, the number of hours per week spent on P2, the number of messages posted, and the frequency of P2-member e-mail contacts off-list, and these findings are corroborated by Parks and Floyd (1996).

Another line of differentiation observed in local scenes is the physical division of the scene space for various kinds of interaction (see Norman Urquia's chapter in this book). Judging by our observations of interaction on P2, there may well be a parallel differentiation within virtual scenes. There are groups of people who occupy different virtual spaces within the flow of messages, in that they read and post on particular topics and not others. As Steve Gardner, a regular contributor, says in response to a new member who says most of the messages aren't interesting: "I've found that I enjoy mailing lists more when I read the threads that I care about and delete the ones that I don't. So, in other words, I try not to worry about the stuff I don't care about. Works for me" (25 July 2001). Most conspicuous among these special topics are posts about technical matters having to do with instruments and the hardware of music making, changes taking place in the music industry, and evaluating alternative country radio station play lists.

The Content of Interaction

Interaction in the typical local scene is richly textured but largely affiliative, as participants show by gesture, word, dress, body adornment, style, and demeanor that they are part of the scene's "neo-tribe" (Bennett 1999). In addition, the risk-free environment, shielded from the gaze of the larger society (see Ken Spring's chapter in this book) and galvanized by hundreds of people in close proximity in places where music is focal, allows a chance to show off while being both highly visible and anonymous. Loud music, dancing, and drugs serve to accentuate this affiliative interaction and tribal identity. Would-be participants who don't exhibit the tribal traits may be ridiculed, ostracized, or excluded entirely.

Such tribal identity markers are absent in the typical virtual scene, since the only mode of communication is the written word. Because of this, one's standing in the group is maintained by the quality and quantity of one's written communication. Having wide-ranging information is valued, and those who chime in without having the facts are quickly contradicted. For example, in October 2001, Dolly Parton announced that a planned New Year's Eve charity concert for young victims of 9/11 was being cancelled. One P2 poster speculated that the reason given by Parton "sounds like spin to me" and went on to suggest that artists were afraid to appear in public because of the fear of terrorism and anthrax. Several people added their speculations until a list member said he had been at the meeting where the decision was made to cancel, and it was made because the acts Dolly wanted to get were already booked for New Year's Eve. According to several of our survey respondents, they like to have others respond to their posts but are frightened by the prospect of someone contradicting what they say. One safe strategy for starting a long and hotly debated thread is simply to ask an opinion question and wait for the debate to begin. Just before the holiday, for example, one radio programmer member asked for views on the best "rootsy" Christmas songs, while another asked for the best Gillian Welch song on death.

In face-to-face local groups, gender, age, and race are generally quite evident and shape interaction. In virtual scenes, age is implied only by the member's musical preferences or recounted life-state experiences. The other factor that comes to the fore in virtual communication is evidence of education, particularly facility with the grammar and vocabulary of written language. Some seem uneasy that this roots-music listserv is the domain of people with higher education. A reference to "deconstruction" or "Adorno" would be followed by an apology, or a retort such as "I'll leave the fancy words to you, but . . . ," and a few members go out of their way to use crude language.

While no one can be seen in a virtual scene, gender is commonly disclosed in the gendered ways of talking (Herring et al. 1995; Ferris 1996), and sexism online is discussed by Ferris (1996) and Markham, 1998). Barbara Ching (2002) has shown the male coding of alt.country in its primary magazine, *No Depression.* Since most P2 members use their own first names, gender is readily recognizable. Questions of gender bias come up in reference to performing in the genre. As Helen Cloud said in a 13 May 1998 message: "I have never felt any gender bias in alt country. I would suppose there might be some but as a woman I just have a blast getting up there with the guys." Some women, and men as well, have objected to the foul and leering language a few male members use in their affiliative remarks. For example, in a set of exchanges on 12 April 2001, Stan Tiller asked: "How many P2 marriages (or relationships . . . not counting drunken mistakes) does that make around here?" To which Stan Heal replied: "I think the number will depend greatly on whether or not we count Jiff Stone's rather sordid relationship history with certain past and present members." To which Stone replied: "You're just jealous. BTW, I'm thinking of making Alfred Fern my newest bitch. Lockman has joined the witness protection program. And besides Alfred has purtier hair. I'll give ya details after Merlefest." Such comments are commonly set off by <g> to show that they are meant in jest.

Social control in local scenes is maintained by a mixture of ostracism, sarcasm and joking, informal persuasion, and, ultimately, bouncers (Goffman 1956). In virtual scenes such as P2 much the same range of controls operates (Smith 1999). The most common tactic for censoring a message is to ignore it. More pointed shaping comments are seen in a message that begins with a note of affiliation, then moves to sarcasm, and finally slams a particular view held by the other and ends on a grace note that reestablishes affiliation. For example: "Good to see you've survived the time-off line lost in the Big Apple, but what did they get you on? You are totally off base calling Lucinda's latest way better than 'Car Wheels. . . .' Let's hope in the clean air of St. Louis that your judgment returns." The parallel to the bouncer is being delisted by the list administrator, which has happened only twice in the history of P2, according to longtime P2 member Barry Mazor.

When Virtual Becomes Local

On a listserv like P2 where people usually know each other's real names and identities, not surprisingly, many want to meet (Jones and Jones 1997). The routine form of establishing face-to-face contact is illustrated by John Wise's (30 January 2001) message regarding Ralph Stanley's appearance in Santa Monica, California: "Any P2ers going to this show, please let me know. We're kind of twang orphans here on the south left coast." There are also messages of the form, "All P2ers in the Detroit area take note . . ." According to Barry Mazor, one such call to meet at a particular bar after a concert led to the organization of a local scene in New York City and eventually to his marriage to one of the people who responded to the call. Such contacts led, in 1998, to a kind of game of tag in which a hat of Western singer Don Walzer went from P2 member to member, each move being duly noted on P2. P2 parties at major music festivals are another form of personal contact. For example, offering to organize a P2 barbeque at the South by Southwest Festival, Chad Hamilton wrote, "I'm trying to put this thing together quickly but want to be sure there is ample demand" (1 March 2001). As with all festivals, this one attracts people from diverse places, so no local scene results, but it does give more P2ers a chance to get to know each other personally.

By far the most important example of how P2 has been energized by face-to-face contact between members is Twangfest, a festival founded by a group of P2ers in the St. Louis area the year after P2 was started. The program for the 2002 event announces: "Twangfest is probably the world's only nonprofit, Internet-generated, community-based music festival. Founded in 1997 by contributors to the Postcard 2 online discussion list, the event is still staffed entirely by volunteers." According to Ray Kasten: "One could say that the first festival six years ago was a modest, even marginal event—the members of a music listserv got together to hear ten bands affiliated with that Internet community" (Kasten 2002). Several members have told us how important their first Twangfest was in drawing them into the P2 community. This is echoed by what Kris Knaus

Data sources (Photo by Richard A. Peterson).

told Ray Kasten: "Non-musically what stands out was a hotel room party in Terry Smith's room. Face-to-face meetings, putting faces to names and (e-mail) signatures, beer, and the relaxing feeling that these folks were all very cool people. People picked up conversations where they left off with the last e-mail–discussions and relationships flowed from the listserv to 'real life' " (Kasten 2002). By 2002 there were twenty bands, bowling, and a CD release party. A goodly number of people at the musical events were not P2 members, but the members were given neighboring motel rooms, and there were late-night parties with music that flowed between rooms. The importance of Twangfest to the virtual community is suggested by the large number of messages just before the event that were devoted to plans for meeting and relating battle stories afterward.

The Life Span of Scenes

How long do music scenes last? Many local scenes are quite short-lived and leave no trace; others start small but gather wider attention in the community and beyond (see the chapters by Paul Hodkinson, Kristen Schilt, and Ken Spring in this book), and if the mass media focuses attention on them they may briefly become huge (Thornton 1995). But in months, or at most a few years, the creative energy of local scenes is spent, the music becomes commodified, and new fans increasingly seek entertainment free of any serious lifestyle commitments. In due course, what remains is a set of performers who play to tourists drawn by the mystique of the former scene (see David Grazian's chapter in this book). Do virtual scenes follow this same trajectory? As observed in the case of P2, at least, the trajectory of a virtual scene can be quite different.

Local scenes typically grow gradually at first, as people drawn to a particular form of music, entertainment, lifestyle expression, and commercial interest gradually come together around a hospitable local site and build a distinct scene identity (see Spring's chapter in this book). In sharp contrast, virtual scenes are created in a day. P2, for example, began with several dozen members who, like a new colony of bees, hived off from another Internet group that had a more narrow focus on two bands. As bees sometimes leave an established hive to follow a new queen, members of a parent listserv who are hiving off flock to a new host site, with one or more members willing to serve as list administrator. Thus, given the availability of computer facilities and at least one dedicated volunteer, a nascent virtual scene can be established at no cost to participants, and it can survive as long as there are interested members and the requisite computer facilities.

Within two years P2 had six hundred members and stabilized at something over seven hundred members writing 600 to 1,100 messages a week through 2001. At six years of age, P2 was strong and apparently little changed, well beyond the time that most local scenes would have faded.

Since the costs of maintaining the scene are so low, it is interesting to ask whether such a virtual scene might remain vital into its second decade. It is too early to tell, but it is possible to look at the factors that are necessary to maintain a scene and learn more about the life span of virtual scenes.

As in all human groups, it is necessary to replace lost members, and new members must quickly become active participants. Our 2001 survey suggests that while membership numbers were being maintained, the 37 percent who report being on the list for at least four years send more messages on average than do those who had been on for less than six months. One might argue that "newbies" hold back until they learn the ropes. And yet the longtime members on average post more messages than all others, spend more hours a week on P2, and contact more members off-list. Taken together, these findings suggest that this core of most active participants tends disproportionately to be longtime members, and that the core is not being replenished with newer recruits.

All scenes need a place to congregate, and, as we have noted, for virtual scenes this means a computer host site on the web. In August 2002, P2 lost the use of its computer host, and a group of people volunteered to take on the administration and moved the host to drizzle.com. As of November 2002, the list had upward of six hundred members. The decline in number, we were told, was due to the number of long-inactive members who never made the shift to the new host. Our informal observations of posts on the new list suggest that the topics and most-active participants have not changed but, as of the first four months, the rate of messaging is down but growing.

As noted earlier, P2 was formed by hiving off from another list. Such hiving is a threat to any virtual scene (Kolko 2000), but with one minor exception there has been no organized hiving off from P2. Both in the statement of purpose and in practice, P2ers are tolerant of discussions on a wide range of topics. There are people who especially like alternative rock and others who especially like bluegrass, but through seven years there was no effort to form a more musically focused list. Instead, we found in our survey, interested members also joined listservs devoted to their genre of particular interest. But in 1999 there was an ongoing discussion of appropriateness of certain kinds of messages. Some didn't like the strongly worded objections to others' musical tastes, while others did not care for discussions of "non twang" music, discussions of social issues, or self-promotion by musician members. About the same time, a number objected to discussions of personal favorites in food, drink, cars, perfume, and the like.

The matter was brought to a head by an extended thread devoted to a debate over the most dreadful seasonal food that came down to a contest between gefilte fish and lutefisk. Wanting to continue the fun but recognizing the irrelevance to alternative country music, the interested members agreed to form a separately hosted list they called the Fluff List for the informal banter about nonmusical tastes and similar observations. An informant has observed that the creation of the Fluff List reduced the large number of brief messages and made P2 a more studious enterprise.

Finally, changes in the music or how it is defined may influence the life span of any kind of scene. Scenes develop around music that is seen as different and special, and they atrophy as that magic is lost. This happens in a number of ways. The novelty of the music may wear off. The music of the leading artists may evolve in different directions. The music may be absorbed into another genre of music, or it may become normalized and incorporated into the ongoing mix of commercial music, as has happened a number of times before in the history of country music (Peterson 1997). Alternative country music is not immune to such developments. A number of the bellwether bands disbanded or evolved to feature another form of music.[5] In addition, there were efforts to incorporate alt.country into the commercial subgenre Americana, and there were parallel efforts to define it as part of a broader movement called roots music. At the same time the remarkable success of the compilation of songs from the movie *O Brother, Where Art Thou* led a number of commercial country music artists to record more traditional-sounding songs and, in so far as this happens, alternative country music may be absorbed into the larger commercial stream of music. Individually or together these changes would mean that P2 would lose its original raison d'être.

The most active P2 members repeatedly told us how much they enjoyed social contacts with other members and cited instances where they had provided psychological support for each other. If the listserv evolves in this direction, it is likely to lose all but the most active core and continue as long as a sufficient number want to maintain contact via a listserv. But there is another possibility: Just as the sites of faded local scenes can have an afterlife as tourist attractions (see Grazian's chapter in this book), the sites of virtual scenes might continue as Web sites where interested people can turn for information, paraphernalia, and music revivals. This is what seems to be happening in the case of the Web site studied by Bennett and documented elsewhere in this book. Already the "twang gang" that puts on Twangfest sells festival records and other items while distancing themselves from dependence on P2. If this trend continues, P2 might eventually live on as a Web site for Twangfest, the festival that P2 created.

Impact of Virtual Scenes on the Music

In concluding, we ask about the impact that P2 has on alternative country music. If some local scenes have helped nurture new genres (Rosenberg 1985; Escott 1991; DeVeaux 1997), can virtual music scenes influence the music as well? We look at the importance of scenes both for musicians and for fans.

Local scenes serve as places where musicians, singers, and DJs can learn their craft and directly see the reactions of fans to their performances. In contrast, alt.country musicians do not present their music on P2. Rather, like other virtual scenes, P2 is focused on fans' reactions to the music and not on creating and experiencing the music itself. Some fledgling alt.country artists crave attention on P2 and write messages to get it, but, according to Barry Mazor, established artists are displeased by the critical discussions on listservs. Echoing this sentiment, the FAQ page of the Postcard list says: "Do the people in Son Volt and Wilco know about the list. Yes they do. . . . Their reaction to the list seems to vary between indifference and slight hostility/annoyance. . . . So if you're looking for a topic to help you strike up a conversation with band members after the show, I wouldn't advise bringing up the Internet; they seem to be quite sick of hearing about it."[6]

When we began the study, we thought that P2 might serve as a means for new fans to learn about alt.country, its performers, their recordings, and shows. It does have this function but, since the membership is relatively small and does not change rapidly, not a large number of people can have been exposed to alt.country through P2 membership.

This said, P2 may still have a considerable impact on the popularity of alternative country precisely because its members are not average fans. As revealed by our survey, fully 28.9 percent of the members work for independent record companies or at record stores, select music at radio stations, or book talent. These people are in a position to help influence which performers are able to make records and to get heard in public. At least as importantly, numerous P2 members are music writers who work for the important fan-oriented music publications and newspapers, ranging from locals to the *New York Times*. These tastemakers serve to inform readers about alternative country music and to shape how it is defined by the public at large. Clearly, such people have influence far beyond their own numbers. Thus, although its membership is small, the virtual scene based in P2 arguably plays a significant role in shaping the development of alternative country music.

Conclusion

Our analysis of P2 as a place apart, where people come to fuel their passion for a kind of music and foster a self-conscious identity and communicate it to others, shows that a Web-based listserv can fulfill the basic functions of a music scene. As with local scenes, it has a loosely defined core and circles of less involved participants, and like a local scene it sharply defines itself against the musical establishment—in the case of P2, the corporate way of producing country music centered in Nashville. It is different from the typical local scene in growing much faster and remaining vital for a longer time. It is also different in sustaining more cognitive interaction and in not depending on drugs or alcohol, as so many local scenes do. Of course, from the study of this one case, it is impossible to tell if a virtual scene could last so long if there were not the chances to make and renew personal relationships at Twangfest, other festivals, and local concerts. Perhaps the virtual scene that remained entirely virtual could not endure as long. Clearly, there is much more to be learned about virtual scenes.

Notes

We greatly appreciate the warm welcome and help extended by many P2 members. Most notably we thank Brad Bechtel, David Cantwell, John Conquest, Chris Corich, Rennee Dechert, Aaron Fox, Steve Gardner, David Goodman, Suzette Lawrence, Barry Mazor, Nina Melechen, Iain Noble, Stacey Taylor, Jeff Wall, Jon Weisberger, and Carl Wilson.

1.   See *lists.drizzle.com/mailman/listinfo/postcard2*
2.   For a further development of this theme see David Goodman (1999) and Peterson and Beal (2003).
3.   There are several other listservs for people who like alternative country music. Most are devoted to one artist or are ostensibly open forums, but in practice are flooded with promotional rave-ups. Postcard and No Depression are the only other notable listservs. In 2002 Postcard had almost a thousand members and there were nine hundred to two thousand posts per month (David Dewey, personal communication, 26 October 2002). It is dedicated to Wilco and Son Volt and traffics in tape trading, which is not allowed on P2. In the

four months for which comparable data is available, P2 messaging was slightly more frequent.
4. All names in messages have been changed to facilitate anonymity.
5. Important early bands that have disbanded include: Uncle Tupelo, Blue Mountain, Whiskeytown, Bad Livers, Beat Farmers, and Cactus Brothers. Those that have evolved out of alternative country include Wilco, Old 97s, Jayhawks, Lambchop, Whiskeytown, and Lucinda Williams
6. *www.postcardfromhell.com/postcard-faq.html.* Some artist-run Web sites solicit fan reactions, but no one has published a study evaluating the influence of such fan feedback.

References

Alden, Grant, and Peter Blackstock, eds. 1998. *No Depression: An Anthology of Review Articles.* Nashville: Dowling. (Selected articles available at *www.node-pression.net*)

Bennett, Andy. 1999. "Subcultures or Neo-tribes? Rethinking the Relationship between Youth, Style, and Musical Taste," *Sociology,* 33(3): 599–617.

————. 2000. *Popular Music and Youth Culture: Music, Identity, and Place.* Basingstoke: Macmillan.

Ching, Barbara. 2002. "Going Back to the Old Mainstream: 'No Depression' and the Construction of Alt.Country." Paper presented at the International Association for the Study of Popular Music, U.S. branch, annual meetings, Cleveland, Ohio, 10–16 October.

DeVeaux, Scott. 1997. *The Birth of BeBop: A Social and Musical History.* Berkeley: University of California Press.

Escott, Colin. 1991. *Good Rockin' Tonight: Sun Records and the Birth of Rock 'n' Roll.* New York: St. Martin's Press.

Ennis, Philip. 1992. *The Seventh Stream.* Hanover, N.H.: Wesleyan University Press.

Ferris, Sharmila Pixy. 1996. "Women On-Line: Cultural and Relational Aspects of Women's Communication in On-Line Discussion Groups." *Interpersonal Computing and Technology* 4, 3/4: 29–40.

Goffman, Erving. 1956. *The Presentation of Self in Everyday Life.* Edinburgh: Social Research Centre, University of Edinburgh Press.

Goodman, David. 1999. *Modern Twang: An Alternative Country Music Guide and Directory.* Nashville: Dowling.

Herring, Susan, Deborah A. Johnson, and Tamra DiBenedetto. 1995. " 'This Discussion Is Going Too Far!': Male Resistance to Female Participation on the Internet." In Kira Hall and Mary Bucholtz, eds., *Gender Articulated: Language and the Socially Constructed Self.* New York: Routledge.

Jones, Steve, and Steven G. Jones, eds. 1997. *Virtual Culture: Identity and Communication in Cybersociety.* London: Sage.

Kasten, Roy. 2002. "Twangfest: It's the Music." In program of the 2002 Twangfest Festival, 24.

Kolko, Beth. 2000. "Dissolution and Fragmentation: Problems in On-Line Communities." In Steve Jones and Steven G. Jones, eds., *Cybersociety 2.0: Revisiting Computer-Mediated Communication and Community*. London: Sage.

Laing, Dave. 1985. *One Chord Wonders: Power and Meaning in Punk Rock*. Milton Keynes, U.K.: Open University Press.

Lee, Steven. 1995. "Re-examining the Concept of the 'Independent' Record Company: The Case of Wax Trax! Records." *Popular Music* 14, 1: 13–32.

Markham, Annette N. 1998. *Life Online: Researching Real Experience in Virtual Space*. Walnut Creek, Calif.: AltaMira.

Parks, Malcolm, and Kory Floyd. 1996. "Making Friends in Cyberspace." *Journal of Communication* 46, 1: 80–97.

Peterson, Richard A. 1997. *Creating Country Music: Fabricating Authenticity*. Chicago: University of Chicago Press.

Peterson, Richard A., and Bruce Beal. 2001. "Alternative Country: Origins, Music, World-view, Fans, and Taste in Genre Formation." *Popular Music and Society* 25:233–49.

Peterson, Richard A., and John Ryan. Forthcoming. "The Disembodied Muse: Music in the Internet Age." In Philip N. Howard and Steve Jones, eds., *The Internet in American Life*. Thousand Oaks, Calif.: Sage.

Rosenberg, Neil. 1985. *Bluegrass: A History*. Urbana: University of Illinois Press.

Smith, Ann Du Val. 1999. "Problems of Conflict Management in Virtual Communities." In Marc A. Smith and Peter Kollock, eds., *Communities in Cyberspace*. London: Routledge.

Smith, Marc A., and Peter Kollock. 1999. "Communities in Cyberspace: An Introduction." In Marc A. Smith and Peter Kollock, eds., *Communities in Cyberspace*. London: Routledge.

Thornton, Sarah. 1995. *Club Cultures: Music, Media, and Subcultural Capital*. Cambridge: Polity Press.

Wellman, Barry, and Milena Gulia. 1999. "Virtual Communities as Communities." In Marc A. Smith and Peter Kollock, eds., *Communities in Cyberspace*. London: Routledge.

11

New Tales from Canterbury: The Making of a Virtual Scene

Andy Bennett

> I am often asked to explain exactly what the essence of
> Canterbury music is and I still struggle to pin it down. A certain
> Englishness maybe . . . a willingness to experiment, perhaps
> . . . consummate musicianship certainly. A loose collection of
> musicians whose paths seem to cross inevitably.
> —Phil Howitt

> It seems to me that the very essence of "Canterbury" is
> the tension between complicated harmonies, extended
> improvisations, and the sincere desire to write catchy popsongs.
> —Canterbury Sound fan

The city of Canterbury is located in the heart of the county of Kent in the south-east corner of England. One of England's most well known and frequently visited "cathedral cities," Canterbury is steeped in historical references, a fact capitalized upon by the local tourist industry. Throughout the year a steady stream of visitors to the city enjoys a range of themed attractions, including the Canterbury Tales (where one can relive the lives and times of such Chaucerian characters as the Wife of Bath, the Miller, and the Pardoner, complete with reproduced fourteenth-century settings), the Heritage Museum, a variety of Ghost Walks, and a carefully preserved Roman mosaic. Such attractions provide tourists to Canterbury with key ways of picturing the many facets of the city's past, both factual and fictional.

Since the mid-1990s, a more recent, if less commonly acknowledged, aspect of the city's local history has become similarly pictured, celebrated, and "mythologized" through the "Canterbury Sound." This was a term briefly used by music journalists during the late 1960s to describe a number of rock groups with Canterbury connections, including Soft Machine and Caravan, whose lineups included former members of local Canterbury rock group the Wilde Flowers. The term was quickly discarded and generally forgotten about for almost thirty years, when a dedicated Canterbury Sound Web site revived interest in the notion of a Canterbury Sound and created a new generation of fans. Within this context, the Canterbury Sound acquired a new resonance as fans set about exchanging views and opinions online as to the defining qualities of the Canterbury Sound and the role of the city in its conception. Indeed, a key feature of such online discussions is the transformation of the term Canterbury Sound from a journalistic device to a descriptive label for what is perceived to be a bona fide local scene. In their online discussions, fans take for granted the existence of a link between the city of Canterbury and the Canterbury Sound, in much the same way as terms such as "Chicago blues" or "New Orleans jazz" assume a seemingly organic link between a musical style and its place of origin.

In this chapter, I consider what the Canterbury Sound contributes to our understanding of virtual scenes and of the relationship between music, space, and place.

The Canterbury Sound

The term "Canterbury Sound" was originally coined by music journalists during the late 1960s to refer to a range of group and solo projects initiated by ex-members of Canterbury-based group the Wilde Flowers (see Frame 1993; Stump 1997; Macan 1997; Martin 1998). The Wilde Flowers, formed in June 1963 by Robert Wyatt, Richard Sinclair, Kevin Ayers, Hugh Hopper, and his brother Brian Hopper, all pupils at Canterbury's Simon Langton Grammar School for Boys, had played a mixture of cover versions and original songs that spanned a range of genres from rock to jazz (Stump 1997). Although the Wilde Flowers achieved a measure of local success, performing at venues such as Canterbury College of Art and the Beehive Club (see Rootes 1997), the group split up in 1965. Robert Wyatt and Hugh Hopper went on to international success with Soft Machine, while Richard Sinclair formed Caravan. Kevin Ayres worked as a solo artist and also fronted the Kevin Ayers Band.

With several notable exceptions, the notion of a Canterbury Sound has never been taken particularly seriously by Canterbury musicians them-selves, who, for the most part, have viewed its associations with the city of Canterbury quite negatively. In a 1999 interview for the U.K. music maga-zine *Mojo*, Robert Wyatt, now a successful solo artist, made the following observation: "[A]lthough it's true that I became interested in music [while in Canterbury] and started playing with other people who were interested in music, this idea of some swinging scene is simply not how I remember it. It was grimmer, and I found Canterbury a rather po-faced sort of town" (Hoskyns 1999, 41). A similar view is offered by Hugh Hopper:

> Canterbury has never really been a good place to play. . . . There are a
> few pubs here, but it's not really a musical hotbed at all. . . . I was born
> in Canterbury and lived here until I was about nineteen and then I lived
> in other places in France and London. . . . And I gradually came back
> this way [but] it wasn't really a plan, it just happened this way. So the
> Canterbury thing, it's a nice idea because it's a nice little town, it's got a
> cathedral and in the Summer it looks good. But not much is happening
> here really. (Calyx, February 1999, 5)

Such observations suggest that the claims for a thriving local music scene inherent in the term "Canterbury Sound" are essentially unfounded. Paradoxically, this is also reinforced by local journalistic accounts of the time, which suggest that both Soft Machine and Caravan were far more centered on the London music scene than on Canterbury. In May 1967 an article in the *Kent Herald* noted that Soft Machine was playing regular fortnightly dates at London's prestigious psychedelic venue the UFO Club, which also hosted gigs by a number of other up-and-coming experimental music groups of the time, including Pink Floyd. In the same article, Robert Wyatt is quoted as saying: "If things don't work out in London, . . . we shall go to San Francisco" ("Progress" 1967). A similarly established London connection exists in the case of Caravan, who became, in Stump's words, "Underground darlings overnight" (1997, 125).

If the notion of a Canterbury Sound is geographically inaccurate, then the term is also highly ambiguous as a stylistic label. Attempts to musically define the Canterbury Sound range from *New Musical Express* journalist Ian MacDonald's reference to the Wilde Flowers' "well-developed Canter-bury biases: a bit of jazz, a touch of rock" (1975) to Stump's commentary on Soft Machine's "fundamentally free-form music," a feature he consid-ers accentuated by the group's decision to rely on organ and saxophone as melody instruments rather than on the standard guitar front line (Stump 1997, 125). Other journalistic accounts identify the Canterbury bands far more readily with the burgeoning jazz-rock and progressive-rock scenes of the late 1960s and early 1970s. In August 1970, Malcolm Mitchell, journalist for the local Canterbury paper the *Kent Herald,* described how Soft Machine was "hailed as one of the leading progressive groups on [the] jazz-rock-pop scene" (1970).

As this brief overview illustrates, even during the height of Soft Machine and Caravan's success, the "Canterbury Sound" was a problematic and contested term. By the mid-1970s, little reference was made to the Canterbury Sound at all, with the exception of occasional retrospective features in British music papers such as *New Musical Express.*

The Revival of the Canterbury Sound

The mid-1990s revival of interest in the notion of a Canterbury Sound resulted partly from the launch of several fanzines, notably *Facelift: The Canterbury Sound and Beyond* and its German equivalent, *Canterbury Nachrichten* (Canterbury News). The Canterbury Sound revival was further consolidated through the establishment of Calyx, a dedicated Canterbury Sound Web site. Launched in February 1996 and based in France, Calyx comprises six main sections: musician profiles, latest releases, upcoming events, lyrics archive, Canterbury discography, and transcriptions and translations of old magazine articles. Additionally, the Web site included a number of special features, such as "What's Rattlin?" a subscriber's newsletter published every three days, and "What Is Canterbury Music?" This latter feature offers fans an open invitation to "define" the Canterbury Sound. Comments lodged here range from semi-sociological observations, in which notions of "Englishness" and English humor are mooted as centrally defining factors of Canterbury bands, to more aesthetically informed points of view, such as, for example, "anti-commercialism" as the essence of an authentic Canterbury band.

A further section of the Calyx Web site, "A Guide to Obscure and Short-lived Canterbury Bands," allows fans to exercise even more specialist levels of knowledge in relation to which groups and artists should and should not be included in the canon of Canterbury Sound music. In recent years Calyx has been joined by a number of other Canterbury Sound Web sites. Among these is Collapso: Canterbury Family Trees, a site built and maintained by a Japanese fan who, adopting a format made popular in Pete

Frame's (1993) book *Rock Family Trees,* plots a genealogy of Canterbury music by tracing a hidden history of obscure and in most cases short-lived Canterbury-based bands.

A particularly significant aspect of this online revival of the Canterbury Sound is the way in which the city of Canterbury itself is positioned within discussions and debates concerning the origins and development of the Canterbury Sound. Given the absence of the physically defined fan base which characterizes geographic scenes, Canterbury Sound fans look for other ways to collectively celebrate their common musical taste and thus forge the sense of "fan community" deemed central to any music scene (Frith 1983). In this sense, the city of Canterbury plays a crucial role. Thus, while physically removed from Canterbury itself, Canterbury Sound fans effectively forge a sense of community through their collective construction of the city in musicalized terms, the online discussions of fans being informed by a shared image of Canterbury as an urban space that provided the necessary stimulus for the birth of the Canterbury Sound and that remains central to its "spirit." The fans inscribe Canterbury's streets, pubs, venues, and other urban spaces with their own fictive interpretations (Chaney 1993), the latter becoming a crucial touchstone for the fans' collective belief in the inherent link between the Canterbury Sound and the city of Canterbury.

At a mundane level, this link derives from the Canterbury Sound musicians' experience of growing up and being friends together in Canterbury—and from their sharing of a locally situated sensibility which found its expression through informal musical liaisons and their gradual maturation into more coherent expressions of song and instrumental improvisation. At a more abstract level, Canterbury's cultural influence upon the Canterbury Sound is judged to manifest itself through, for example, the expression a "certain Englishness" and "a uniquely English lyrical and vocal content" (Calyx, February 1999, 4). From the point of view of the fans then, Canterbury becomes an important physical point of reference around which to collectively discuss the significance of the Canterbury Sound and its relationship to a particular set of people in a given time and space.

As interest in the Canterbury Sound has grown, such online debates concerning the nature of Canterbury music have been enhanced through the availability of new inspirational resources. Like other young musicians in the United Kingdom and elsewhere anxious to experiment with their craft, the Wilde Flowers and other local Canterbury bands of the mid-1960s recorded much of their early work on cheap, domestic, reel-to-reel tape recorders. For the most part, these early recordings were little more than rough experiments or rehearsal sessions, of variable quality both audibly and musically. In recent years, however, a number of these crude, lo-fi recordings have been resurrected and belatedly introduced into the "public sphere" (Reimer 1995) in the form of the *Canterburied Sounds*, a four-volume CD set that features tracks by the Wilde Flowers and Caravan, as well as musical liaisons between members of these groups and other, often unidentified, local musicians.[1] That such a resurrection of these early recordings was feasible at all is largely due to the possibilities offered by state-of-the-art digital recording equipment. Thus, as Brian Hopper, brother of former Soft Machine bassist Hugh Hopper and the person behind the *Canterburied Sounds* project, explains in the sleeve notes to volume 1 of the series:

> Although most of the tapes had survived three decades of storage in various lofts and cupboards, some were obviously showing signs of deterioration with several bits of detached tape floating around in the boxes holding them. These were painstakingly spliced together where this was possible and the long and somewhat tedious process of transference to DAT [digital audio tape] embarked upon. . . . Using DAT copies it was then easier to assess not only the content but also the recording quality [and choose] potential tracks; . . . employing the wonders of Sadie/Cedar [digital sound-processing equipment] and other modern audio editing technology, we were able to clean up the tape hiss, mains hum and other extraneous noise and at the same time enhance the wanted sounds.[2]

The *Canterburied Sounds* series is, in many respects, a unique document of the musicalization of everyday life in a local urban context; a sonic statement of what Finnegan refers to as the shared "pathways" via which local musicians negotiate the "impersonal wilderness of urban life" (1989, 306). While local musicians may often talk about previous musical collaborations and play private copies of early recordings to each other and to friends (see, for example, Cohen and McManus 1991; McManus 1994), it is highly unusual for such a local history of music making to be reconstituted and publicly showcased in this way.

Hopper's claim in the sleeve notes of the *Canterburied Sounds*, Volume 1, is that the collection represents some "unfinished business," yet it seems clear from Hopper's subsequent use of the descriptive term "Canterbury-ism" and its implication of a developing cult aura around the notion of the Canterbury Sound that this was also a motivation for working on the project. In essence then, the *Canterburied Sounds* project could be taken as a response to the revived interest in the Canterbury Sound and the increasing belief among fans in an organic link between the music and the city of Canterbury. Moreover, the *Canterburied Sounds* project's realization further enhances the potential connections which the new generation of fans are apt to make between the Canterbury Sound and its perceived city of origin, providing, in effect, a stock of foundational recorded work which fans can use as a basis for assembling a canon of Canterbury Sound bands and music.

The creative imagination of fans is further fired by the packaging of the *Canterburied Sounds* CDs. The cover of each CD case in the *Canterburied*

Cover design of Canterburied Sounds CD collection featuring painting of Canterbury Cathedral (Artist: Leslie Hopper)

Sounds series features a painting by Leslie Hopper, father of Brian and Hugh Hopper, of Canterbury Cathedral, nestling among trees and meadows in a rustic-style setting, an image that evokes a "vision of pastoral England" (Morley and Robbins 1989, 16), resonating with fans' beliefs in the deeply ingrained "Englishness" of the Canterbury Sound. The imagery extends to the CDs themselves, each of which are decorated with a silhouetted profile of the cathedral tower, its black spires sharply contrasting with the silver finish of the disk. The *Canterburied Sounds* series can, then, be seen to provide two main functions in the construction of the Canterbury Sound. The music contained on the CDs serves to reinforce in the minds of dedicated fans the authenticity of the Canterbury Sound as a distinctive local musical style with historical roots and a pattern of development. Similarly, the packaging of the CDs further forges the connection between the Canterbury Sound and the "Englishness" deemed by fans to be at its heart.

In themselves, the tracks and experimentations featured on the *Canterburied Sounds* have little in common, being nothing more than an ad hoc grouping of musical improvisations, rough rehearsal sessions, and early live performances. Unremarkable as these early recordings may be, however, their value in the geo-sonic mapping of the Canterbury Sound is literally immense. Due to their "ready-made" connection with the virtual scene that has grown up in their absence from the public sphere, the "lo-fi" experimentations featured on the *Canterburied Sound* CDs have automatically become a central point of reference for Canterbury fans in their Internet discussions and fanzine correspondence relating to the nature and essence of the Canterbury Sound.

Selling Canterbury by the Sound

Despite the resurgence of interest in the Canterbury Sound, its history, and its development as a part of the local identity of Canterbury, the point remains that such interest is shared by a relatively small translocal group of hardcore fans. A wider interest in the Canterbury Sound would no doubt have led to moves on the part of the local tourist industry to capitalize on this in some way, for example, through organized tours to significant local sites, like the Beatles tours in Liverpool. Similarly, there is insufficient local and tourist interest in the Canterbury Sound to make it profitable for any local bands to recreate Canterbury Sound music or for local clubs to feature Canterbury Sound nights. Indeed, it is likely that any attempt to commodify the Canterbury Sound at this level would remain over-shadowed by tourist attractions for which Canterbury is better known, notably the award-winning and highly profitable Canterbury Tales Exhibition, which attracts thousands of tourists every year. Nevertheless, in recent years local businesses and individuals have sought ways of weaving the concept of the Canterbury Sound into the city's tourist gaze (Urry 1990). Rootes's book, *Images of Canterbury*, a collection of black-and-white photographs that document the history of Canterbury between 1930 and 1970, includes a section on the "Canterbury Scene" that features the Wilde Flowers and Caravan and an author's note which reads: "The city [Canterbury] made musical history in the 1960s with the development of what became known as the Canterbury Scene (or Sound)" (1997, 157–58). Similarly, a number of local record shops now feature Canterbury Sound sections whose coverage varies from "acknowledged" Canterbury bands, typically Soft Machine, Caravan, and Hatfield and the North (the group formed by Canterbury-born musician Richard Sinclair following his departure from Caravan), to groups with altogether more tenuous Canterbury links, such as Gong, whose only real Canterbury connection is original-group guitarist Steve Hillage, a former student at the University of Kent at Canterbury during the late 1960s.

According to Hugh Hopper, whom I interviewed in 1999 regarding his connections to the Canterbury Sound, the use of the term "Canterbury Sound" by local record shops as a marketing device is a very recent development. It is significant, and perhaps inevitable, in this respect that the recently produced *Canterburied Sounds* CDs are used as the centerpiece of local record shops' Canterbury Sound sections. From the point of view of Canterbury Sound fans visiting the city, the fact that the *Canterburied Sounds* CDs are centrally featured in this way by local record shops is further suggestive of an inherent connection between Canterbury and the Canterbury Sound. Indeed the marketing of the Canterbury Sound in this way also serves to spread the myth of "Canterburyism," particularly among tourists who have no previous knowledge of the Canterbury Sound and who are thus even more inclined to accept uncritically the notion of a locally acknowledged and culturally inscribed link between the music and the city. Thus, as a local record shop owner explained to me: "People from all over the world come into my shop and see my Canterbury Sounds CDs. Some are fans already, but often people will say, 'I've never heard of this before.' So they buy a CD or two and take them home, and that's what keeps it [the Canterbury Sound] growing, really."

As this observation suggests, while the majority of visitors to Canterbury have no existing knowledge of the Canterbury Sound, a number of visitors, especially from overseas, arrive in the city with preformed ideas about Canterbury's rock musical heritage. This is supported by Hugh Hopper's account of occasionally running a record stall owned by a friend at a local market: "You get people coming over from France and Belgium on day trips or whatever and asking, 'Where's it happening? Where's the music?' " Similarly, in an article which appeared in the German fanzine *Canterbury Nachrichten,* a Dutch fan expressed surprise at the apparent lack of interest in the Canterbury Sound among local music fans he met and talked to while visiting Canterbury. The same fan attended a Caravan concert in the Midlands region of England and was again surprised by lack of interest in and knowledge about the Canterbury Sound. Thus he observed: "In the Midlands Caravan is a completely unknown band with as big a reputation as every amateur band. . . . At the concert I attended the audience were there more because they remembered the era [the late 1960s] than because of the band [Caravan]" (Smit 1997, 24).[3]

The response of certain local musicians to the growing interest in the Canterbury Sound is also serving to authenticate its perceived association with the city. For example, in the section of the Calyx Web site entitled "What Is Canterbury Music?" former Caravan and Hatfield and the North member Richard Sinclair offers the following opinion:

> People say, what is the Canterbury scene? I think you have to come to Canterbury and see it and hear it! I think Kent has got a particular sound. We've sung in our schools here, we were all at school in this sort of area. I was part of the Church of England choir: up to the age of sixteen I was singing tonalities that are very English. Over the last three or four hundred years, and even earlier than that, some of the tonalities go back. So they are here, and they are a mixture of European things too. The history is very much that. A very historical centre of activity is Canterbury for the last hundred years. So it's quite an important stepping stone of whatever this thousand years have covered. I think it's not to be mocked because it's a centre of communication here and it's a meeting point—many nations come here to visit the cathedral, so you get a very unique situation happening.

In 1992, Sinclair released an album entitled *Richard Sinclair's Caravan of Dreams,* his first recorded work for some years. In one of the first direct references to the Canterbury Sound to appear in the local media, the *Kentish Gazette*, produced in Canterbury, featured an article on Sinclair on 16 April 1992 suggesting that *Caravan of Dreams* would be "instantly familiar and welcome to Caravan and Canterbury scene fans." As with the production of the *Canterburied Sounds* CDs and their use by local record shops as a merchandising tactic designed to confirm Canterbury's central- ity both to the origins and essence of a body of music which has already been seamlessly woven by fans into an imagined history of music making in the city, references by the local media to the Canterbury Sound play their part in forging a circularity between myth and reality by providing further evidence, from the point of view of fans, of a longstanding and locally ac- knowledged link between the city and the Canterbury Sound.

The late 1990s saw the re-forming of Caravan and their first album and live performances for a number of years. Similarly, in the summer of 2000, the first Canterbury Sound Festival took place. In addition to Caravan and Gong, the lineup for the three-day event included a wealth of other sixties British progressive-rock favorites, among them, Coliseum, Man, and the Crazy World of Arthur Brown. Interestingly, while this concert represented a significant step toward the commodification of the Canterbury Sound on "home ground," the venture has a considerable way to go if it is to match the imaginative way in which the Canterbury Sound concept has been integrated into comparable festivals elsewhere in Europe. The following extract is taken from a German fan's account of a visit to an annual music festival in the Dutch town of Harlingen during 1997. Included on the bill of the three-day event was former Caravan and Hatfield and the North front man Richard Sinclair. To celebrate Sinclair's appearance, an elaborate series of Canterbury Sound themes had been organized:

In the back part of the [festival] tent there was the café where one could get food and drink . . . and there was, appropriately enough, a bar with typical English beer. For historical effect there was the "music museum" in which rare record sleeves, musical equipment, such as the old amplifier of Dick Sinclair, Richard's father (a 1950's model) or rare and ancient black and white photos of the Canterbury-legends Wilde Flowers as well as Soft Machine and various other things were exhibited. And above the stage hung a big picture [with the title]: "Canterbury music in Harlingen" which combined the symbol of Canterbury, the Cathe- dral, with the symbol of Harlingen, which is the harbour. ("Harlingen" 1997, 7)[4]

Telling Tales about the Canterbury Sound

The Canterbury Sound is in many ways a unique phenomenon. First, it brings together a globally diffuse community of fans. Second, it involves these fans in an attempt to categorize and authenticate as true examples of the Canterbury Sound a series of musical liaisons which took place, in most instances, more than thirty years ago. Third, this revived interest in the Canterbury Sound has given rise to a series of attempts by local musicians and entrepreneurs to buy into the myth of the Canterbury Sound as an "authentic" aspect of Canterbury's recent local history with identifiable origins in the city and surrounding area.

The Canterbury Sound displays many of the properties associated with what are now commonly referred to as virtual scenes. Fans conduct most of their communication over the Internet, rarely, if ever, meeting face-to-face, save for chance meetings, for example, at record fairs or at music festivals. Moreover, it is clear that much of the substance of the current Canterbury Sound scene has been built up online. As studies that deal with particular genres of popular music illustrate (see, for example, Laing 1985 in relation to punk and Gillett 1991 in relation to rock 'n' roll), of central importance for fan discussions of any musical style is a sense of its historical development. In the case of the Canterbury Sound, such historical development is currently a major part of the online discussion engaged in by fans.

Moreover, given the relative absence of official journalistic material on the Canterbury bands, particularly since the early 1970s, fans have taken a more active role in defining the Canterbury Sound than is common with other scenes. Through applying their knowledge of Canterbury Sound bands, for example, particular musical liaisons between individual musicians, rare and "bootleg" recordings, or obscure bands that perhaps lasted little more than a few weeks, fans effectively contribute to the writing of the Canterbury Sound's history. Competing narratives thus assume the form of alternative "takes" of the Canterbury Sound, as fans read each other's online interpretations or "versions" of the scene and rewrite pieces of the latter to accommodate their "knowledge" of Canterbury music or their personal views on a particular group, album, or song.

Indeed, through their incorporation into the Web site, even recent developments and events are creatively recontextualized in ways that give them a sense of historical *belonging*. For example, in reviews of the Canterbury Sound Festival posted on the Web site, fans had written "Canterbury

Sound Festival 2000 ~~1970~~," deliberately crossing out the "1970" and replacing it with "2000." This simple romantic gesture could be seen as an attempt both to locate the Canterbury Sound Festival within the "rock" era, when Caravan and Soft Machine were established touring bands, and to suggest a thirty-year unbroken history of Canterbury Sound music. For those with no previous knowledge of the Canterbury Sound, this image on the Web site suggests an annual local festival with a history comparable to more established and well-known festivals, such as Glastonbury. Again, it could be argued, the exercise of such creative license on the part of fans is crucial to their collective sense of "sceneness," something which is all the more important given the lack of a physical basis for Canterbury Sound scene.

The Canterbury Sound then is very much a scene of "ideas" that both define and contextualize Canterbury music and provide a sense of its history and continuation. Indeed, in this respect the recently established Collapso Web site performs a crucial role, charting the development of Canterbury music through the 1980s and up to the present principally in terms of new projects by Canterbury musicians such as Richard Sinclair and reunion tours and albums by Caravan, Gong, and others. As we have seen, however, the collective investment of fans in the notion of a Canterbury Sound extends beyond discussions of music. Also integral to online communication between fans is an attempt to construct a narrative of Canterbury that involves representations of the city, its inhabitants, and the everyday culture in which they share.

As shown here, the collective narrativization of Canterbury engaged in by fans involves a rich collection of images and preconceptions about Canterbury and about England more generally. Canterbury is represented as a place where typical "English" traits of humor and irony combine with a sense of history to produce a particular English sensibility that articulates itself through music and text. It is tempting to speculate on the extent to which this image of Canterbury is inspired by Chaucer's *Canterbury Tales,* itself a fictionalized account of Canterbury in which the city is represented in a particular way to suit the narrative intentions of the author. As with the Canterbury Sound, albeit on a much grander scale, *The Canterbury Tales* has played a major role in perpetuating myths about Canterbury and has attracted tourists to the city through the ages.

Ultimately, however, the Canterbury Sound provides a compelling example of music's richness as a resource in the construction of narratives of the local (Bennett 2000). Chaney (1993) has suggested that urban life, rather than complying with a commonly acknowledged, "objective" social narrative, comprises a series of competing fictive interpretations of particular urban spaces. A similar point is made by Massey: "If it is now recognized that people have multiple identities, then the same point can be made in relation to places" (1993, 65). Although both Chaney and Massey are referring here to the way in which fictional narratives of space are constructed by those who occupy and experience such spaces on a day-to-day basis, it is possible, through the example of the Canterbury Sound, to see how such fictive interpretations of space and place are more widely engaged in. Through their online discussions, Canterbury Sound fans with no direct everyday experience of the city itself create rich narratives of space and place, tracing the origins of the Canterbury Sound, mapping its history and development in the context of local circumstances deemed unique to Canterbury. In effect, a new tale of Canterbury is being told, one that portrays the recent history of the city in musicalized terms through the creation of a narrative which embeds the Canterbury Sound in the everyday happenstance of Canterbury itself.

Notes

Some of the material presented in this paper is drawn from an article published in the journal *Media, Culture, and Society* (see Bennett 2002). The first chapter epigraph quotes Phil Howitt (1998), the editor of *Facelift: The Canterbury Scene and Beyond*. The second is drawn from Calyx: The Canterbury Web site, 5, accessed February 1999.

1. The term "lo fi" (short for "low fidelity") describes a form of DIY recording that was typically done by amateur musicians on cheap, domestic recording appliances, such as cassette or reel-to-reel tape machines, in home settings such as the bedroom or living room. Due to the conditions under which they were made, lo-fi recordings were generally of a much poorer quality than the hi-fi recordings made by professional musicians in professional studios. In recent times, however, the availability of cheap, high-quality digital home-recording units has resulted in an increasing turn to lo-fi recording by groups and musicians without recording contracts, who use such technology, in conjunction with independent distribution channels, to record, produce, and market their music.
2. The term "mains hum" refers to noise generated by current passing through electrically powered equipment.
3. English translation by Monika Schuster.
4. English translation by Monika Schuster.

References

Bennett, Andy. 2000. *Popular Music and Youth Culture: Music, Identity, and Place.* London: Macmillan.

————. 2002. "Music, Media, and Urban Mythscapes: A Study of the Canterbury Sound." *Media, Culture, and Society* 24, 1: 107–20.

Calyx: The Canterbury Web Site. www.alpes-net.fr/~bigbang/.

Canterbury Nachrichten, no. 32, March 1997.

Canterburied Sounds. Vols. 1 and 2. CD. Houghton le Spring, U.K.: Voiceprint.

Chaney, David. 1993. *Fictions of Collective Life: Public Drama in Late Modern Culture.* London: Routledge.

Cohen, Sara, and Kevin McManus. 1991. *Harmonious Relations: Popular Music in Family Life on Merseyside.* Liverpool: National Museums and Galleries on Merseyside.

Collapso: Canterbury Family Trees. www.macgraphic.co.jp/ich/index.html.

Finnegan, Ruth. 1989. *The Hidden Musicians: Music-Making in an English Town.* Cambridge: Cambridge University Press.

Frame, Pete. 1993. *Rock Family Trees.* London: Omnibus Press.

Frith, Simon. 1983. *Sound Effects: Youth, Leisure, and the Politics of Rock.* London: Constable.

Gillett, Charlie. 1983. *The Sound of the City: The Rise of Rock and Roll.* 2d. ed. London: Souvenir Press.

"Harlingen: Das Festival und die CDs." 1997. *Canterbury Nachrichten* 32: 6–15.

Hoskyns, Barney. 1999. "8 out of 10 Cats Prefer Whiskers." *Mojo,* March, 38–46.

Howitt, Phil. 1998. "Sleevenotes: *The Canterburied Sounds.*" Vol. 2. CD. Houghton le Spring, U.K.: Voiceprint.

Laing, Dave. 1985. *One Chord Wonders: Power and Meaning in Punk Rock.* Milton Keynes, U.K.: Open University Press.

Macan, Edward. 1997. *Rocking the Classics: English Progressive Rock and the Counterculture.* Oxford: Oxford University Press.

MacDonald, Ian. 1975. "Lookin' Back: The Soft Machine." *New Musical Express,* 25 January, 32.

Martin, Bill. 1998. *Listening to the Future: The Time of Progressive Rock.* Chicago: Open Court.

Massey, Doreen. 1993. "Power-Geometry and a Progressive Sense of Place." In Jon Bird, Barry Curtis, Tim Putnam, George Robertson, and Lisa Tickner, eds., *Mapping the Futures: Local Cultures, Global Change.* London: Routledge.

McManus, Kevin. 1994. *"Nashville of the North": Country Music in Liverpool.* Liverpool: Institute of Popular Music, University of Liverpool.

Mitchell, Malcolm. 1970. "Whither Goest the Soft Machine." *Kent Herald,* 19 August, 11.

Morely, David, and Kevin Robbins. 1989. "Spaces of Identity: Communications Technologies and the Reconfiguration of Europe." *Screen* 30, 4: 10–34.

"The Progress of the Soft Machine." 1967. *Kent Herald,* 10 May, 5.

Reimer, Bo. 1995. "The Media in Public and Private Spheres." In Johan Fornäs and Göran Bolin, eds., *Youth Culture in Late Modernity*. London: Sage.

Rootes, Andrew. 1997. *Images of Canterbury*. Derby: Breedon Books.

Smit, Jasper. 1997. "Caravan: Back on the Tracks." *Canterbury Nachrichten* 32: 24–25.

" 'Spirit of Caravan' Takes New Turning." 1992. *Kentish Gazette*, 16 April.

Stump, Paul. 1997. *The Music's All That Matters: A History of Progressive Rock*. London: Quartet Books.

Urry, John. 1990. *The Tourist Gaze: Leisure and Travel in Contemporary Societies*. London: Sage.

12

The Fanzine Discourse over Post-rock

James A. Hodgkinson

This chapter will show how the virtual scene of post-rock is discursively created in music fanzines. The term "post-rock" was coined as a catch-all for exploratory music said to be going "beyond rock" in the mid-1990s and is perhaps particularly interesting for an anthology of scene-based work, as it was said to involve a rejection of community or scene when in fact post-rock necessarily depended on certain components inherent in the idea of a scene, notably a shared discourse.[1] An especially prominent discourse about post-rock, for instance, was that this was music which went beyond language/description; but in this very method of attempting to highlight an individual piece of music's difference to everything else, fanzine writers who focused on post-rock were collectively distinguishing themselves from those writing about other types of music, and suggesting the commonality of their musical taste with other writers who utilized a similar discourse, thus creating the shared discourse they were claiming was impossible.

Post-rock music was created across the world but had clear local variations, especially in parts of the United Kingdom (for example, Bristol, Birmingham, rural Wales, Glasgow), Germany, Canada (Montreal), the U.S.A. (notably Chicago, Detroit, and cities in Texas), Japan, and New Zealand, often relating to the activities of a few individuals. Still, despite their geographical isolation from one another, the participants in one area might collaborate with others, play alongside them at certain festivals, and release records on particular labels (in this sense, post-rock was a translocal scene), though this tended to happen only in the later stages of post-rock, by which time the term had come to be associated with a quite specific variety of guitar-derived instrumental music that was altered or treated using effects or studio techniques and backed up by analogue synthesizers and nonconventional rock instruments (rather than meaning exploratory music that was different from anything which had gone before).

The concept of scene is approached then as one created through discourse, where shared use of language about music serves itself to construct a musical community (collaboration made possible by a sense of musical community only arising once the virtual scene of post-rock had been *discursively* constructed). The discourses of post-rock (including indescribability itself) established a common ground by which to describe the supposedly indescribable. The analysis used in this chapter is based on Thornton's classification of media scenes as discourse streams. This approach argues that the media actively construct subcultures. Thus, suggests Thornton: " [T]he music press construct subcultures as much as they document them. . . . They are central to the process of subcultural formation, integral to the way we 'create groups with words' (Bourdieu 1990, 139)" (1995, 117).

It is difficult to generalize about a typical audience for post-rock, due to the diversity of the music, but it is fair to say its members are typically older than the average pop concert attendee (from undergraduate age to late twenties), usually white and college educated, but with a fair proportion of women as well as men. Often these are people who have maintained their enthusiasm for new music from their teenage years but "outgrown" both mainstream and commercially successful alternative musics (such as nu-metal and Britpop), and perhaps more often than not, they are people actively engaged in the music world, either playing in bands or writing fanzines themselves. Fanzine writers thus make up a far higher percentage of the overall audience of post-rock than of most music scenes, and so zines can be seen as more representative of the audience view of this music.

The Scene without a Location

The term "post-rock" was coined by journalist Simon Reynolds. Reynolds explicates the term (after using it the first time in a review of an album by Bark Psychosis) in an article published in *The Wire* in May 1994 (issue 123). This was originally part of a series of articles by various authors on the theme "Music in the 21st Century." It is worth noting that the term has its basis in the idea of a future music, a sonic fiction or at least an ideal type of current practices that are imagined as developing into something more definite in the years to come. Reynolds begins his article: "Today's more adventurous rock groups are embracing technology and the avant garde to forge a new genre: Post-Rock" and later continues:

> What to call this zone? Some of its occupants, Seefeel for instance, could be dubbed 'Ambient'; others, Bark Psychosis and Papa Sprain, could be called 'art rock.' 'Avant rock' would just about suffice, but is too suggestive of jerky time signatures and a dearth of melodic loveliness, which isn't necessarily the case. Perhaps the only term open ended yet precise enough to cover all this activity is 'post-rock.' (1994a, 28)

In the first article to feature post-rock, under the headline "R U Ready to Post-rock?" Reynolds wrote:

> Imagine, if you will, a scene without a location, a community of misfits, a loose confederation of exiles and prophets without honour. Bands . . . who are gradually linking up into a network as they drift further out from the indie mainstream. . . . For want of anything snappier, I call this phenomenon 'post-rock' because, technically and ideologically, that's precisely what it is. (1994b, 42)

The type of music generalized as post-rock is extremely hard to define, precisely because it attempts to escape mere classification by genre and because it does not represent any subculture. Post-rock does not merely lack a cohesive scene, but is inherently opposed to the very idea of scenes, according to Reynolds. He contends that

> post-rock severs itself from rock 'n' roll ideas like 'youth,' 'community,' 'populism.' Post-rock bands have responded, consciously or unconsciously, to the industry-sponsored monolith of mediocrity that is 'alternative,' by reviving the old ideals of 'independent music' (back before indie labels became merely a farm-system for the majors). They have given up the idea of mass success or even indie cult-hood, and accepted the idea of being marginal forever. (Ibid.)

As one enthusiastic fanzine editor (Dave Howell, of *Obsessive Eye*) gushingly declares:

Opposed to the generalizations of any scene, this is rather music
as a myriad of sparkling possibilities. Each of these bands exist
autonomously, alone in its own vision. The affect of each is different: a
series of tiny revolutions . . . post-rockers find themselves Marginalised
[sic] precisely because they choose innovation rather than lining up in
the stale discourse of rock. (Howell, *Obsessive Eye,* no. 3 [1995]: 3)

Howell, who like Reynolds is influenced by poststructuralist theory,
wishes precisely to oppose the notion of a scene as applicable to post-rock
music. Yet there existed many local post-rock scenes, varying in the type
of music being produced in Birmingham, Glasgow, Bristol, Detroit, New
Zealand, Montreal, Japan, Paris, the Ruhr, Houston, Chicago, rural Wales,
Austin, and Cheltenham. These were or are centers of local activity that
often generated, or continue to generate, their own record labels and fanzines. This much is not controversial, but what may be is the generalizing
of such localized activity into the concept of a whole new genre, a translocal scene of music: post-rock. The amount of international collaboration
highlights the links between the scenes attached to specific places, but it is
accepted that there would be no understanding of a wider post-rock scene
without media intervention, or as one zinester sardonically describes it, the
process of "the music press hastily shuffling these groups into the ambiguous category "post-rock" for consumers' ease" (Paul Dickow, *Perfect Sound
Forever,* February 1996).

However, by linking certain contemporary bands together, by suggesting a common set of ancestors, by using the term "post-rock" itself, and by
suggesting what these acts have in common, Howells is clearly contributing to the formation of a scene, even as he is stating his opposition "to the
generalizations of any scene" (*Obsessive Eye,* no. 3 [1995]: 3). He is himself
creating a particular cultural phenomenon, much as he may be loathe to
admit it. His attempts to discuss the music(s) in question obviously go beyond "pure description" anyway, but the essential point is that even such a
descriptive approach itself would serve to actually construct that which it
claims it is merely trying to give a voice to. Thus the zine writers, as much
as the professional music journalists, create "the generalization of a scene,"
in Howells's words.

In the very short zine *What Is This Thing Called Post-rock?* the anonymous author(s) recognize the dangers of classifying by genre or scene, like
Howells, but argue that this also has a positive dimension: "Yet the general
grouping of similar bands within a 'scene label' is useful—allowing the

audience to discover new bands that operate within a broadly comparable musical environment." This is perhaps the other side of Dickow's rather disapproving comments about the "consumer's ease." It demonstrates one way of bringing something novel and uncommercial to a wider audience without needing to compromise on its substantive qualities. When alternative communities / local scenes link up in some way, they became more noticeable and powerful. In addition, the rise of post-rock allowed music fans to rediscover aspects of their musical heritage, from lost gems of the "krautrock" scene to early electronic experimentalists such as the Silver Apples from the late 1960s (and the number of re-releases that occurred in the late 1990s suggests that there was suddenly a good market for these former obscurities).[2] This was all the more important because there was nowhere to hear this new, different-sounding music in the mid-1990s, before bands began to record sound clips on Internet sites, other than on the John Peel show and Radio 3's *Mixing It* (at least in terms of nationwide coverage in the United Kingdom).

Fanzine Culture

Fanzines, or zines, are generally considered to provide an independent voice, distinct from the major publications on so-called alternative popular and contemporary music such as *Melody Maker* and *New Musical Express*. As they are often written either by fans or sometimes by the musicians themselves, they provide an excellent insight into how the music is constructed discursively by leading players in the scene who are not professional journalists.

The diversity in design and subject matter of zines is such that it is difficult to make effective generalizations about the character of what Duncombe calls these "scruffy, homemade little pamphlets. Little publications filled with rantings of high weirdness and exploding with chaotic design" (1997, 1). Duncombe provides a fuller definition of zines as "noncommercial, nonprofessional, small-circulation magazines which their creators produce, publish and distribute by themselves" (6). The combination of economic independence and the norms of the fanzine culture, which allow for the revelation of the intensely personal, provide for reading matter decidedly contrary to that of the mainstream publications, even when the subject matter is ostensibly the same. As Duncombe suggests, "[Z]ine writers insert the personal into almost any topic," and he contends that "viewing a topic through a highly subjective lens, then sharing those personal insights, experiences and feelings with others, making it clear that the teller is as important as what is being told," constitutes a "*convention* of zine writing" (26, 27, my italics).

Nevertheless, a key element in fanzine culture is the network of zines, emphasized at the end of almost every zine by the numerous reviews of other zines, the promotion of fanzine festivals, the frequent "Do It Yourself" articles urging readers to start their own zines, and the fact that the common currency in zine culture is the zine itself. A clear ideal of community and a respect for others engaged in the same process of creating and publishing exists, and there is a concomitant desire to spread the word about popular cultural tastes and activities that remain underrepresented, as well as to provide an individual perspective on more mainstream subjects.

Zine suspicion of mainstream culture is accurately portrayed more as a hostility to order and structure than as a movement with a more avowedly political purpose. The commitment to self-expression is absolute, for "saying whatever's on your mind, unbeholden to corporate sponsors, puritan censors, or professional standards of argument and design, being yourself and expressing your real thoughts and real feelings—these are what zinesters consider authentic" (Duncombe 1997, 33). This privileging of self-expression above all else can result in zines that are not only bizarrely packaged, unconstrained from traditional publishing practices, but indecipherable to the point of being literally unreadable. Thus "what matters is unfettered, authentic expression, not necessarily making sense" (ibid). Such a preference for meaninglessness can also be found in many of the song titles chosen by many post-rockers, who either try to avoid language altogether, or opt for surrealism or pure nonsense. Duncombe draws parallels with both the Dadaist and anarchist traditions, and contends that the nonsense created in many zines is the conclusion to the ideal of pure expression. He opines:

> By eschewing standards of language and logic the zine creator refuses to bend individual expression to any socially sanctified order. That this nonsense communicates nothing (except its own expressiveness) to the reader of the zine matters little, for the fact that no one except the creator can understand it means that something absolutely authentic has been created. (34)

Post-rock Zines

There is a vast variety of fanzines which, while having an eclectic musical coverage, feature post-rock strongly, and from the end of 1996 onward in particular, as post-rock and space rock have gotten their own sections in independent music stores, a number of publications which concentrate on post-rock solely. The diversity of post-rock is revealed in the number of fanzines which have a particular musical focus but still feature post-rock acts as if they were part of their own scenes. Thus the industrial and experimental music magazines *Music from the Empty Quarter* and *Electric Shock Treatment* cover much of the ground of early post-rock (1992–1996) in their writing, as the psychedelia zines *Wig Out!* and *Ptolemaic Terrascope* continue to do. The more professional-looking and intellectual zines tend to focus on the experimental branches of electronica as much as on post-rock (*Immerse, Sound Projector, Obsessive Eye, Space Age Bachelor, Lizard*), following the influential *The Wire.* The classic image of the fanzine—handwritten or photocopied, a cut-and-paste black-and-white format—is represented strongly too, with zines such as *Kill Everyone Now, Drunk on the Pope's Blood, Hedonist, Velvet Sheep,* and *Manana Baby* taking a strong interest in post-rock, as well as the more usual alternative indie/punk/"lo-fi" (meaning not having a high-fidelity sound, being rawly produced) guitar bands, who tend to be particularly overrepresented in zine culture generally, as Duncombe also found (1997, 118–19). Latterly, there have been zines devoted solely to post-rock, such as *Monitor, Comes with a Smile,* and *Easy Pieces.*

The variety of musical styles associated with fanzines that have a strong interest in at least some aspects of post-rock is matched by the variety of places of origin of the zines. The United States and United Kingdom are well represented, but so is Canada (*Space Age Bachelor* and *Frequency*), as well as France and Japan, which both have thriving post-rock scenes of their own. *Opprobrium* from New Zealand concentrates primarily on the free-noise scene of that country, providing an excellent insight into the local color of a part of post-rock on the other side of the world. Fanzines are primarily locally based and are often associated with the mini-scenes of post-rock, providing insight into how such mini-scenes conceptualize themselves.

It is also important to note who the fanzine writers are. Some fanzines are the work of ordinary fans, teenagers and students sufficiently enthused by what they have heard to feel they want to say something about it to the world at large. Others are by professional journalists. Some are written by people who later go on to become professional music journalists, supposedly a fairly common route into the profession. Thus Brian Duguid of *Electric Shock Treatment* now regularly writes for *The Wire*. The authors of *Sound Projector* are cartoonists, and those of *Immerse* are similarly in the art and design business. A number of the writers are, or become, very active players in the scene more generally, such as *Ptolemaic Terrascope's* Phil McMullen. Dave Howells, of *Obsessive Eye,* has DJed at a number of post-rock gigs. Many fanzine writers are in bands themselves, mostly total unknowns, as in the case of the *Cool your boots!* writer, and Donald Anderson of *Space Age Bachelor.* There are label-fanzine links, as between *Wig Out!* and the Ochre label, and between *Speeder* and the Kylie label. Some fanzines have their own labels, such as *Boa* (run by Gayle Harrison, half of Electroscope, a well respected post-rock act) and *Hedonist.* The best known post-rocker to be running a fanzine is perhaps Ryan Anderson of Füxa, who edits *Mass Transfer,* as well as contributing to *Monitor.* A number of other musicians write in the professional magazines—David Keenan (Telstar Ponies), Sasha Frere-Jones (Ui) and Paul Schutze all write for *The Wire,* and Keenan for *Melody Maker* too.

The virtual aspect of post-rock centers on its use of fanzines, newsletters, and the internet—which reflects the desire to circumvent the influence of the established mass-media, (the group Godspeed, for instance, refuses to be interviewed by commercial magazines, only by fanzines) and to reduce the barrier between audience and performer. Since my original research into post-rock fanzine culture was undertaken, a number of Net zines that cover musical ground emphasizing post-rock have proliferated, including *Strange Fruit* (which also puts on gigs and DJ events), the *Trout Cave,* and the *Green Dolphin.* In addition, some former print-only zines have converted entirely to the Net, such as *Opprobrium* and *The Lizard* (known as *Silencer* on the Web), and there are Internet versions of *The Satellite, Space Age Bachelor, Perfect Sound Forever,* and *Brainwashed.*

The Discourses of Post-rock:
Fanzine Discourses about Labradford

In considering what exactly led reviewers or interviewers to classify something as post-rock, I identified a number of discourses that served to construct post-rock (Hodgkinson 2000)—both in terms of the way the music was described by professional music journalists (especially in *New Musical*

Express, the now defunct *Melody Maker,* and *The Wire,* which gave most prominence to post-rock) and fanzine writers, and also in the words used by the bands and songwriters themselves, as shown through their lyric titles (it was only possible to do this because much post-rock is instrumental and thus titles correspond to the music in some way, rather than the lyrics). In these discourses, notions of insubstantiality and indescribability were particularly prominent, as was the usage of terms of reference akin to a public expression of a private language. Also prominent was the use of metaphors from outer space and space travel, and discourses of drug use, discourses that suggested going against nature, and those that stressed harmony with the natural world, scientific and technological discourses, and discourses of movement. By highlighting the use of such discursive forms across a spectrum of individual writers and publication types, it is possible to illustrate the discursive construction of the post-rock scene. This, in turn, necessitates a consideration of how the discourse of indescribability (the factors in common in protestations of the impossibility of representing the music to others in a way they can understand, that is, socially and rationally) is itself a socially established form of description created through a series of discourses of post-rock that have solidified over time and become socially agreed upon in the virtual scene.

The huge number both of post-rock releases and fanzine reviews makes it impossible in a short chapter to discuss the range of discourses across them all. Instead I shall use the example of reviews of the group Labradford's first two albums. Labradford has been chosen, as this band is considered particularly significant and influential in post-rock circles and hence is one of the most widely reviewed and interviewed of all post-rock acts.

One of the most prominent meta-discourses identified was the discourse of insubstantiality. Descriptions of the music of Labradford as being in some way insubstantial are legion across the range of publications examined. Thus, their "songs have a haunting, dreamlike quality" (*Music from the Empty Quarter,* no. 12, August–September 1995) and are "in a delicate, haunting fashion" (*Vox,* August 1995), and the word "haunting" is also considered particularly apposite by *Wig Out!* and *Obsessive Eye.* Tom Ridge in *The Wire* remarks: "What vocals there are to be heard are way back, . . . semi-recited whispers, adding to the music's dream-like qualities" (no. 136, June 1995), and Graeme from *Kill Everyone Now* concurs that "the introspective spoken vocals convey dreamlike moods" (issue 3). Lucy Cage in *The Lizard* finds the music so conducive to the dreaming state that she recounts an actual dream experienced while "dreaming to Labradford" (no. 5, summer 1995).

She then goes on to write that there is something in the music of the group "that suggest[s] the practically unhearable, the almost imperceptively [*sic*] faint sounds." Such music, Cage seems to suggest, is so lacking in solidity that it is almost not there at all, a point echoed in Simon Reynolds's *Melody Maker* review, as he comments on the "barely enunciated whisper, buried deep within the instrumental fog," and later remarks that one track reaches us "smudged and indistinct, like sunlight refracting under the sea surface" (24 June 1995). David Howell, whose approach in his *Obsessive Eye* fanzine is to eschew the conventional interview or review for an extended commentary about a band, argues that in the case of Labradford: "There's none of rock's flesh or drive here, none of its grinding insistence. Instead the form is thoroughly filleted and feminised, abstracted to a gorgeously gaseous shimmer and swirl, a pale glow" (*Obsessive Eye,* no. 4 [1996]: 38).

Some of the most frequent discourses used in the reviews of Labradford's music are not surprising, such as reference to the instruments used by the band members, background information about the group (their previous records, where they come from), and attempts to describe their sound by reference to other groups—all of these discourses are common in describing any contemporary music, not just post-rock. However, the frequency of usage of some discourses is quite revealing. The number of references to the act of reviewing itself, and to other reviewers, is abnormally high, which can be seen as testament to the difficulty of adequately doing justice to the music using conventional vocabulary. *Kill Everyone Now*'s Graeme begins his review with the observation,

> I don't think I can recall another band accruing such a diverse collection of reference points in reviews. Labradford have been compared to (deep breath) Main, Spaceman 3, Einsturzende Neubauten, Kraftwerk, Brian Eno, Stereolab, Flying Saucer Attack, Can, Neu, Telstar Ponies, My Bloody Valentine, Codeine, Suicide, The Aphex Twin and even Slowdive and The Cure. This means that either the critics don't know what they're talking about . . . or Labradford are doing something totally unlike anything else. (Issue 3)

A number of reviewers seem to be taking particular care to avoid simplistic classifications and comparisons with this music. Graeme ends his comments on Labradford with the parenthetical remark "and I didn't use the word "ambience" once." The editor of issue 12 of *Music from the Empty Quarter* similarly rails against what he calls the "a-word" (that is, "ambient") used as a catch-all generalization by latecomers to lump together the differing strands of experimental music he enjoys and considers to be part of his scene. The reviewer of Labradford's work in the same issue pointedly comments, "And sorry, but I fail to see the Stereolab comparisons," in an effort to refute ignorant claims of correspondence, and earlier worries that "it's probably a cliché but 'David Lynch soundtrack' frequently comes to mind." Indeed, it does seem to be something of a cliché, as the entry on Labradford in *The Rough Guide to Rock* (Penguin, 1996) utilizes the same reference point, as does *The Wire's* Tom Ridge, who contends the music is "similar to the soundtrack of David Lynch's *Eraserhead*" (no. 136, June 1995). This corresponds with my wider finding of a "filmic" discourse around some post-rock, and the fact that two of the reviewers of Labradford's work compare it to the soundtrack music of Ennio Morricone only serves to confirm this.

It is also noteworthy that there are a large number of personal references, that is, references to the reviewers themselves. Lucy Cage's writing about her dream has already been mentioned, but the personal pronoun is used recurrently through a number of reviews, as we have seen already in the reviews taken from *Music from the Empty Quarter* and *Kill Everyone Now.* Taken in conjunction with the desire to avoid cliché and the difficulty of pinpointing adequate points of comparison, this can be seen as evidence of the problematic nature of simply getting on with the job of describing the music itself. That the reviewers feel a need to simultaneously stress the subjective (how they themselves relate to the music) and the collective (how others have described the music, either as possible allies or simply to stress the difficulty of such a procedure in this case) reveals they perceive such a task as far from straightforward. This clearly relates to the emphasis in zine writing on the personal and subjective, and the idea of a community of zinesters linked by a fanzine network.

The use in reviews of title tracks as some kind of guide to the nature of the music, as an attempt to find an appropriate set of linguistic descriptions, similarly suggests a feeling that one is rather groping in the dark to find the right words to suit the sounds in question. Hence the comment "That two tracks have the word 'listening' in the title also conveys some of Labradford's static yet skyward reaching intent" (*Kill Everyone Now,* issue 3) comes across as a perhaps flawed attempt to justify a claim about the music by rooting it in the less ambiguous realm (compared to music, and especially this apparently so insubstantial brand of music) of language. The reviewer in *Speeder* concludes his comments: "There is no stable reference;

this floats, 'Balanced on its Flame' [sic], and the effect is to create an ambient masterpiece" (issue 2). He not only includes one song title explicitly, though inaccurately, but also uses it as a prime way of summing the album up by referring to its actual title, namely *A Stable Reference*. The difficulty of describing new music is illustrated particularly effectively on the occasions when the comments of reviewers seem little more than a listing of the song titles of an album.

Continuing the detailed examination of reviews of Labradford, one finds that words are on occasion used to evoke the music, as opposed to merely describing it. Thus the music is said to be "*tiptoeing* into the realms of Morricone's westerns" (*Vox*, August 1995, my emphasis) and contended to be a "*weave* of soft vocals and resonating strings" (*Lizard*, no. 5, summer 1995; my emphasis). Perhaps in a similar vein, many writers use an array of rather fanciful phrasing. So they talk of "[t]he genesis of a unique sound" (*Kill Everyone Now*, issue 3), rather than more simply "where it all began." Lucy Cage argues that

> there's something in the timbre of the notes, their extenuated vibrations, that suggest the practically unhearable, the almost imperceptively [sic] faint sounds of micro-harmonics shimmering skywards. The beauty lies in the cross-texturing of guitars and keyboards, the stately progressions towards and through each other's harmonies, like aural aerial acrobatics. (*Lizard*, no. 5, summer 1995)

Meanwhile Simon Reynolds in *Melody Maker* (24 June 1995) compares one track to "the subcutaneous threnody of inner-body music."[3] Arguably, this use of impressive or pretentious vocabulary reflects or attempts to suggest a quality about the music that may imply its difference from mainstream popular music.

In post-rock reviews there is much use of what I have termed the "one thing and its opposite" language device (Hodgkinson 2000). This is evidenced in a number of reviews of Labradford's work, as in "they somehow manage to sound simultaneously dense, sombre and minimal" and indeed are "at once desolate and uplifting" (*Music from the Empty Quarter*, issue 12 [August/September 1995], 94); are "both ice-cold and golden-warm" (*Speeder*, issue 2); and have a "static yet skyward reaching intent" (*Kill Everyone Now*, issue 3, 1995–96). And one *Wire* reviewer (no. 126, August 1994) writes: "The surrounding sound hovers between an exhilarating high and a low end swamp, populated by indecipherable drones. This unresolved tension proves highly attractive, straddling both melody and noise on 'Everlast,' and capturing calm and turbulence on 'Splash Down' "—an entire series of contrasts that nonetheless operates to perform as a whole. Reynolds is explicit in his description of Labradford's music as a "unique, paradoxical sound (cloistered expanse, thunderous hush)" (*Melody Maker*, 24 June 1995). In my opinion, this language device is used by the writers as a way of suggesting the indescribability of the music: It is simultaneously one thing and the precise opposite of that thing. How, then, can one provide "a stable reference" (ironically itself the title of Labradford's second album) to adequately sum it up?

Local References

Though post-rock is a scene that is discursively generated and perpetuated via music media, rather than one that encompasses a specific location, the paradoxical way discourse can reference geographical specificities (for example, a "Chicago style," or mention that a band is from Austin, Texas, or from the South Island of New Zealand as part of an author's attempt to indicate something of the aural qualities of the tracks being discussed) is one of the most commonly used discourses in the attempt to conjure up an idea of how something sounds to its readership. In so doing, it can be argued that in this most nonsocial or virtual of music scenes, the concept of the *local* as well as a *shared* discourse of indescribability and insubstantiality remains paramount.

A certain category of discourse used about post-rock highlights the continued importance of place of origin of musicians as a method of partially describing their sound. Articles have tried to identify specific local post-rock scenes, with their own musical approaches, in Texas (with subscenes in Denton and Houston), New York, Chicago, Canada, France, the South Island of New Zealand, Glasgow, Birmingham, Bristol, and even a small town in Germany named Wellheim. Place of origin is often supposed to be directly related to the type of music an artist makes, even if concrete proof to support this claim is scarce. While Roy Montgomery has released an album entitled *Scenes from the South Island* to evoke the part of New Zealand he originates from, he is the exception, not the rule. In an interview with Scenic, whose *Incident at Cima* album was to some extent inspired by the Mojave Desert, multi-instrumentalist Bruce Licher remarks: "People have written to us from the green hills of Kentucky to Manhattan, all saying that we've managed to capture a sense of their surroundings" (*Melody*

Maker, 14 September 1996, 14). This pleases him, and he is quoted as saying that "the fact that people have reinterpreted it for themselves transcends what it's all about."

The place of origin of a group may be significant for appreciating what musical sounds it creates, but for a reason wholly different from the idea that the environment artists grow up in will impinge on their work. Non-mainstream music, including all that could be classified as post-rock, is frequently released on small-scale independent labels run by one individual or a group of friends with a specific aim in mind, and often based in a restricted geographical area (due to financial constraints). Such labels frequently have a particular musical identity, and in such instances for a journalist to refer to the label of a particular release may be highly implicative of what the music being described will sound like. Labels which are concentrated in certain areas, run by friends whose own releases may in certain cases comprise the entire roster, give the lie to—while apparently supporting—the view that geography and musical sound are related. Some of the more significant locally based labels include Germany's Kitty Yo-Kollaps-Payola axis, New Zealand's Corpus Hermeticum (with its clearly defined free-noise philosophy), and Chicago's Thrill Jockey/City Slang. As the labels become more financially viable, they are able to expand to include more overseas artists, as has been done by the English-based Earworm and Enraptured labels, the U.S. label Kranky, and the band Stereolab's own Duophonic, which has released the latest album by Wellheim-based the Notwist. Just as certain labels are viewed as post-rock, others are perceived as primarily concerned with other varieties of music. An example of such a label is the "intelligent techno" label Warp, based in Sheffield, U.K., which now plays host to Birmingham post-rockers Broadcast and Plone. These last two bands now find themselves increasingly reviewed in the "dance" sections of the music magazines, without a discernible change in their sound or approach to music.

The significance of the local context confirms the findings of Bennett (1995, 2000) of important diversity between hip-hop as constituted in different cities, but also within a given city—scenes within a scene, in a sense. Thus locality must be recognized as important, but a definite relationship between musical style and a given location certainly cannot be assumed.

Conclusion

"Post-rock" originally functioned primarily as a musical attitude, a wish to go beyond the limitations of rock, and was a term intended to generalize little more than that. That it *now* functions as something quite musically specific appears an extraordinary evolution, as the term has come to stand for precisely what it was earmarked to oppose. Nevertheless, it is precisely such a fate that also befell psychedelia, punk, indie, and industrial music. Even the term "alternative" has been used to market a particular type of music, with its own definite aural identity, and artists have been known to reject the terms "avant-garde" and "experimental" because they feel such categories are too suggestive of a certain sound that they do not wish to be identified with. However, the lack of an associated subculture with post-rock makes it a particularly significant case, in terms of a sociology of music scenes. Post-rock is, at most, a postmodern subculture or "post-subculture" in the sense indicated by Muggleton (1997), privileging ephemerality, fragmentation, and incoherence, and shaped by media representations. Without the discourses of post-rock, the phenomenon could not truly be said to exist; it would seem to have no basis in social structure, in wider social change, at all (which punk and psychedelia certainly have been claimed to have). The discourses that surrounded it in fact constructed it. Those self-same discourses, as they solidified, then served to delimit that which they created, preventing it from fulfilling its original protocol. Post-rock, it may be observed, was truly hoisted by its own petard—a "music of the future" which came to occupy a significant, and very specific, section of the present.

Notes

1. There is no published book on post-rock. However, Toop 1995 on the history of "ambient," Thompson 1994 on space rock, Cope 1996 on krautrock, DeRogatis 1996 (and Melechi 1997 and Reynolds and Press 1995, section 2) on the development of psychedelia, and, in particular, Reynolds 1990 on the more experimental aspects of the indie scene in the late 1980s, provide some insight into the musical background to post-rock.
2. A 1970s scene of German experimental rock groups.
3. "Subcutaneous threnody" translates as "an ode or song of lamentation from under the skin."

References

Beezer, Anne. 1992. "Dick Hebdige, Subculture: The Meaning of Style." In Martin Barker and Anne Beezer, eds., *Reading into Cultural Studies*. London: Routledge.

Bennett, Andy. 1995. "Hip-hop am Main: The Localisation of Rap Music and Hip Hop Culture." Paper presented at "Contested Cities," the Sociological Association Annual Conference, University of Leicester, U.K., 10–13 April.

————. 2000. *Popular Music and Youth Culture: Music, Identity, and Place*. Basingstoke, U.K.: Macmillan.

Bourdieu, Pierre. 1984. *Distinction: A Social Critique of the Judgement of Taste*, trans. R. Nice. London: Routledge and Kegan Paul.

————. 1990. *In Other Words: Essays towards a Reflexive Sociology*. Cambridge: Polity Press.

Cope, Julian. 1996. *Krautrocksampler*. London: Head Heritage, KAK.

DeRogatis, Jim. 1996. *Kaleidoscope Eyes: Psychedelic Rock from the '60s to the '90s*. Secaucus, N.J.: Citadel Underground.

Dickow, Paul, W. 1996. "Can: Godparents of Current Crop of 'Indie' Avant-garde?" *Perfect Sound Forever*, February *(www.furious.com/perfect/can.html)*.

Duncombe, Stephan. 1997. *Notes from Underground: Zines and the Politics of Alternative Culture*. London: Verso.

Hall, Stuart, and Tony Jefferson, eds. 1976. *Resistance through Rituals: Youth Subcultures in Post-War Britain*. London: Hutchinson.

Hebdige, Dick. 1979. *Subculture: The Meaning of Style*. London: Routledge.

————. 1988. *Hiding in the Light: On Images and Things*. London: Routledge.

Hodgkinson, James. 1995. "Consumed!" M.Sc. dissertation, University of Surrey, U.K.

————. 2000. "An Unstable Reference." Ph.D. thesis, University of Surrey, U.K.

Laing, Dave. 1985. *One Chord Wonders: Power and Meaning in Punk Rock*. Milton Keynes, U.K.: Open University Press.

Melechi, Antonio, ed. 1997. *Psychedelia Britannica*. London: Turnaround.

Muggleton, David. 1997. "The Post-Subculturalist." In Steve Redhead, Derek Wynne, and Justin O'Connor, eds., *The Club Cultures Reader: Readings in Popular Cultural Studies*. Oxford: Blackwell.

Redhead, Steve. 1990. *The End of the Century Party*. Manchester, U.K.: Manchester University Press.

Redhead, Steve, Derek Wynne, and Justin O'Connor, eds. 1997. *The Club Cultures Reader: Readings in Popular Cultural Studies*. Oxford: Blackwell.

Reynolds, Simon. 1990. *Blissed Out*. London: Serpent's Tail.

————. 1994a. "Music in the 21st Century, Part 4: Main, Seefeel, Disco Inferno." *The Wire* 124: 28.

————. 1994b. "R U Ready to Post-rock?" *Melody Maker*, 23 July, 42–43.

Reynolds, Simon, and Joy Press. 1995. *The Sex Revolts*. London: Serpent's Tail.

Thompson, Dave. 1994. *Space Daze: The History and Mystery of Electronic Ambient Space Rock.* Los Angeles: Cleopatra.

Thornton, Sarah. 1995. *Club Cultures: Music, Media, and Subcultural Capital.* Cambridge: Polity Press.

Toop, David. 1995. *Ocean of Sound—Aether Talk, Ambient Sound, and Imaginary Worlds.* London: Serpent's Tail.

"Post-rock" Discography / Recommended Listening

As post-rock is so diverse, it is difficult to recommend representative albums, but compilations by post-rock labels are one route in.

Post-rock Label Compilation Albums

A Rocket Girl Compilation. 2001. Rocket Girl.
Freischwimmer. 2000. Kitty-Yo.
Infrasonic Waves. 1999. Ochre.
Monsters, Robots, and Bugmen. 1996. Virgin.
Kranky Kompilation. 1998. Kranky.
The Tell-Tale Signs of Earworm. 1999. Earworm.
Will our Children Thank Us? 1999. Foundry.

Individual Artist's Albums

Bark Psychosis. 1997. *Game Over.* Compilation (1989–1994). Third Stone.
Broadcast. 2000. *The Noise Made by People.* Warp.
Dadamah. 1993. *This is Not a Dream.* Compilation (Majora, 1992). Kranky.
Disco Inferno. 1994. *D.I. Go Pop.* Rough Trade.
Godspeed You Black Emperor! 1998. *F# A#.* Reissue (Constellation, 1997). Kranky.
Labradford. 1996. *A Stable Reference.* Kranky.
Laika. 1994. *Silver Apples of the Moon.* Too Pure.
Main. 1992. *Hydra-Calm.* Compilation (1991–1992). Beggars Banquet.
Olivia Tremor Control. 1996. *Dusk at Cubist Castle.* Flydaddy.
Piano Magic. 1999. *Low Birth Weight.* Rocket Girl.
———. 2001. *Seasonally Affective: A Piano Magic Retrospective, 1996–2000.* Rocket Girl.
Slint. 1991. *Spiderland.* Touch and Go.
Techno Animal. 1995. *Re-Entry.* Virgin.
Tortoise. 1996. *Millions Now Living Will Never Die.* City Slang.

13

Kate Bush: Teen Pop and Older Female Fans

Laura Vroomen

> I'm not a member of any Kate Bush fan clubs—why would I
> be? So I can get my free "signed" photo and badge?? No thanks.
> Same goes for email discussions about the relative merits of
> Never Forever [sic]. Can't be arsed, frankly. . . . I'm not really
> interested in fan behavior, because. . . . Well, why would I be?
> Without sounding too snotty, isn't it more teenage girls who get
> together and talk about how gorgeous Ronan is?
> —Robin

> You can't really categorize/pigeonhole a Kate Bush fan. They
> don't look a certain way, i.e., a punk would look "punk."
> —Barbara

This chapter offers a case study of the fan practices of a group of mature, largely middle class and female Kate Bush fans.[1] It is part of a larger study that aims to challenge essentialist understandings of popular-music fandom and scenes through a consideration of a group of fans who, mainly because of their gender, age, and class position, are seldom considered legitimate objects of study but who can nevertheless be seen to constitute a scene on the basis of their common feelings and shared knowledge. It demonstrates that in spite of a limited involvement in, for instance, club or concert-based activities, older female fans continue to invest strongly in popular music and that, moreover, these investments are a complex mixture of resistance and conformity to social norms.

The choice of case study was informed both by my own interest in Kate Bush and by her achievements in an industry that has long been male dominated. Kate Bush (b. 1958) has been a commercially and critically successful performer since the late 1970s and has challenged certain stereotypical conceptions of the female performer by writing and often producing her own material and by presenting a complex performance of femininity that can be read as both inviting and rejecting the male gaze. She first emerged on the music scene in 1978 when, at the age of nineteen, her debut single, "Wuthering Heights," became the first single written and performed by a British woman to reach the top of the U.K. charts. Accompanied by a video that showcased her distinctive visual style—a combination of dance and mime—it was seen as a novelty hit at the time. However, an equally successful album, *The Kick Inside* (1978), soon followed, as did many hit singles and albums such as "The Man with the Child in His Eyes" (1978), "Babooshka" (1980), "Running up That Hill" (1985), *Never for Ever* (1980), and *Hounds of Love* (1985) (see also Vermorel 1983; Bolton 1987; Cann and Mayes 1988; and Juby 1988).

Methods and Methodology

In this chapter I focus on three respondents whose experiences were representative of the wide range of fan expressions that emerged in the research in order to gain a deeper insight into their individual and shared fandom. The analysis, however, is part of a larger study that draws on data from forty-five questionnaires and sixteen semi-structured interviews (conducted by e-mail and face-to-face) with self-selected and self-identified Kate Bush fans.[2] This questionnaire and interview material was complemented by analysis of those Kate Bush lyrics and images that best illustrate the fans' views and that can be seen as her most iconic ones.

My choice of Kate Bush was potentially problematic because she has not released any new albums since *The Red Shoes* in 1993, and, although she continues to pick up new fans, the absence of new material to listen to and discuss exasperates some and places pressure on the continuation of the scene. Besides, Kate Bush, although popular, is perhaps not the kind of "hip" or "transgressive" performer that popular-music scholars are often most interested in.[3] But perhaps most importantly, Kate Bush has not toured since her 1979 European tour, and there is no "Kate Bush field" to which I could gain easy access, and this made it difficult to undertake "ethnographic research" in the anthropological sense of the term. Fan clubs, of course, do potentially offer such a field and I had hoped to advertise in the fanzine published by the United Kingdom's largest Kate Bush fan club, Homeground. However, citing bad experiences with journalists and "serious" researchers in the past, its organizers were distrustful of my motives and declined to place my advertisement asking for fans to complete my questionnaire. Thus, forced to find alternative means to gain access to fans, I advertised instead in two British music magazines (*Q* and *Mojo*), on an e-mail discussion list (Love-Hounds), and on a German Web site dedicated to Kate Bush (Irgendwo in der Tiefe), all of which can be seen as potential alternative fields.[4] I also personally requested a few fans I met during the course of the research to participate. The women who participated in the research, most of whom had first become fans between the late 1970s and mid-1980s, constituted a relatively homogeneous group of women who were largely in their late twenties, thirties, and early forties, white, middle and lower-middle class, and heterosexual. Geographically, however, they were much more varied, hailing not only from the United Kingdom, but also from continental Europe, North America, Australia, and Asia.

The fan club's rejection had an unforeseen but fortunate effect on the research in that it allowed me to look at fans who were markedly different from those usually privileged by studies of subcultures and scenes or feminist studies of fandom. I gained access to women who, instead of being heavily involved in a fan community, were for the most part relatively isolated fans who had few opportunities—and often little inclination—to gather or to display their fandom publicly. They were rather invisible and did not constitute a scene as it is usually understood. A look at these fans, then, defamiliarizes our notion of "scene" as highly visible and locally specific and raises questions about, for instance, the constraints experienced by women who have family and career commitments and the interaction between older age and gender when women invest in a performer. The fact that these women were keen to take part in the research and to share their experiences with me—encouraged by our mutual recognition as fans—suggests the possible existence of a scene, albeit a more loosely defined one based on shared feelings and knowledge. These women also enabled me to see "resistance" as located not in class discontent or generational rebellion, but rather in their articulation of popular music and maturity, their refusal to be included in the abject category of the "eroticized" female fan, and their feminist beliefs. Finally, the research also pointed to the ways in which Internet technologies may allow socially and geographically dispersed fans to create and maintain a virtual scene.

Research Data

In the remainder of this chapter I want to look more closely at the experiences of Barbara and Liz, with whom I conducted e-mail interviews, and of Jasmine, whom I met for a face-to-face interview. Occasionally I shall refer to the responses of some other fans as well. My primary focus here will be on the ways in which the women's roles as mothers, partners, or both affected their interaction with other fans, their use of fan media (in particular their experience of the Love-Hounds discussion list), and the empowerment they derived from their fandom.

Liz was an American woman in her early forties who worked as a university counselor and lived with her husband, two-year-old son, and two teenage stepchildren. Liz was aware that while Kate Bush is a household name for many in the United Kingdom (and Western Europe), she remains perhaps more of a cult figure in the United States (see also Kruse 1990). In the following exchange I tried to find out more about how Liz saw herself and other fans within this context.

> Laura: Do you think that Kate's fans in the U.S. have something in
>   common besides their interest in Kate?
> Liz: I don't know, to tell you the truth. I can't answer that because, besides
>   me, I know NO OTHER Kate fans. I mean that seriously. My brother
>   bought a couple albums because he heard me play them and my one
>   roommate in college bought *The Dreaming* for the same reasons.
>   My husband is not a fan, though he will listen if I am playing her
>   music—though as background noise, if you know what I mean. So
>   . . . I really cannot answer this question! No data other than my own!

I picked up on this in our subsequent e-mail conversation.

> Laura: You mentioned that you don't know any other Kate fans. Does
>   that bother you at all? Would you prefer to know other Kate fans?
> Liz: I think I would like to know other Kate fans, but I am so used to
>   being the island that I don't really think about it that much anymore.
>   I have sort of been an oddball when it comes to taste & have always
>   liked artists—musicians or actors or authors—that most of my

friends never heard of or were not interested in, so not knowing
other Kate fans is a non-issue really.

Liz, who had responded to my message to the Love-Hounds mailing list,
did not acknowledge the list as a place for fans to convene or as a kind
of "support group" for isolated fans. Indicating that she had subscribed to
the list only for information about new releases, she did not feel any connection to other fans online nor did she attempt to form any relationships
with them. Liz suggested that time played a significant role in this; she
and her friends, who were all in their thirties and forties, had relatively
little time to invest in popular music, hence little time to "chat" online to
other fans.

Over and above such time constraints, many of the fans who were in
their thirties and forties also felt a certain ambivalence about their popular-
music investments and questioned what is "right and proper" to listen to
at a particular age. The following quote from Karen, a Kate Bush fan who
also—unusually—liked the Spice Girls, illustrates this dilemma well. Karen
was around forty at the time of the interview and lived with her partner
(who shared her enthusiasm for Kate Bush) and thirteen-year-old son.

> I find myself in regular arguments with people (only adults) about
> the talents of the Spice Girls and the appropriateness of someone my
> age liking them. I accuse them of being dull and trapped in the adult
> mentality of sticking with what's safe and known to be OK within the
> social circle. I think liking the Spice Girls is probably extreme in terms of
> age difference.

Equating an "adult mentality" with corroboration with dominant culture, Karen appeared to confirm the association of popular music with
youth (as a style or spirit if not a physical age), because she is either unwilling or unable to articulate a link between popular music and adult
sensibilities. Others, however, did articulate such a link, seeing Kate Bush's
work—in particular her more recent releases such as *The Sensual World*
(1989) and *The Red Shoes* (1993)—as particularly meaningful expressions
of adult experiences and emotions, including relationships with long-term
partners and the death of parents. For instance, Liz, who became a fan
when she was in her early twenties, appreciated the later albums because
they are "lyrically refined" and express "mature concerns" and wrote that
"something like 'You're the Only One I Want' [off *The Red Shoes*] with its

Procol Harum organ track & lyrical allusions and topic about a long term relationship's break-up—that is a 30's/40's age group song!"

Involvement in music-based subcultures and scenes has often been characterized as an attempt to delay adult responsibilities, as a way of resisting "social ageing" (see Thornton 1995; Bourdieu 1998). In other words, it is thought that only when young people let go of their "extreme" involvement in music and style and take up their destined social roles that they can become proper adults. Consequently, the older fan either is seen to remain within his or her scene to live an extended "youth" or is dismissed as a reluctant exile who is not interesting as a subject for study. Weinstein, for instance, dismisses the older heavy-metal fans in her study as "wistful emigrants" from the subculture they were once a part of (1990, 111). Despite evidence of continuing investment in the music, they are ignored because their practices are less visible and unspectacular. This opposition between participation in a scene and social aging suggests, on the one hand, that such participation is temporary and a mark of immaturity, and, on the other hand, that aging is a process of increasing incorporation into dominant culture. Consequently, there is an assumption that intense popular-music investments cannot be carried over into adult life, and that contradictory identifications and practices cannot be sustained.

On the evidence of what they say, my respondents (with the possible exception of Karen) do not offer any strong evidence of resistance either against growing up or against dominant social norms. Their investment in Kate Bush entails neither a pessimistic resignation nor any overoptimistic sense that they are challenging the world and the aging process. Instead, the women use the resources offered by their Kate Bush fandom—such as the lyrics that speak of (adult) women's experiences—to function in everyday life. Their fandom, then, helps enable maturity, in the sense that it enables the respondents to maintain a sense of self-worth and strength, which in turn enables them to deal with the demands of work and intimate relationships. Kate Bush provides a soundtrack to the respondents' lives, but one which leads neither to spectacular resistance nor necessarily to what Karen called "being dull and trapped." Indeed, their contradictory identifications and practices—suggested by, for instance, the women's feminist beliefs on the one hand and their relatively conventional roles within the family on the other—may in fact enable investment in popular music to be sustained in adult life. The scene, then, is characterized less by highly visible and extraordinary displays and more by relatively mundane expressions of fandom that agree with the women's lifestyles.

Liz's fandom played a key role in her life, even if she had little time to spend on music. Indeed, her musical tastes appeared central in establishing her position within the household.

> Laura: How old are your children? What kind of music do they listen to? Do you ever listen or talk about music with them?
>
> Liz: I have two stepchildren for whom I have been the only "Mom" for 10 years—they are a 20 year old girl and a 16 year old boy. I also have a 2 year old son with my husband. My step-daughter definitely benefited from living with me—my husband's tastes run Top 40 with a strange affinity for the Moody Blues! And the kids' biological mother likes country & western (which I hate). So . . . my step daughter came to me loving New Kids On the Block (sort of a Hanson pre-cursor). I like many things, all of which I deem "quality." I know trivia about artists and songs from long ago, like Carole King, Gerry Goffin, etc in the Brill Building in the early 60s just churning out hit after hit. She liked that kind of stuff from me and asked questions and stuff. We talk a lot about artists & intent and interpretation. The result: she has CDs of everyone from the Chieftains to Aretha Franklin to the Kinks (she loves *Preservation Act 2*). An openness to lots of different music and a somewhat discriminating ear are my gifts to her. My step-son, on the other hand, likes everything that the majority of other kids his age at school seem to like. And he can tell you that—"I dunno why I like it—everybody has this CD." Still he shows promise—left alone over the summer, he has started picking out CDs from my collection and seems to be addicted to Patti Smith's *Gone Again* at the moment.

By passing her Kate Bush fandom and other music tastes on to her children, Liz not only secures the ongoing existence of the scene, she also establishes a relationship with her stepchildren and, significantly, distinguishes herself from their biological mother. She carved out a role as a kind of musical "educator" within her family, or as Bourdieu (1996) would argue, she takes on a role typically performed by women, namely the display and transmission, and thereby preservation, of family cultural capital. In this respect, Liz conformed to social expectations, while by defying the youth focus of popular music she simultaneously resisted them.

The somewhat conservative quality of Liz's practices finds further expression in what many perceived to be Kate Bush's "tasteful" femininity. Many respondents disliked what they considered to be overtly sexual performances from artists such as Madonna, the Spice Girls, and Tina Turner. In her questionnaire Liz explained why she sees Kate Bush as a role model for women: "She never sets herself up as some sort of sex object (à la Madonna), but presents herself as intelligent, thoughtful—yet she is still attractive and feminine." Barbara wrote in her questionnaire that Kate Bush "is not a 'pop tart' like the Spice Girls! She doesn't come across as a sex object."[5] This rejection of the more overtly sexual in favor of the more "intellectual" was also evident in the women's attempts to distinguish themselves from other fans—particularly from the stereotypical male fan with his prurient gaze and from the stereotypical teenage girl fan who, as suggested by Robin's quote at the start of this chapter, was seen as liking (male) performers for the "wrong" (i.e., sexual) reasons and was associated with mindless, hysterical crowds.

It is difficult not to succumb to the temptation to find signs of resistant or progressive readings, especially when looking at women's practices in a largely male-dominated genre. In my case, when embarking on the research, I was particularly keen to "rehabilitate" the oft-disparaged female fan and to identify any feminist allegiances in my respondents; Kate Bush's achievements, I thought, would lend themselves particularly well to such a reading. However, if my respondents' practices were to some degree informed by feminist ideas, this was less straightforward than I had anticipated, and at times I was taken aback by what I perceived to be "unfeminist" practices. While the women's practices challenged both the idea that mature women are indifferent to popular music and the association of women fans with passivity or bad taste, the latter was accompanied by a rearticulation of precisely those qualities in others. Thus, the respondents did not challenge the derogation of the female fan, but rather their own inclusion within that abject category.

However, as illustrated by the following exchange with Barbara, who was in her early thirties at the time of the interview and married, these more reactionary views were often coarticulated with feminist beliefs. Originally from the United Kingdom, Barbara and her husband had relocated to the United States, where she was now a student and financially dependent on her husband. Since she identified as a feminist ("feminism = female empowerment") and greatly valued women's independence, this was a cause of frustration. In many of our exchanges, Barbara referred to Kate Bush's independence and expressed her appreciation of those lyrics that speak of women's power and autonomy. In her questionnaire she wrote:

I get the feeling that the lyrics [of "The Sensual World"] are about the sexual power that women have over men. It's so rare to hear about sexuality from a woman's point of view. You always hear about male sexuality in the form of porn, media, etc. ("how to satisfy your man" articles in magazines) so it is refreshing to hear about female sexuality in Kate's lyrics.

In our interview, I followed up on this issue:

Laura: The fact that Kate sings about female experiences seems very important to you and you expressed disappointment at hearing that she's not a feminist. Could you elaborate on this?

Barbara: My impression of Kate is that she is "pro-female," not anti-feminist. There aren't many female songwriters that have the same independence/autonomy that Kate has. She produces her own albums, has her own recording studio, is quite wealthy and has the clout to attract "names" to help with recording.

This may be the 90s but there are still a lot of women who are dependent on a man's support to get somewhere, me included. I am financially dependent on my husband, which I am not happy about but I have to deal with it.

This financial dependence, however, did not prevent Barbara from investing in Kate Bush, both emotionally and financially (she was an avid collector). Paradoxically, her husband's money enabled her to make these investments in an artist who inspired her to strive for independence.

However, admiration for Kate Bush's autonomy and power did not always translate into powerful positions. Jasmine was in her late twenties at the time of the interview, of French/North African parentage, and resident in the United Kingdom. She worked as a research assistant and part-time lecturer and was married without children. Inspired by Kate Bush, Jasmine had become involved in contemporary dance during her teens and had worked as a semi-professional dancer for some time. Her fandom, then, had had a considerable enabling effect that appears to be canceled out in the following exchange during our interview on 27 October 1998.

Laura: Did you try and persuade your partner to like Kate Bush?

Jasmine: Yeah, I have often . . . he liked, he quite likes Kate Bush, he likes some things, but he is . . . no way is he even vaguely a fan and he would never . . . he didn't own anything by Kate Bush before he met me. No, I don't try and convince him, but we do have a few arguments actually over who gets to play their own music. . . .

The thing actually is that in a way he does win a lot, because I don't actually like to listen to it with him around. It doesn't work, it's not something I . . . especially Kate Bush, I mean . . . Kate Bush I don't actually play with him around very much, because . . . I don't know. I need to be on my own, and I need to be sort of thinking, you know, it makes me kind of dream, and I can't do that with someone in the room. At all! . . .

It's an excuse for my space and this is my time, my space, and I need, as a teenager I needed that a lot, my own space where you, I don't know what you do, but . . . you know, that thing. With music, you can do a lot with music, and I still—I don't need that very much now, I don't do it very often, but Kate, if I do it it's with Kate Bush. Kate Bush is what I'll put on. If I have time.

Significantly, Jasmine uses Kate Bush to recapture her independent identity, to distance herself, to a certain extent, from her partner. Yet at the same time her words suggest a degree of powerlessness on Jasmine's part, which demonstrates clearly that active consumption need not equal power or resistance. However, in response to my question whether she also refrains from playing the Throwing Muses, her other favorites, when he is around, Jasmine explains:

No, the Throwing Muses I put on when he is around. It's more, Throwing Muses is more, it's a bit more angry. It's a specific mood where . . . it's not exactly about that space where you need . . . where you can dream. It's too aggressive I think. But Kate Bush, she is . . . and Kate Bush is what I'll put on when I'm alone in the house. And I've got some time.

This response suggests that Jasmine's withdrawal from the shared sound space may be informed less by a lack of power than by a changed relationship to the music and other fans. While Jasmine had been in close contact with other fans during her teens, her fandom had now by and large become a private affair and she felt little need to go public with it. Indeed, few of my respondents would take their fandom into the public arena. In this respect they were similar to the Smithton women in Janice Radway's study of romance reading (1991). The women in her study used their reading as an "escape" from their daily routines of housework and care for their family and would assuage their feelings of guilt and objections from their partners by highlighting the educational aspects of the romances (such as their historical facts and geographical locations). Their claims to distinction depended largely on their partners' and children's lack of knowledge of what counts as legitimate cultural capital and their ignorance of the low status of romance reading in the field of reading generally. Yet in spite of this lack of "official" recognition, the women managed to translate their reading practices into both a degree of power within the family and "time out" for themselves.

Respondents like Jasmine, however, would not bring their fandom even into the public arena of the home. They were "private listeners" whose claims to distinction often appeared to be made as much for themselves as for anyone else. Jasmine's desire to keep Kate Bush to herself suggests that she does not need the kind of acknowledgment of her cultural capital that Liz, for instance, strove for within her household. Perhaps the fact that few of my respondents were full-time housewives like Radway's romance readers and were therefore less dependent on their partners for legitimation of their tastes explains why they may have found it easier to forgo the support and acknowledgment of a fan community.

Jasmine's private fandom also suggests that despite many shared feelings this scene is far from secure and always threatening to disappear altogether. At the same time, however, the scene also knows some more noticeable manifestations. The following exchanges with Barbara, for instance, illustrate the key role of Internet technologies in scene creation and continuance, particularly for fans and consumers who live far from like-minded people or who appreciate a performer who has ceased to tour or release records (see also Kibby 2000). Barbara, whom I described earlier as having invested strongly in Kate Bush, subscribed to the e-mail discussion list Love-Hounds.

> Laura: As far as I know Kate is not as well known in the US as she is here in the United Kingdom. Do you know any other people in the US who are fans? Would you like to?
>
> Barbara: Yes, but I don't know many! I buy Kate rarities online using an auction website which puts me into contact with other Kate fans. I regularly go through rec.music.gaffa, which gives me a chance to buy/trade and chat with others. I've only met two Kate fans, the first one was at a record fair. I saw this young woman buying the

"Running Up That Hill" single and I homed in on her. . . . The second fan I met was working at a local record store. I had found a copy of the HOL [*Hounds of Love*] album and had put it on the counter to buy when the young man who took the money asked me if I was a Kate fan as he was too.

I went on to ask her about her experiences with the mailing list.

Laura: When you chat with others through rec.music.gaffa what do you tend to talk about?

Barbara: I used to chat quite a bit with other "lovehounds" when I first discovered rec.music.gaffa. I always answered questions that people had about Kate. "What's her fan club address," "when is her birthday," "where was she born," that sort of stuff. I still regularly "lurk" on the group but rarely post these days. Most of the lovehounds are American, therefore most of them know little about her because of her cult status in the USA. Sometimes, the conversation does get a little petty, I usually keep away from any "flaming" or negativity. Some fans get a little frustrated because Kate hasn't released an album since 1993 and their testiness shows in their posts. Others want to discuss the meaning of songs. I see the newsgroup as a "support group," albeit I don't see it as a major influence on me. I find it better to just let the music "do all the talking." I occasionally buy things from the people who advertise there. You are more likely to pick up some real rarities, especially from people who know what it is they are selling.

Where Liz's subscription to the mailing list was fuelled by little more than a desire for information, Barbara's responses highlighted the support and communal feelings that are potentially engendered by online contact. My observation of the list bears this out. I subscribed to the Love-Hounds list for two years during the research, occasionally posting messages though mostly lurking. Although the list tended to be dominated by a relatively small group of long-term contributors who all knew one another well and often shared personal information and long-running jokes, they usually extended warm welcomes to newcomers, and occasionally threads would bring out and unite the many lurkers with the regulars. One such thread centered on the ages of Kate Bush fans and inspired many previously "hidden" fans to disclose their ages. The contributions suggested that being an older and, by implication, long-term fan can confer distinction, while they also momentarily united contributors who were either younger or newer fans, or older and more established fans, thereby highlighting the subdivision of a scene into smaller groups with potentially distinct interests.

That such a virtual or online community has the potential to develop into an offline one is illustrated by Barbara's comments on U.S. fans and the events surrounding Kate Bush's birthday:

> They are usually extremely eager to meet/know other fans. Most of them know very little about Kate and they are always wanting to find out things. On rec.music.gaffa they organise "Katemas" gatherings, which usually consist of one person inviting others for a bit to eat, drinks, playing Kate music, showing off their Kate collection. They usually organise these events around Christmas or on Kate's birthday, 30th July. I've come across some websites specifically put together in order to inform others of meetings.

Some of these "Katemas" gatherings are one-time events, while others, such as the Katemas organized in Glastonbury by the Homeground fan club, have become somewhat of a tradition. It already had a ten-year history when I attended in 1998, and it brought together some thirty-odd men and women, some of whom had traveled from continental Europe, and many of whom had met at previous gatherings.

Barbara's participation in the mailing list did not extend to any of these Katemas events; in fact, her responses seem to betray some ambivalence about involvement. While she corresponded and traded with other subscribers, like Liz she claimed not to know any Kate Bush fans other than those she had met offline. Despite evidence to the contrary, then, chatting online may be seen as having less real effects, which suggests the need for a certain degree of caution about its potential.

Conclusion

As Peterson and Bennett suggest in the introduction to this book, rather than drawing a hard line between scenes and nonscenes it may be more appropriate to say that groups exhibit varying degrees of "sceneness." This chapter, then, has described a scene that, despite a strong degree of shared feelings and knowledge, appears to be in constant danger of disintegration on account of its members' geographical dispersion, conflicting family, career and fan affiliations, and a quest for distinction that prevents many of them from going public with their fandom. This means that they were relatively "invisible" and "unspectacular"; as Barbara put it, Kate Bush fans "don't look a certain way."

The fluidity of the scene, its constantly shifting configuration in terms of size, location, and degree of involvement, was illustrated particularly well by the way in which contributors to the Love-Hounds mailing list moved in and out of discussion threads and by my respondents' reservations about participation. While the list certainly suggests the viability of a virtual scene, many respondents continued to see contact with other fans in terms of formal networks such as fan clubs (often associated with exploitation, teenage fandom, or both) rather than more informal and sometimes ephemeral networks initiated and controlled by fans themselves. Virtual scenes may cater more directly to fans' needs, yet this cannot be divorced from the sense that their effects may be perceived as less real. Traditional, romantic notions of "community"—as involving face-to-face and locally specific contact—appear to endure beyond the perceived ephemeral nature of Internet scenes, as do ideas about fandom as a teenage pursuit. While Barbara's responses, for instance, clearly indicated that she enjoyed the contact with other fans and that her fandom functioned as a resource through which she could strive for more confidence and independence, I believe reservations about fandom generally—fuelled by media reports of "excessive" and "obsessive" fans—held her back. The women's quest for distinction—which sees fan activities and involvement in music scenes as too "fannish" and "teenage"—required them to downplay the importance of any scene affiliation, and "to just let the music do all the talking." Yet, having said this, the women's responses clearly demonstrated the continuing importance of popular music in their lives. They attributed strength and self-confidence to their investments in an artist whose work they felt voiced the concerns of their own mature lives with the contradictory demands of work and family commitments, social standing, and independence.

Notes

1. Names of respondents have been changed.
2. The majority of the questionnaires were completed during the autumn of 1997 and a few during the early months of 1998. The interviews were conducted between June and December 1998.
3. It is worth noting in relation to this lack of "hipness" that early on in Kate Bush's career the media frequently criticized her precociousness, suburban

roots, and sexy image. Although more recently she has come to be recognized as an innovative and influential artist, her fans continue to be disparaged; for instance, their continuing and "excessive" loyalty, in spite of the lack of new releases, is frequently mocked.

4. The Web site for the German fan club, Irgendwo in der Tiefe, was found at *itsnova.mach.uni-karlsruhe.de/~meiswink/katebush/* but no longer exists at this URL.

5. My respondents' view of Bush's image as "sensual" and "tasteful" rather than as overtly sexual overlooks the ambiguities in some of her visuals. Early publicity material, such as the infamous "leotard" pictures to promote her debut album and the videos for "The Man with the Child in His Eyes" (both 1978) and "Babooshka" (1980), suggest that Bush can also be read as inviting the male gaze. On the other hand, the respondents seldom acknowledge Madonna as someone who knowingly manipulates her image.

References

Bolton, Cecil, ed. 1987. *Kate Bush Complete.* Woodford Green, Essex, U.K.: EMI Music Publishing.

Bourdieu, Pierre. 1996. *The State Nobility.* Cambridge: Polity Press.

———. 1998. *Distinction: A Social Critique of the Judgement of Taste.* London: Routledge.

Cann, Kevin, and Sean Mayes. 1988. *Kate Bush: A Visual Documentary.* London: Omnibus Press.

Frith, Simon, and Andrew Goodwin, eds. 1990. *On Record: Rock, Pop, and the Written Word.* London: Routledge.

Juby, Kerry, with Karen Sullivan. 1988. *Kate Bush: The Whole Story.* London: Sidgwick and Jackson.

Kibby, Marjorie J. 2000. "Home on the Page: A Virtual Place of Music Community." *Popular Music* 19, 1: 91–100.

Kruse, Holly. 1990. "In Praise of Kate Bush." In Simon Frith and Andrew Goodwin, eds., *On Record: Rock, Pop, and the Written Word.* London: Routledge.

Radway, Janice. 1991. *Reading the Romance: Women, Patriarchy, and Popular Literature.* Chapel Hill and London: University of North Carolina Press.

Thornton, Sarah. 1995. *Club Cultures: Music, Media, and Subcultural Capital.* Cambridge: Polity Press.

Vermorel, Fred. 1983. *The Secret History of Kate Bush (and the Strange Art of Pop).* London: Omnibus.

Weinstein, Deena. 1991. *Heavy Metal: A Cultural Sociology.* New York: Lexington Books.

Discography

Bush, Kate. 1978. "Wuthering Heights." EMI.

————. 1978. *The Kick Inside*. EMI.

————. 1978. "The Man with the Child in His Eyes." EMI.

————. 1980. "Babooshka." EMI.

————. 1980. *Never for Ever*. EMI.

————. 1985. *Hounds of Love*. EMI.

————. 1985. "Running up That Hill." EMI.

————. 1989. *The Sensual World*. EMI.

————. 1993. *The Red Shoes*, EMI

Index

ABBA, 75
Adams, Ryan, 188
Afro-Celtic-funkabilly, 157
Aguilera, Christina, 85
Allman Brothers, 31
alternative country music:
    defined, 188–90
    music, 188–90
    virtual scene, 190–201
alternative music industry, 171, 172–73,
    176–77
alternative rock, 189
Alternative Tentacles Records, 169, 171,
    173, 176, 180n1, 180n6
American Music Center, 154
Americana music, 188
anarcho-punk:
    music, 170
    politics, 170
    scene, 8, 169–71
Antheil, George, 151
anti-music:
    karaoke as, 64
archival methodology, 191
art world, 3
Atlantic Records, 171
authenticity, 2, 3, 17, 31–46, 163, 172, 189,
    190, 212
    and DIY production, 173
    fabrication of, 32
    and fans, 178–79
    in fanzines, 226

natural ambiance of, 45
sliding scale of, 34, 38–42
in a specific genre:
    —alternative country music, 90
    —blues, 32, 34, 38–42, 45–46
    —Canterbury Sound, 212, 216
    —punk, 174
    —rock, 174–75
staged, 46
symbolic economy of, 34
and tourist attraction, 45, 46

B-52s, 52
Babbitt, Milton, 151, 154
Babes in Toyland, 52
Backstreet Boys, 80
bars:
    biker, 52
    neighborhood, 25
Basie, Count (William), 21, 23, 26
Beatlemania, 9
Becker, Howard S., 3, 12n3, 17–27, 48
Bennett, Andy, 6, 10, 200
Berry, Chuck, 37
Biafra, 181n15
Bikini Kill, 116, 118, 119, 123, 125, 126
Black Flag, 162, 169, 175, 176, 180n4
"Black Lone Ranger, The," 43
Blink 182, 160
bluegrass, 188, 190, 199
blues, 188
    Chicago, 31–47, 206

"*Blues Brothers, The*," 31
Bluurgh Records, 169, 173
BMX:
 bikes, 10
 exhibition, 160, 165n1
bouncers, 57, 60
boundary work, 151–52, 156–57, 160–61
Bourdieu, Pierre, 3
Brando, Marlon, 175
Bratmobile, 116, 119
Britpop, 222
Brown, James, 37
Brown, Les, 21
Brubeck, David, 19
Bush, Kate, 11, 238–51
 career, 239
 tasteful femininity, 239, 244–45
 Web site, 240
Butthole Surfers, 176
BYO Records, 159

Calloway, Cab, 21
Calyx Web site, 208
Canterbury, UK, 205–06, 208
Canterbury Sound, 10, 206–8, 215
 authenticity, 212, 216
 Englishness of, 209, 212, 217
 festival, 215
 marketing of, 213
 Web sites, 208
"Canterbury Tales," 205, 217
Canterburyism, 210–11
capital, subcultural, 11
Caravan, 206, 207, 210, 213, 215, 217
Cash, Johnny, 188
Chainsaw Records, 119
Chaucer, Geoffrey, 205, 217
Chess Records, 171
Chieftains, The, 244
city authorities, 59, 61
Clapton, Eric, 31
Clash, 168
class conflict, land of, 175, 176, 177
classical music vs. serious music, 150–51,
 152–54

club kids, 50, 62
clubs:
 blues, Chicago, 35–45
 Canterbury, UK, 206
 jazz, 18, 20–22
 —Chicago, 25
 —Kansas City, 18
 karaoke, 64, 67–69, 71–72
 techno dance, 51–59
cocaine, 58
Codeine, 230
Cohen, Sara, 3, 7, 69
Collapso Web site, 208, 217
community, 8, 32
 Chicago black, 24
Copland, Aaron, 151, 152, 153
Corpus Hermeticum Records, 234
country music, 188–89
Cowell, Henry, 152
Crass (the band), 168, 169
Crass Records, 169, 173, 178, 181n10
Crosby, Bob, 21
culture, global and local, 45–46

D.O.A., 176
Dale, Jimmie, band, 23
dance club:
 culture, 48
 salsa, 98–102
 techno, 52
 underground, 54
dance, striptease, 26
Davis, Miles, 21
Dead Kennedys, 169, 170, 176, 179, 181n9,
 181n15
Deadheads, 10
Dean, James, 175
DeMent, Iris, 188
digital recording, 5
Dischord Records, 169, 171, 173, 180n1,
 180n6
disk jockey (DJ):
 dance, 50, 54, 55, 56, 57, 61, 62
 goth, 134, 136, 137
 in local scenes, 201

distribution, record, 171, 172
Dixieland jazz, 20
DIY (Do-It-Yourself):
    advice on, 194
    ethos, 119, 163, 168–69, 172, 173, 174
    fanzines, 226
    festival, 155–56
    music industry, 5, 170, 171–72, 176–78
    recording, lo fi, 218n1
Dorsey, Tommy, 21
Dowd, Timothy J., 10, 149–67
Drew, Rob, 64–79
drugs:
    availability of, 57, 58
    dealers, 49, 55, 57, 62

Ecstasy (E), 51, 58
Earl, Steve, 188
Earthworm Records, 234
Ellington, Duke (Edward Kennedy), 21
emcee, karaoke, 67, 70
Englishness, 209, 212, 217
Eno, Brian, 230
Enraptured Records, 234
Epitaph Records, 160
ethnographic methodology, 35–36, 49,
    65–66, 132–33
ethos, alternative country music, 190
    blues, tourist, 34, 37–42
    DIY, 119, 163, 168–69, 172, 173, 174
    punk, 179
    rebel, 175

Factory Records, 172
fannishness, 251
fans:
    adult, 238–50
    age of, 240
    alternative country music, 192, 193
    anti-tourist, 39
    and authenticity, 178–79
    construct scene, 209, 216
    demographic characteristics of, Kate
        Bush, 240

female, eroticized, 240–41
    and genre formation, 190
    local scene, 36–42
    newbie, 199
    private, 240, 248
    of a specific genre:
    —alternative country music, 198–99
    —Kate Bush, 238–51
    —Chicago blues, 36–42
    —Chicago jazz, 21
    —goth, 131, 134–35
    —rave, 50, 62
    —skatepunk, 159, 162
    —post-rock, 227–28
    —teen-pop, 80–95
    virtual scene, 240, 251
    write fanzines, 115, 117–19; 227–28
fanzine:
    create scene, 224
    culture, 225–26
    defined, 12n2, 225–26
    DIY, 226
    self-reflexive, 231
    of a specific genre:
    —Canterbury Sound, 208, 212, 214
    —goth, 138, 142, 143
    —post-rock, 10, 227–28
    —punk, 162
    —Riot Grrrl, 115–16, 117–19, 120
    written by, 115, 117–19; 227–28
fashion:
    goth, 131, 134–35
    punk, 168, 169
    Riot Grrrl, 125–26
femininity, 239, 244–45
feminism, 118–19, 155, 243, 245
feminist consciousness, 86–90, 94, 117–
    19, 121–23, 154–58, 245
    teen; 86–90, 94
festival:
    attendees, 152, 154, 157–58
    commercial, 160–63
    defined, 9–10, 149–50, 163–65
    as scene, 9-10, 149–65

festival, *continued*
  specific venue:
  —Canterbury Sound, 215
  —Glastonbury, 217
  —Ladyfest, 128
  —Merlefest, 195
  —Michigan Womyn's Music Festival,
    154–58
  —Midlands Carnival, 214
  —SXSW (South by Southwest), 196
  —Twangfest, 196–98
  —Whitby Gothic Weekend, 136
  —Yaddo, 150–54
  of a specific genre:
  —anarcho-punk, 170
  —country music, 196
  —hardcore, 159, 162
  —rock, 10
  —serious music, 151–54
  —skatepunk, 150, 158–63
  —womyn's music, 150, 154–58
  sponsorship, 161, 162
field, 3
Finnegan, Ruth, 69
Flux of Pink Indians, 169
Flying Saucer Attack, 230
focus-groups, 81–83
Franklin, Aretha, 244
Fugazi, 169, 175, 180n1

Gaines, Donna, 3
gaze:
  male, 239, 245, 252n5
  tourist, 2, 213
gender:
  contested, 157
  equality, 86
genre atrophy, 200
  formation and fans, 190
  and scenes, 187
Getz, Stan, 26
ghetto, Chicago black, 45
  as tourist attraction, 42–45, 46
gig, 24
Gill, Vince, 188

Gillespie, Dizzy (Charles Burks), 26
girl power, 86–88
Goffman, Erving, 48
Gong, 213, 217
Goodman, Benny, 21
Goo-Goo Dolls, 52
Gosling, Tim, 5, 8, 168–83
gospel music, 189
goth:
  fans, 131, 134–35
  fanzines, 138
  identity, 133–35
  music, defined, 131
  music, in record stores, 139
  style, 131, 134–35
Graham, Jory, 44
Grateful Dead, 10
Grazian, David, 2, 31–47, 193, 198, 200
Guy, Buddy, 35

Hancock, Wayne, 188
Hanson, 244
hardcore punk, 169
  festival, 159, 162
Hawkins, Erskine, 24
Heavens to Betsy, 119
Herman, Woody (Woodrow Wilson),
    21, 23, 26
Heywood, Eddie, 24
Hill, Ubaka, 157
Hodgkinson, James A., 8, 221–237
Hodkinson, Paul, 10, 131–48,198
Homeground, Kate Bush fan club, 240
honky tonk, 189
house music, 190
House of Blues, Chicago blues club, 35,
    39, 40
Husker Du, 176

industry:
  alternative, 171, 172–73, 176–77, 194
  See DIY (Do-It-Yourself)
  mainstream, 171
  —Nashville, 189, 194

Internet, and goth scene, 142, 143, 144
    surfing for information on acts, 81, 82
    and virtual scenes, 10–11, 187–202,
        208–9, 216, 228
Internet-based music scene, 4, 6, 10–11,
    187–204, 205–18
Ives, Charles, 152, 153

Jackson, Alan, 188
jam session, 25
jazz, 17–27, 190
    clubs, 18, 20
    specific locale:
    —Chicago, 20–25
    —Kansas City, 18
    —New Orleans, 206
    on college campuses, 19
    scene, 18
    straight, 23
John, Elton, 74
Johnson, Robert, 31

K Records, 119
karaoke music, 7, 67–69, 71–73
    and Chinese immigrants, 74
    emcee, 70
    performance, 67–69
    and punk sensibilities, 76
    scene in the US, 64–79
    —formed, 67
    —unique characteristics, 67
    and Vietnamese immigrants, 74
Katemoms, fan club, 250
Keen, Robert Earl, 188
Kenton, Stan, 23, 24
Kevin Ayres Band, 206
Kid Rock, 52
Kill Rock Stars, 119, 179
King, Albert, 37
King, B.B. (Riley B.), 37
King, Carol, 244
Kinks, 244
Kitty Yo-Kollaps-Payola Records, 234
Koko Taylor's Celebrity, Chicago blues
    club, 36

Kraftwerk, 230
krautrock, 225
Kruse, Holly, 9, 133

Labradford, 229–33
Ladyfest, festival, 128
Le Tigre, 157
Lee, Steve S. 6, 10, 187–204
lesbian consciousness, 154, 156
Liddle, Kathleen, 10, 149–67
lifestyle, marketable, 164
listserv, defined, 190
"Living Blues," 44
local scene. See scene, local
lo fi (low fidelity) recording, 218n1
Lounge Ax, New York karaoke club, 64
Love-Hounds Web site, 240, 242, 248,
    249
Lowe, Melanie, 11, 80–95
lurking, 192, 193
Lyman, Kevin, 160, 161

Madonna, 245
male gaze, 239, 245, 252n5
marijuana, 58
marketable lifestyle, 164
Marley, Bob, 37
McCready, Mindy, 73
media:
    global, 9
    niche, 11, 141
    and Riot Grrrl scene, 124–27
methodology:
    archival, 191, 227–28
    ethnographic, 35–36, 49, 65–66, 132–
        33, 239–40
    focus-groups, 81–83
    interview, 239–41
    interview via Internet, 241–42
    participant observation, 20, 49, 191
    survey, 191, 239–41
Michigan Womyn's Music Festival,
    154–58
Mighty Mighty Bosstones, 160
Minor Threat, 169

Moto-X exhibition, 160, 165n1
MTV (Music Television), 46, 50, 81
  TRL (Total Request Live) teen
    program, 82, 94
music festival. *See* festival
music genre:
  atrophy, 200
  formation, 190
music genres:
  acid rock, 190
  —alternative, 189
  —Liverpool, 4
  Americana, 188
  anarcho-punk, 170
  Assyrian, 22
  Austin, Texas, 3, 7
  bhangra, 4, 6
  bluegrass, 188, 189
  blues, 188
  —Chicago, 31–47
  commercial, 26
  country, 188–89
  dance, 4, 6, 22
  —house, 51, 190
  —jungle, 51
  —salsa, 7, 96–97
  —swing, 21
  —techno, 49–51
  —trance, 51
  Dixieland, 20
  electronic, 51
  extreme metal, 4
  gospel, 189
  goth, 8, 131
  Greek, 22
  honky tonk, 189
  house, 51, 190
  jazz, 17–27, 190
  jungle, 51
  karaoke, 74
  Polish, 22
  post-rock, 10, 222–25, 235
  punk, 168, 174
  —anarcho, 8, 170

  —skate, 10, 159
  —thrash, 10
  rap, 4
  rockabilly, 189, 190
  salsa, 7, 96–97
  serious, 150, 151–54
  skatepunk, 10, 159
  techno, 49–51
  teen, 80–81, 91–93
  thrash punk, 10
  trance, 51
  western swing, 189
  women's, 154, 156
music industry. *See* industry
My Bloody Valentine, 230

'N Sync, 80
Nelson, Jenna, 10, 149–67
New Kids on the Block, 244
newbies, 199
Nirvana, 123
No Doubt, 160
nostalgia, 10

O'Neil, Jim, 44
objectification of women, 88
Owens, Buck, 188

P 2 (Postcard Two), list serve, 190–91
  as virtual scene, 187–202
Parker, Charlie, 21, 26
Parker, Junior (Herman), 31
Parsons, Gram, 188
participant observation, methodology,
  20, 191
Parton, Dolly, 194
Picket, Wilson, 37
place, 4, 20, 26, 34, 65, 144, 209, 211,
  233–34
  defined, 20, 26
  and jazz, 17–27
Plone Records, 234
plug-and-play, 159

politics in scenes:
  anarcho-punk, 170, 171
  punk, 174
  Riot Grrrl, 116–20, 121–23, 124–28
  salsa, 96, 99–102, 109–11
  techno, 59–60
  women's, 86–90, 116–20, 121–23, 124–
      28, 150–58
Postcard, 202n3.
Postcard Two. *See* (P 2)
postmodern slumming, 39
post-rock, 10, 221–35
  fanzines, 10, 227–28
  local scene, 221
  locus of, 233–34
  music, 221–22
  —defined, 222–25, 235
  —hard to define, 223
Presley, Elvis, 74
Pretenders, The, 125
Prince, 74–75
Prine, John, 10
promoters, 54, 56–57, 62
Puente, Tito, 24
punk:
  defined, 168, 174
  ethos, 179
  —in post-rock, 228
  fashion, 168, 169
  politics, 169
  sensibilities, 76, 190
  types of:
  —anarcho, 8, 170
  —hardcore, 117
  —skate, 10, 159
  —thrash, 10

Quarashi, 160

race:
  stereotypes, 38
  and Chicago blues scene, 43–45
  mixed band, 23
  and Riot Grrrl scene, 121, 127–28

Radway, Janice, 247–48
rebel ethos, 175
record stores, goth music in, 139
resistance, 80, 90–93, 94
  and Britney Spears, 90–93, 94
  of Kate Bush fans, 240–41, 243
  and social aging, 243
Riot Grrrl, 8
  defined, 119–20, 121–24, 125–27
  meaning contested, 119–27
  as fashion trend, 125–26
  scene, 115–28
  formed, 115–19
  —ends, 127
  —leader, 126
  —and race, 121, 127–28
risk-free environment, 50, 57, 60, 194
rock:
  acid, 190
  alternative, 189
  rockabilly, 189, 190
  Rough Trade Records, 172
  Ruggles, Carl, 152

salsa, music, 7, 96
  gay, 111
Sam and Dave, 37
sampling, 5
scene:
  defined, 1–4
  journalistic, 2, 206–8
  See also scene, local
  See also scene, translocal
  See also scene, virtual
scene, local:
  and city authorities, 59, 61
  communication in, 195
  core and periphery, 193
  defined, 6, 7–8
  DJs in, 201
  and drug dealers, 49, 55, 57, 62
  falls apart, 18, 26, 45–46, 61–62,
      108–10
  fan characteristics, 192, 195

scene, local, *continued*
fans construct, 209, 216
faux, 209, 216
and fire marshals, 55, 59
formation of, 17–18, 50–53, 67, 198
illicit activity in, 57–58, 59
interaction in, 191–92
interaction, quality of, 194
international tourist, 36
locale:
—Austin, Texas, 3, 7
—Birmingham, UK goth, 132, 136, 137
—Canterbury, 207–8, 216
—Chicago; blues, 31–47, jazz, 20–26
—Detroit; Motown, 65, techno, 49
—Frankfurt rap, 4
—Kansas City jazz, 17, 20
—Leeds, UK goth, 132, 137
—Liverpool rock, 4, 48
—London salsa, 7, 98–102
—Memphis rockabilly, 65
—Milton Keynes, UK, 69
—Newcastle, 4, 6
—New Orleans jazz, 48
—Olympia, WA Riot Grrrl, 115–17
—Plymouth, UK goth, 132
—San Francisco psychedelic rock, 48, 65
—Seattle grunge, 48
—Washington, DC punk, 117
longevity of, 198
and the media, 62
in music genre:
—aboriginal Australian, 75
—be-bop jazz, 48
—dance, 4, 6, 49–62
—goth, 141
—jazz, 17–20, 20–26
—karaoke, 7, 64–77
—post-rock, 10, 221
—rap, 4
—rave, 5, 48–62
—Riot Grrrl, 8, 115–28
—serious music, 151–53
—skatepunk, 10
—techno, 49–62
—tween, 80–95
—womyn's music, 154–58
music genre, impact of, 201
not for adults, 243
official protection of, 59, 60, 61
physical setting, 51–52, 55, 104–07
and police, 53, 59–60, 61
recruitment to, 192
Riot Grrrl, 115–17
risk-free environment, 50, 57,60
social control, 195
and tourism, 212
for tourists, 32, 36–37, 39–42, 200, 212
scene, translocal, 8–10
college campus, 19
and commerce, 138–39
defined, 4, 6, 8–10, 133
ends, 127
formation, 115–19, 133
and identity, 133–35
and the Internet, 142, 143, 144
leader,126
and media, 141–42
in music genre:
—anarcho-punk, 169–80
—skatepunk, 159–63
—Canterbury Sound, 212
—jazz, 19
—psychedelic rock, 48
—Riot Grrrl, 115–28
—skatepunk, 159–63
—teen, 83
role of fanzines in, 10, 117–19
and style, 134–35
and travel, 135–37
scene, versus subculture, 146n1
scene, virtual, 4, 6, 10–11, 77
communication in, 195, 228
as community, 251
core and periphery, 193

defined, 6, 10–11
end of, 199–201
fans, 192, 194, 195, 209, 216, 251
faux local, 209
formation of, 198–99, 208, 221, 229
and gender, 195
impact on music genre, 201
interaction in, 191–93
—face-to-face, 196
—quality of, 194
and the Internet, 187,190–91, 208–9, 228
local references in, 233–34
longevity of, 198–99
lurkers in, 192, 193
and marriage, 196
media-made, 233
member turnover in, 199
in music genre:
—alternative country music, 187–202
—Canterbury Sound, 205–18
—goth, 141–43
—Kate Bush, 251
—post-rock, 231, 233–34
—teen, 83
newbies in, 199
recruitment to, 192
and sexism, 195
social control, 195–96
for tourists, 200–1
sceneness, 11, 250
of virtual scene, 191–96, 202
Schilt, Kristin, 8, 115–30, 198
security guards, 57, 60
selling out, 122–24, 162, 168
serious music: ·
defined, 151, 152
scene, 151–53
vs. classical music, 150–51, 152–54
sexism, 117, 195
Shank, Barry, 3, 7
Silver Apples, 225
Sisters of Mercy, 132

skateboarding, 159, 160
skatepunk festival, 150, 158–63
music, 158–59
Slimelight, goth club, 143
Slobin, Mark, 9
slumming, 39
Smashing Pumpkins, 52
Smith, Patti, 244
Smith, Richard and Tim Maughan, 5
social aging, 243
Soft Machine, 206, 207, 217
Son Volt, 188, 201, 202n3
Sonic Youth, 125
Spears, Britney, 11, 80
image, risqué/slut /whore, 85, 88, 94
liberation through, 94
as Lolita, 94
negative role model, 89
and resistance, 90–93, 94
Spice Girls, 75, 86, 242, 245
Spiderleg Records, 169, 173
Spring, Ken, 4, 48–63, 194, 198
SST Records, 159, 169, 171, 173, 176, 180n6
stereotypes, race, 38
straight-edge, 169
Straw, Will, 3, 8
subculture, 3
versus scene, 146n1
subcultural capital, 70, 71
Subhumans, The, 169
survey methodology, 191
Suture, 116
symbolic economy, 31

techno music, 49
defined, 50
teen-pop, 81, 91–93, 239
and Kate Bush, 239
teeny-bopper, 11
Telstar Ponies, 230
Thornton, Sara, 11
thrash punk, 10
thread, defined, 191, 194
Thrill Jockey Records, 234

tour sponsorship, 161, 162
tourist:
    attraction, ghetto as, 42–45, 46
    gaze, 2, 213
    slumming, 39
tourists:
    Canterbury Sound, 213
    Chicago blues, 32, 36–37, 39–41
tours, Beatles in Liverpool, 212
translocal scene. *See* scene, translocal
tribe, 194
Tristano, Lennie, 26
tween scene, defined, 80, 94

UFO, London rock club, 207
Uncle Tupelo, 188, 203n5
Urquia, Norman, 96-112, 193

Van Halen, 175
Vans Inc., 158, 161
Vans Warped Tour, 10, 158–63
Vinton, Bobby, 69
vinyl records, 50, 54
virtual scene. *See* scene, virtual
volunteerism, 155
Vroomen, Laura, 10, 238–53

Warp Records, 234
Waters, Muddy (McKinley Morganfield),
    31, 37
Web site:
    Canterbury Sound, 208
    Kate Bush, 249
    Love-Hounds, 240, 242, 248, 249
Welch, Gillian, 188
western swing, 189
Wheeler, Cheryl, 157
Whitby Gothic Weekend, festival, 136,
    139
Whitman, Walt, 17
Wilco, 188, 201, 202n3, 203n5
Wilde Flowers, 206, 207, 209, 210, 213
Williams, Lucinda, 188, 196, 203n5
women, objectification of, 88
women-only space, 157
womyn's music scene, 154–58
womyn-born-womyn, 157
working class, girls in London, 86
Wuthnow, Robert, 76
Wyatt, Robert, 206, 207

Yaddo Music Festival, 150–54